...cel

...ng changing lives

Edexcel A2 PE

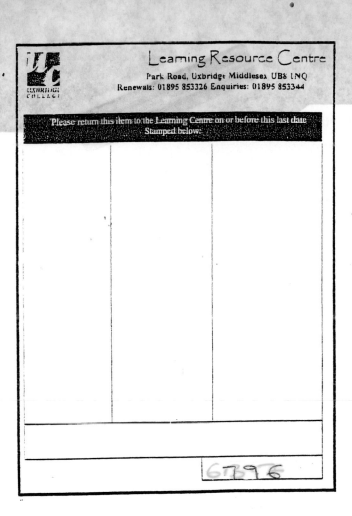

Mike Hill

Colin Maskery

Gavin Roberts

A PEARSON COMPANY

Published by Pearson Education Limited, a company incorporated in England and Wales, having its registered office at Edinburgh Gate, Harlow, Essex, CM20 2JE. Registered company number: 872828

www.heinemann.co.uk

Edexcel is a registered trademark of Edexcel Limited

Text © Pearson Education Limited 2009

First published 2009

12 11 10 09
10 9 8 7 6 5 4 3 2

British Library Cataloguing in Publication Data is available from the British Library on request.

ISBN 978 0 43550060 3

Designed by Wooden Ark Studios
Typeset by 𝘛 Tek-Art, Crawley Down, West Sussex
Original illustrations © Pearson Education Limited 2009
Cover design by Wooden Ark Studios
Cover photo © Masterfile
Printed in China (SWTC/02)

Websites
The websites used in this book were correct and up to date at the time of publication. It is essential for tutors to preview each website before using it in class so as to ensure that the URL is still accurate, relevant and appropriate. We suggest that tutors bookmark useful websites and consider enabling students to access them through the school/college intranet.

Disclaimer
This Edexcel publication offers high-quality support for the delivery of Edexcel qualifications.

Edexcel endorsement does not mean that using this material is essential to achieve any Edexcel qualification, nor does it mean that this is the only suitable material available to support Edexcel qualifications. No endorsed material will be used verbatim in setting any Edexcel examination/ assessment and any resource lists produced by Edexcel shall include this and other appropriate texts.

Copies of official specifications for all Edexcel qualifications may be found on the Edexcel website: www.edexcel.com

CONTENTS

UNIT 3 PREPARATION FOR OPTIMUM SPORTS PERFORMANCE   1

UNIT 4 THE DEVELOPING SPORTS PERFORMER   185

INTRODUCTION

UNITS 3 AND 4

Your A2 Physical Education course is divided into two units:

- *Preparation for Optimum Sports Performance* and
- *The Developing Sports Performer.*

This Student Book provides an exact match to the Edexcel specification and as well as teaching and learning material it includes features such as suggested tasks, examiner tips and stretch and challenge opportunities.

The Edexcel A2 PE Student Book is divided into four sections:

- Unit 3 Preparation for Optimum Sports Performance: Part A Short-term Preparation
- Unit 3 Preparation for Optimum Sports Performance: Part B Long-term Preparation
- Unit 3 Preparation for Optimum Sports Performance: Part C Managing Elite Performance
- Unit 4 The Developing Sports Performer.

The first three sections cover the part of your qualification that is assessed by examination and the fourth section covers the part that is assessed by coursework.

Unit 3 is worth 50 per cent of the Advanced Level award and is marked out of a total of 90

Unit 4 is worth 50 per cent of the Advanced Level award and is marked out of a total of 90.

LEARNING STYLES

The key to success at A2 level is to understand that you need to learn the concepts, definitions and examples required to answer the questions in the exam. The information you are given in your lessons and the words and case studies presented in the text are only that – information. You will need to go over the chapters several times and attempt all the tasks if you really want to learn the information. It is also important to find out what is the best way for you to learn. We have offered a range of tasks and activities in this Student Book and you may find some are easier to complete than others.

Generally each person will have a preferred style of learning and research suggests that there are three main types of learning:

- through sight (visually)
- through sound (auditory)
- through physical movement (kinaesthetic).

If you are not sure which is your preferred learning style there are a range of short online tests that you can do to identify your preferred style.

Learning style	Strategies for revision
Visual style	Use tables and diagrams to summarise key points Use colour or highlighters to reinforce the most important points Use the pictures and photos in the book to create a 'visual' case study Put information into timelines or picture boards to help understand the links between concepts
Auditory style	Where possible discuss the topics you are learning with friends Record lessons or notes on an MP3 player for re-listening later and repeat/chant facts/information/ examples over and over to retain
Kinaesthetic style	Write out notes several times – each time try to reduce the number of words you are using Make your own charts and tables Trace keywords and phrase with your fingers Try to do things with your hands while you are revising – squeezing a squash or tennis ball, for example

Although using your preferred style of learning will help you revise for exams most effectively it is equally important to try lots of different techniques. If we can use all three styles of learning we will be able to learn more effectively, retaining up to 90 per cent of information presented. Compare that to 60 per cent if doing solely practical activities, 50 per cent using solely visual stimuli or 20 per cent using solely auditory cues.

So when learning or revising make sure you try to present the information in the following ways:

- **Draw it!** (visual) – use mind maps and posters
- **Describe it!** out loud if necessary (auditory) – use audio tapes, podcasts and mnemonics
- **Do it!** (kinaesthetic) – make models, role-play or even move around while learning.

FEATURES OF THE BOOK

LEARNING OUTCOMES

These help to ensure you understand fully the content of each chapter. When you have completed a particular topic area, make sure you can achieve each learning objective stated. When preparing for your examination you should collate all the learning objectives from the beginning of the chapters and tick them off as you prepare.

> **LEARNING OUTCOMES**
> By working through this chapter, you should:
> - know the four basic requirements for physical activity...

KEY TERMS

Throughout the text you will find explanations of important key terms and concepts that may be new to you. These are a useful reference source.

> **KEY TERM**
> **health-related fitness**
> a basic level of physical fitness components...

TASKS

You will find a range of motivating activities to help you practise what you are learning, including opportunities for small-group discussions. These also help to reinforce learning.

> **TASK**
> *Record your daily activities in a diary...*

REMEMBER

These features will help to highlight key concepts.

> **REMEMBER**
> - A high risk profile for diabetes is an inactive, overweight individual...

APPLY IT!

These activities will encourage the application of concepts to real-life contexts. They will reinforce how theory is used in practice.

> **APPLY IT!**
> *Vigorous cycling will burn between 500 and 700 calories per hour...*

HOTLINKS

Website-related activities throughout the text will direct you to extra exciting resources and encourage further research on topics.

> **HOTLINKS**
> Research osteoporosis at **www.nos.org.uk**...

EXAM TIP

Essential bits of exam technique and advice that will improve your examination performance.

EXAM TIP

Practise answering past paper questions as often as possible...

COURSEWORK TIP

Advice and reminders of the best approach to compiling your portfolio of evidence on all the four major coursework tasks.

COURSEWORK TIP

You will need to reference the work you submit...

STRETCH AND CHALLENGE

These activities will provide opportunities for you to undertake further work on a topic and strengthen your understanding.

STRETCH AND CHALLENGE

Close your eyes and create a mental picture of a significant success that you wish to achieve in the next 12 months.

CASE STUDIES

New and up-to-date case studies provide real-life examples of the topics you are studying. Questions on the case studies will enable you to explore the topic further, understand the key issues and deepen your understanding of the topic.

CASE STUDY
NOTATION IN TENNIS

Let's look at the data collected...

EXAMCAFÉ

In our unique ExamCafé you'll find lots of ideas to help you prepare for your Unit 3 exams, as well as your Unit 4 Coursework. For example, there is handy advice on **Getting started, Revision checklists** at the end of each chapter to check that you have taken on board all the concepts within the chapter and are aware of what you need to know and understand, and **Get the result** that gives you sample questions and answers together with model answers accompanied by examiners' tips. These sections have been specifically written to help you improve your examination performance.

Exam**Café**
Relax, refresh, result!

ExamCafé
Relax, refresh, result!

Relax and prepare

What I wish I had known at the start of the year…

Lamar

Hand in your work on the designated days – make your deadlines. If you don't understand something then get help from your tutor or teacher – otherwise you'll fall behind. Every evening go over your work covered in the lessons that day, making extra notes from your text.

Asha

Your coursework is a large part of the course and carries a high weighting, so it's good to put a lot of effort into all aspects of this. Do your coursework and hand it in before the deadlines and make the most effective use of your teachers. This will enable you to make adjustments and this will make your coursework the best it can be. Do not leave any work or revision to the last minute.

Student tips

Mark

Look at as many resources as you can and do your preparation sooner rather than later. Go back and check over your work carefully before you hand it in. For your exams, start your revision early, always ask for help and do not waste your free time.

Getting started …

Transition from AS to A2:

Once you have completed Units 1 and 2 of the AS (Advanced Subsidiary) course you are required to build on your PE knowledge and understanding by working through Unit 3: Preparation for Optimum Sports Performance, and extend your practical experiences by undertaking Unit 4: The Developing Sports Performer.

In Unit 4 you will have to complete four assessed coursework task. Each task builds onto and further develops the ethos of an applied specification that involves you in developing your own personal performance pathway and in further applying your theoretical knowledge and understanding to the performance arena. In addition, you will be required to carry forward and apply the knowledge and understanding gained from the completion of Unit 3. You will construct a portfolio of evidence that will reflect your experiences and final task submissions.

Get the result!

examiner's tips

Before answering the question make sure you read the question to or three times first. When you are happy that you know what the question is asking underline or highlight all the question cues and key words; only then should you put pen to paper and attempt an answer. The table below lists some common question cues, or doing words, together with an idea of the requirements from the candidate in their answer.

Question cues doing word(s)	What you need to do ...
Account for	Explain, clarify, give reasons
Analyse	Resolve into its component parts, examine critically
Assess	Determine the value of, weigh up
Compare	Look for similarities and differences between examples perhaps reach conclusion about which is preferable and justify this clearly
Contrast	Set in opposition in order to bring out the differences sharply
Compare and contrast	Find some points of common ground between x and y and show where or how they differ
Criticise	Make a judgement backed by a discussion of the evidence of reasoning involved, about the merit of theories or opinions or about the truth assertions
Define	State the exact meaning of a word or phrase, in some cases it may be necessary or desirable to examine different possible or often-used definitions
Describe	Give a detailed account of
Discuss	Explain, then give two sides of the issue and any implications
Distinguish/ Differentiate between	Look for differences between

Evaluate	Make an appraisal of the worth/validity/effectiveness of something in the light of its truth or usefulness
Explain	Give details about how and why something is so
To what extent	Usually involves looking at evidence/arguments for and against and weighing them up
Illustrate	Make clear and explicit, usually requires the use of carefully chosen examples
Justify	Show adequate grounds for decisions or conclusions and answer the main objections likely to be made about them
Outline	Give the main features or general principles of a subject, omitting minor details and emphasising structure and arrangement
State	Present in a brief, clear form
Summarise	Give a concise, clear explanation or account of the topic, presenting the chief factors and omitting minor details and examples
What arguments can be made for and against this view	Look at both sides of this argument

examiner's tips

- Try to use up-to-date examples in your examination answers to support the points you are making. Always try to explain the science behind any examples you include.

- Be specific when answering any examination question. Identify the number of points you need to make, and the facts required to score for each point. Then write accurately and without waffle. If you are struggling to express yourself as well as you would like, provide an example to support or illustrate your point.

- To get good marks in your coursework, you must improve on the personal performance you achieved in the AS course. So, look at the assessment criteria for the A2 course and discuss with your centre staff how you can obtain the best marks possible – devise and action plan.

UNIT 3
PREPARATION FOR OPTIMUM SPORTS PERFORMANCE

PART A
SHORT-TERM PREPARATION

The first part of this book looks at the concepts behind optimum preparation for the athlete, with a focus on the elite performer. Short-term preparation is considered from the physiological, psychological and technical points of view. The final sections of this part look at the support that exists to aid performers.

In Chapter 1 we look at short-term physiological preparation, including the physiological responses experienced by the body in response to various stresses. We look at how these stresses can be manipulated by the performer to ensure their performance is enhanced. The positive effects of correct diet on performance are studied, along with the potential dangers of failing to give this element the consideration it deserves. Finally, we examine the role the environment plays in performance, and what athletes can do to minimise any potential adverse effects.

Chapter 2 focuses on short-term psychological responses, and how these can affect performance both adversely and positively. We look at how the environment can affect an individual's ability to perform to their optimum level, and examine the strategies and techniques available to coaches and performers so that they can manipulate the environment to their advantage.

Chapter 3 focuses on technical aspects that can affect the performer, and how these can be manipulated in the short term. Here we look at how the choice of equipment can affect performance, and how changes in the environment need to be reflected with adapted equipment. We also examine the different ergogenic aids that are available to athletes as they seek to gain an edge over their rivals – both legally and illegally.

Chapter 4 looks at the importance of the anabolic phase of an athlete's training programme. By being aware of the anabolic stages, the coach and athlete can maximise training so that levels of fitness and performance are attained and maintained. They can also anticipate likely responses to different types of training, allowing them to plan appropriate recovery stages and activities. By understanding recovery, athletes can maximise their training while avoiding the consequences of getting it wrong.

CHAPTER 1 SHORT-TERM PHYSIOLOGICAL PREPARATION

LEARNING OUTCOMES

By working through this chapter, you should:

- understand the aims and objectives of the warm-up: stages, types of stretching, intensity and duration
- know the main sources of energy for exercise and their manipulation through diet, carbohydrate loading, hydration and creatine loading
- understand the need for short-term acclimatisation: environmental factors influencing preparation and competition, heat adaptation, hydration planning, increase in plasma volume, increased sweat rate and effects of altitude

For elite athletes to be fully prepared, they will have considered the **synergy** of the sport and of their performance, paying a great deal of attention to all the factors that can aid or limit performance.

KEY TERM

synergy
two or more separate influences or agents acting together to create an effect greater than that of the separate parts

These factors include:

- physical conditioning
- the fuel required
- the environment in which they are to perform
- the clothing they need to wear
- the duration of their event
- the role they must perform.

In the context of sport, the term 'warm-up' is synonymous with preparation. But for an elite athlete, preparation for an event does not begin just minutes before, and does not consist simply of physical exertion and/or psychological focusing. For elite-level athletes, preparation will have begun several months or even years before. So we need to understand that there are both short- and long-term preparations, and to be able to distinguish between the two.

Long-term physiological preparation is covered in Chapter 5. The terms 'short' and 'long' are subjective, so it is easier to distinguish between them if we consider the concepts of responses and adaptations. Both involve changes, but:

- **responses** are changes that occur quickly, and are temporary
- **adaptations** take longer to occur, and are more permanent – at least until the environment changes.

If we apply that understanding to short- and long-term preparation, we see that short-term preparation can encompass the last few weeks, days or hours before an event.

APPLY IT!

Before reading this chapter, describe your current warm-up routine. Describe what you do, and specifically what you expect to happen as a result of each activity.

Rate out of 10 the benefit that your warm-up routine offers to your performance, and justify your rating.

THE WARM-UP

Warming up is a topic of some debate – the biggest question is about why, and how, to do it.

Previously, warming up was not considered to be an essential element necessary for sporting success. Consequently, it was usually a token few minutes' pre-match activity. But now it seems to have become an essential activity for some groups of athletes, and many now spend far more time warming up than on their actual competitive performance. For example, a 100-metre sprinter may spend several hours preparing for a 10-second event. Since the introduction of the National Curriculum in 1988, warming up has been taught in schools, and youngsters are actively encouraged to do so.

Is it a coincidence that the growing trend among elite-level athletes to perform a warm-up has accompanied the rapid growth and acceptability of sports psychology? It could be argued that the time spent undertaking pre-activity physiological activities is really time generated so that the athlete can get their mindset and focus right (see Chapter 2).

When you are about to undertake competitive sport against an opponent, would seeing your opponent perform an extensive warm-up, consisting of apparently strange and new activities, give them an edge over you? Is this new trend essential for effective physiological functioning – or is it a psychological placebo?

In attempting to examine the relevance and effectiveness of warming up, a number of questions need to be considered. It is probably useful to start at the end:

- what are you attempting to achieve from a warm-up?
- what are your objectives?
- is it possible to achieve these objectives?
- what activities will need to be done to ensure your objectives are achieved?

The human body will develop a status or level that allows it to function effectively with the minimum of effort. While at rest, or during prolonged maximum exertion, it will attempt to function at its most efficient level.

A simple example might be that a healthy 20-year-old adult would have an approximate *maximum* heart rate of 200 beats per minute (bpm), while *at rest* the average adult heart rate in the UK is 72 bpm.

The body has calculated that with the demands that are being made on it at rest, it can function effectively at just over one-third of its capacity. A heart rate over that level would be unnecessary while the body is at rest, and so would be a waste of effort and energy. The body effectively puts many of its systems on standby. While we are sleeping, there are fewest demands on the body so it can function at its lowest level, allowing energy to be focused on growth and repair (see Chapter 4).

When a stress is experienced, the body has to respond – and it will respond in a way that enables it to meet the demands made on it with the least amount of effort. For example, after sitting and resting, standing up and walking around will place additional stress on the body, which will respond to meet those demands.

Initially, an increased level of carbon dioxide (CO_2) will be detected. This will lead to an increase in heart rate which will:

- speed up removal of the additional CO_2
- Increase the delivery of oxygen (O_2) in order to provide energy for the additional workload.

If the stress increases further and extra O_2 is required, the body will respond by restricting blood flow to certain areas of the body, enabling more O_2 to be delivered to where it is needed.

The body has responded in a way that enables it to meet the demands placed on it. By responding, it is still performing efficiently, but at an increased level. It is this understanding that physiologists are attempting to utilise when we warm up.

WHY WARM UP?

The objectives of a warm-up are to:

- prepare the body both physiologically and mentally for performance
- improve performance
- reduce the risk of injury.

If at the end of the warm-up these three objectives have been achieved, it is safe to say that warming up is a beneficial activity. The difficulty comes when attempting to prove whether the objectives were achieved as a direct consequence of the warm-up activities – or despite them.

Let's examine each objective in a little more detail. Are they realistic objectives – and are they attainable?

▶ *Warming up is now taught in schools*

TO PREPARE THE BODY PHYSIOLOGICALLY AND MENTALLY FOR PERFORMANCE

As the warm-up occurs before the activity itself, it is logical that its major purpose is preparation for the activity – it is therefore a desirable and attainable objective. But the success of the warm-up in meeting this objective depends on how the warm-up is performed:

- the choice of activities
- the manner in which they are carried out
- the time allowed to carry them out
- the perceived success of carrying them out by the performer.

If the performer fails to be successful here, the net result of the warm-up would be a feeling of not being ready or prepared, with a likely outcome of poor performance.

TO IMPROVE PERFORMANCE

Warming up is not a mode of training designed to increase an athlete's one-repetition maximum (1-rep max, 1RM), or their personal best time for a given event. It will not improve your performance in that context. But by performing certain activities, you will be better able to perform at your current optimum level.

TO REDUCE THE RISK OF INJURY

This is perhaps the most contentious objective of a warm-up – and the hardest to prove. The view is that by gradually introducing the body to a changing environment, it is less likely to experience trauma. But the subjectivity of any test to measure the effectiveness of pre-sport activity, and the lack of reliability of such a test, means that there are few credible data to prove or disprove whether this objective is feasible or attainable.

So we have identified the objectives of a warm-up. The next stage is to examine whether achieving these objectives is realistic and likely. To do this, we will consider the activities undertaken and the responses that are targeted, as well as the responses that will actually occur. Finally, we will examine the effects of these responses on the athlete's performance.

All warm-ups should be specific to the activity that is to follow. They should include exercises that prepare the muscles to be used and activate the energy systems required for that particular activity.

To ensure the athlete gains as much as possible from the warm-up, the following stages have become accepted as the most appropriate.

STAGES OF A WARM-UP

STAGE 1: INITIAL PREPARATION: GROSS MOTOR SKILLS AND PULSE-RAISER

Gross motor skills begin this phase. The purpose is to introduce stress to the body in a gradual and controlled manner, which is safer for the athlete, effectively lowering the risk of injury. This phase also raises the temperature of the body's core and of specific muscles, which in turn encourages several other responses to occur.

> ### KEY TERM
> **gross motor skills**
> skills that involve the movement of large body parts or of the whole body

This stage of the warm-up can be achieved by performing some kind of cardiovascular exercise, such as jogging, cycling, rowing, swimming, etc.

Pulse-raising refers to raising the heart rate gradually to the level that will encourage the necessary physiological responses. Once these responses have been achieved, the performer will seek to elevate their heart rate to the level needed for performance.

▶ *Initial preparation raises core body temperature as well as that of specific muscles*

STAGE 2: INJURY PREVENTION

Now that muscle temperature has been raised, the athlete can perform some mobility exercises. Whether the ultimate objective is to reduce the risk of injury or to increase flexibility by increasing localised muscle elasticity, the most common types of activity in this stage are stretches.

The benefit of pre-exercise stretching has been challenged recently. Static stretching, the most common type of stretch used, lacks sports specificity, and there is potential to injure a muscle if stretches are done when the muscle fibres are colder. So some sports scientists have questioned whether stretching should be included in pre-sport activities.

Stretching is covered in more detail later in this chapter (pages 6–9).

STAGE 3: SKILL PRACTICE

This next stage of a warm-up should involve a skill-related component, where the neuromuscular mechanisms related to the activity to follow are worked. Examples include practising serving in tennis, tumble-turns in swimming, or shooting baskets in basketball.

STAGE 4: SPORT-SPECIFIC

Often included with the previous part of the warm-up (skill practice), this phase includes practising specific skills and exertions similarly to how they will be experienced in a game situation.

APPLY IT!

Design a warm-up for your preferred sport that is specific for you, including each of the four stages.

Stage 1 Light/gentle jogging

Stage 2 Static quad and hamstring stretch, followed by dynamic hamstring stretch

Stage 3 Control and passing

Stage 4 Jogging, turn and sprint (to simulate losing a marker) – receive ball, change direction at speed, pass ball to a teammate

Fig. 1.1 The four stages of warming up – this illustration is for soccer

EFFECTS OF A WARM-UP

In a warm-up routine, why do we do what we do? What short-term changes do we want to occur? Will the activities that we do produce them?

First we need to look at the effects on the body of each of the four stages.

IMMEDIATE RESPONSES TO EXERCISE

Increase in:	Other effects
Heart rate	Vasodilation* of some blood vessels
Stroke volume*	Vasoconstriction* of some blood vessels
Cardiac output*	Vascular shunting*
End-diastolic volume*	Decrease in end-systolic volume
Venous return*	Thermoregulation* begins
Localised and core heat generation	Localised muscular metabolism speeds up
Ventilation rate* – becoming quicker, deeper, more active and heavier	Dilation of capillaries
Carbon dioxide build-up	Reduced muscle viscosity
Activity of the sympathetic nervous system*	
Production, utilisation and transportation of lactic acid	
Production of synovial fluid	
Production and release of adrenaline	
Muscle elasticity	
Production of synovial fluid at the joint	
Speed of nerve impulses	

*See Key Terms.

Table 1.1 Immediate responses to exercise

KEY TERMS

cardiac output
the volume of blood pumped by the left ventricle in one minute

end-diastolic volume
the volume of blood in the heart at the end of filling (diastole)

stroke volume
the volume of blood pumped by the left ventricle of the heart in one contraction

sympathetic nervous system
the link between the cardiac acceleratory system and the heart, that results in an increase in heart rate

thermoregulation
the ability of an organism to keep its body temperature within certain boundaries

vascular shunting
the process of directing blood to where it is most needed

vasoconstriction
narrowing of the blood vessels

vasodilation
widening of the blood vessels

venous return
the flow of blood back to the right atrium of the heart

ventilation rate
the rate at which gas enters or leaves the lung

STRETCHING

Stretching is often used to increase the elasticity of muscle and connective tissue. This increases the range of movement at a joint, and so improves the flexibility of the joint and of the athlete. As the majority of sporting injuries are muscle and joint injuries, the idea is that after increasing the localised temperature of the muscles, specific stretches will aid elasticity, reducing the risk of injury during performance.

It is becoming increasingly accepted that stretching to increase muscle elasticity and joint flexibility needs to be targeted – just like any other training adaptation. As muscle elasticity increases more effectively when the muscle temperature is at its optimum, stretching following activity – during a cool-down – may be a better opportunity than pre-activity stretching during a warm-up.

But it is very difficult to find reliable and accurate data to either support or challenge the advantages

TASK

Categorise the immediate responses to exercise shown in Table 1.1 under the following headings:

Skeletal system	Muscular system	Circulatory system	Respiratory system

List the responses, and for each one identify the functional benefit to the performer.

Try to identify in which stages of the warm-up the immediate effects of exercise would occur.

Response	Functional benefit	Stage/s of warm-up

of pre-activity stretching in relation to preventing injury. So its inclusion in any warm-up should be analysed critically and any risk assessed. Does the risk of undertaking stretching outweigh the risk of not doing so?

The specific types of stretch and their benefits and risks need to be examined in relation to the specific sport. Stretching is thought to benefit flexibility by increasing muscle elasticity. Would increasing the muscle elasticity, and subsequent joint flexibility, aid a performer in this specific activity? If the answer is yes, then the types of stretch to be performed would need to be considered.

STATIC STRETCHING

Static stretching is what many people consider to be 'traditional' stretching. As the name suggests, there is a lack of movement. The performer stretches a muscle to its safe limit and then holds that position for up to 30 seconds, relaxes and repeats.

This is possibly the safest way to stretch, as the performer is always in control of the movement. But it is perhaps the least sports-specific, so if performed as the only method of stretching within a warm-up it would not be considered ideal preparation.

▶ *Is pre-exercise stretching beneficial – or not?*

DYNAMIC STRETCHING

Dynamic stretching consists of controlled movements taking the joint through its full range of movement. This type of stretching is more sports-specific than static stretching. The muscle and joint must be warm before undertaking dynamic stretching, and the movements must always be performed under the control of the performer. Examples include slow, controlled leg swings, arm swings and torso twists.

BALLISTIC STRETCHING

Ballistic stretching also involves movement, but unlike dynamic stretching, this method uses momentum or bouncing to help forcibly stretch the muscle. This momentum, or bouncing action, means the performer is increasing the risk of injury and also increasing the potential for delayed-onset muscle soreness (DOMS) – the pain or discomfort that may be experienced some 24–48 hours after the cessation of exercise. Ballistic stretching alone is unlikely to allow your muscles to adjust to, and relax in, the stretched position. Instead, it may cause them to tighten up by repeatedly activating the stretch reflex.

So ballistic stretching has often been identified as a mode of stretching not to be used in warm-up. On the other hand, ballistic stretching is specific for a great many sports, as these bouncing, explosive movements are replicated as we run, jump, throw, etc. Static stretching, considered safe in comparison, is not particularly sports-specific. The answer is to use a combination of modes of stretching, building up to ballistic stretching if the activity requires it, in order to safely and effectively prepare the muscle for the subsequent activity.

PROPRIOCEPTIVE NEUROMUSCULAR FACILITATION (PNF)

PNF is considered to be an advanced form of flexibility training, rather than a method to be included in a warm-up routine. It involves passive stretching followed by **isometric** contractions of the muscle group being targeted. So it is very good for increasing flexibility and improving muscular strength. An isometric contraction is performed when the muscle is at its greatest length – when it has been stretched – so it is important that the athlete has undergone some prior training.

> ### KEY TERM
> **isometric**
> a type of exercise in which the joint angle and muscle length do not change during contraction

Fig. 1.2 Stretching – (a) active static; (b) active dynamic; (c) passive static; (d) PNF

PASSIVE AND ACTIVE STRETCHING

These are not so much methods of stretching as different ways of performing those methods.

A passive stretch is one where you assume a position and hold it with some other part of your body, or with the assistance of a partner or some other apparatus. For example, when a partner lifts your extended leg and then holds it in place.

Active stretches are when you actively stretch the muscle yourself. For example, if you sit with your legs outstretched in front of you and move your body towards your straight legs yourself, you are being active; if you relax and allow a partner to push your body towards your legs, you are being passive.

SHOULD STRETCHING BE PART OF A WARM-UP?

The recent debate about the value of warming up prior to physical activity really centres on whether an athlete or performer should include any form of static stretching in their warm-up routine. There is research from a small number of studies supporting the theory that long bouts of static stretching may induce temporary *losses* in strength.

But stretching is just one element of the warm-up, and static stretching is likely to be one of several modes of stretching used.

CASE STUDY   PERFORMING A PNF STRETCH

The muscle group to be stretched is positioned so that the muscles are stretched and under tension. The individual then contracts the stretched muscle group for 5–6 seconds while a partner, or immovable object, applies sufficient resistance to inhibit movement. The effort of contraction should be relevant to the level of conditioning.

The contracted muscle group is then relaxed, and a controlled stretch is applied for about 30 seconds. The muscle group is then allowed 30 seconds to recover and the process is repeated between two and four times.

| *Athlete and partner assume the position for the stretch – the partner extends the athlete's limb until the muscle is stretched and tension is felt.* | *The athlete then contracts the stretched muscle for 5–6 seconds, and the partner must inhibit all movement. The force of the contraction should be relevant to the condition of the muscle. For example, if the muscle has been injured, do not apply a maximum contraction.* | *The muscle group is relaxed, then immediately and cautiously pushed past its normal range of movement for about 30 seconds. Allow 30 seconds' recovery before repeating the procedure two to four times.* |

Table 1.2 PNF stretching

Different people make different recommendations about the amounts of time for PNF stretches. Although there are conflicting ideas about how long to contract the muscle group, and how long to rest between each stretch, the above timing recommendations should provide the maximum benefits from PNF stretching.

■ Design PNF exercises that would be safe and suitable for other body parts.

WHAT INTENSITY, AND FOR WHAT DURATION, SHOULD MY WARM-UP BE?

These questions should now be easier to answer. Let us once again go to the end of the warm-up. The objective is to cause suitable physiological (both anatomical and structural) responses so that the athlete:

- is mentally and physically prepared for the activity
- has potentially improved their performance level
- has reduced their risk of incurring injury.

The athlete needs to work at the intensity that will lead to all the responses needed for optimum performance in their chosen activity. So the duration of the warm-up is set not in minutes, but in objectives. When these objectives have been met, the warm-up is complete.

For example, before a 60-minute time trial in the Tour de France, Lance Armstrong would warm up for up to 90 minutes. (This means that he allows up to 90 minutes to achieve his objectives, rather than that he specifies 90 minutes and sticks to it regardless of the results.)

Armstrong knows that he will:

- need to perform at his optimum level from the first second of the race to the last
- be working anaerobically for a significant amount of time
- need his muscles to generate a significant amount of power for quite a long time
- experience high levels of lactic acid
- generate significant amounts of heat.

So his warm-up must prepare him fully for this event. He will begin at a low intensity to generate localised heat so that his muscles can perform effectively. He will gradually increase the intensity until he attains what he perceives will be his race pace for the duration of the race. His body will be generating heat, so it will begin to effectively thermoregulate itself. He will perform some maximal exertion efforts within the warm-up in order to simulate the race, encouraging lactic acid build-up and its consequent transportation, utilisation and breakdown. This will ensure that at the beginning of the race he can perform optimally.

To summarise:

Question	How intense should my warm-up be?
Answer	How intensely will you be working during your performance?
Question	How long should my warm-up last?
Answer	Until you have achieved what you need to achieve.

REMEMBER

We warm up to:
- improve performance
- prepare mentally and physically
- reduce the risk of injury.

▶ Lance Armstrong has specific warm-up practices for specific goals

SOURCES OF ENERGY FOR EXERCISE

The body needs to convert energy-providing food groups into a chemical compound called adenosine triphosphate (ATP), which fuels muscular contraction. The role of the different food groups is covered in detail in the AS units.

Carbohydrate, fat and protein (macronutrients) are the only sources of food energy – so they are called 'energy nutrients'.

Food also contains other nutrients – minerals and vitamins (micronutrients) – but these do not provide energy.

ACCESSING STORED ENERGY

When energy has been stored in the body, there are three mechanisms we can use to convert it back from its stored state into a usable form of ATP – the body's energy currency. These are:

- the aerobic energy system (Figure 1.4)

- the ATP– phosphocreatine (PC) system – also known as the alactic energy system (Figure 1.5) ⎫
- the lactic acid system (Figure 1.6) ⎬ anaerobic

Different mechanisms are dominant at different durations of exercise (see Figure 1.3).

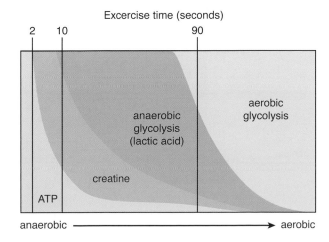

Fig. 1.3 Dominant energy pathways for exercise of different durations

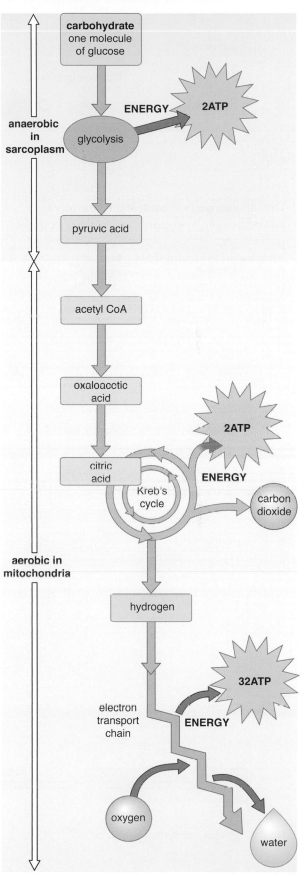

Fig. 1.4 The aerobic system

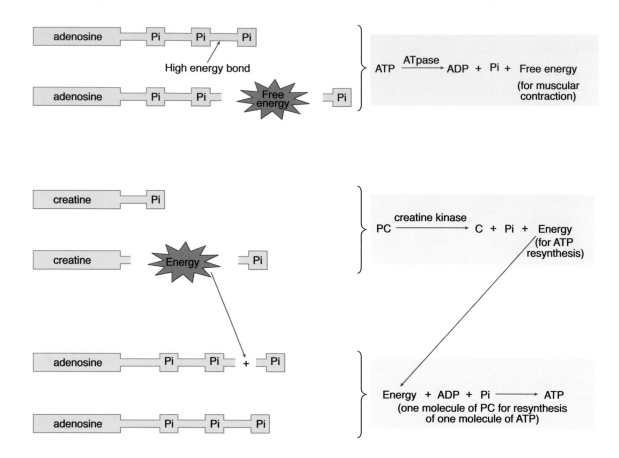

Fig. 1.5 *The ATP–PC system where energy is used for muscular contraction and ATP resynthesis*

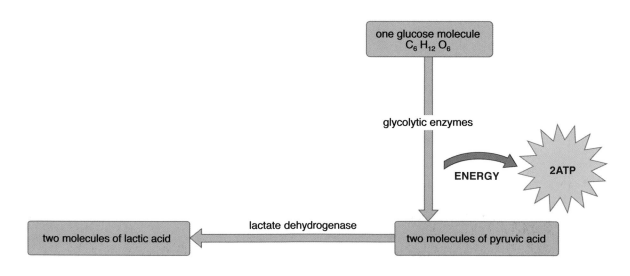

Fig. 1.6 *The lactic acid system*

CARBOHYDRATES

There are three kinds of carbohydrate, as shown in Figure 1.7.

monosaccharides	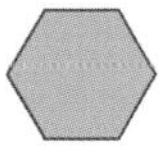	glucose, fructose and galactose		fruit
disaccharides	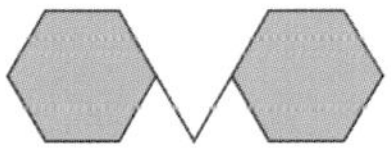	sucrose and maltose	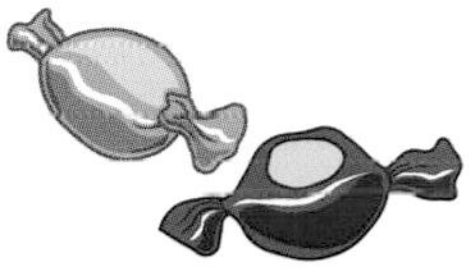	sweets
polysaccharides		glycogen and starch		bread

Fig. 1.7 *The three types of carbohydrate*

Glucose, which is the basic usable form of carbohydrate in the body, is formed as a natural sugar in food, or is produced in the body as a result of the digestion of more complicated carbohydrates. Glucose can be used directly by the cell for energy, stored as glycogen in the muscle and liver, or converted to fat as an energy store.

Blood glucose levels are regulated mainly through the glycogen stored in the liver. A constant blood glucose level, within a narrow physiological range, is important as this is the primary energy source for the nervous system. Glycogen metabolism in the liver regulates the blood glucose level. After meals, glucose is taken up by the liver with the help of a hormone called insulin, leading to storage of liver glycogen. During the night or during fasting, liver glycogen is broken down, with the help of a hormone called glucagon, by a process called glycogenolysis, which maintains a normal blood glucose level. Muscle glycogen is designed to serve as a rapid energy source, which can be made available in a situation of sudden, intensive muscular work.

STORAGE AND RELEASE

Glycogen is made up of chains of glucose molecules, and forms the carbohydrate stores for the body to utilise during exercise. In a process known as glycolysis, these glycogen molecules are broken down in both aerobic and anaerobic exercise.

This process involves the glucose molecules (which constitute glycogen) being removed one at a time, and released into the bloodstream or muscle cells so that they may be further broken down to release energy.

In the bloodstream, glucose (derived from fats and carbohydrates) may be:

- sent directly to the muscles for the release of energy
- converted into glycogen for storage in the muscles or liver
- converted into lipids and stored as fat.

If the body does not need the glucose, it enters the fat metabolic system, where it is converted to fatty acids and glycerol, and is stored in the body as triglycerides (body fat) in adipose tissue and skeletal muscle. When energy is required from the fat reserves, the triglycerides are broken down into glycerol and free fatty acids, which are then transported to the liver, where they are converted to glucose. The majority of the body's glycogen is stored in the liver, with the remainder being stored in the muscles.

So a function of the liver is to convert glycogen into glucose when it is needed for energy production during periods of prolonged exercise.

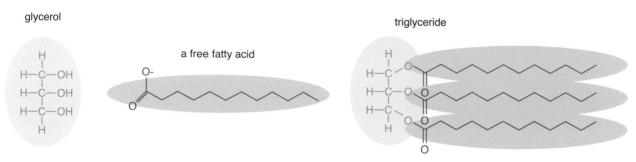

Fig. 1.8 *A triglyceride – one molecule of glycerol and three molecules of free fatty acids*

Other hormones that take part in the conversion of fat into carbohydrate are adrenaline and glucagon.

Adrenaline is secreted by the adrenal glands, and is associated with the 'fight-or-flight' reaction in stressful situations. One effect of this reaction is to promote the conversion of fats into glucose for use as an immediate energy source.

Glucagon has the opposite effect to insulin – it promotes the conversion of fats and glycogen to glucose. It is utilised by the body when blood sugar levels are low.

FATS

Fats, or lipids, are present in the body mainly as triglycerides, fatty acids and cholesterol.

The basic structure of triglycerides is one molecule of glycerol and three molecules of free fatty acids (Figure 1.8). Stores of triglycerides are found in the adipose (fat) tissue and in the skeletal muscle.

A free fatty acid that has its carbon atoms saturated with hydrogen atoms is referred to as a saturated fatty acid (Figure 1.9). Consumption of large amounts of saturated fats is thought to lead to high blood cholesterol levels and coronary heart disease. Saturated fat includes most animal fat, such as pork, beef and lamb.

Unsaturated fats are fatty acids that do not have their carbon atoms saturated with hydrogen atoms. These fats are in a liquid state at room temperature. They are found in vegetable oils such as peanut oil, corn oil and soybean oil.

As with glycogen, the synthesis of fat or its breakdown depends on the concentration of the building blocks, in this case fatty acids. This concentration is determined mainly by uptake or release of free fatty acids, in and from triglycerides, and their withdrawal for energy metabolism. When energy production is low, the supply of fatty acids after a meal will lead to an increase in the fatty acid concentration in the cell. If the energy requirement increases, fatty acids will be used in energy production. This results in a decrease in the fatty acid concentration, which stimulates the breakdown of triglycerides into glycerol and free fatty acids to compensate. This process is caused by a large number of interactions, in which hormonal and nervous influences play a major role.

Two major fuel forms of fat available to the muscle during exercise are free fatty acids mobilised from adipose tissue, and triglycerides from within the muscle cells.

saturated fats			animal fats
unsaturated fat			vegetable oils

Fig. 1.9 *Saturated and unsaturated fats*

PROTEINS

The basic structural units of proteins are amino acids. Foods that are richest in essential amino acids are animal proteins and milk. Common sources of protein are cereal, cheese, eggs, fish, lean meat and liver. The proteins in the body are either part of tissue structures (structural proteins), or part of metabolic systems such as transport, hormone or enzyme systems (functional proteins).

We do not have a protein store, as is the case with carbohydrate (stored in the liver and muscles as glycogen), or fat (stored in the adipose tissue as triglycerides). Although the role of protein in providing energy has not been considered important for most forms of muscular activity, it is becoming increasingly clear that protein metabolism is increased during endurance exercise.

SOURCES OF ENERGY – SUMMARY

- Carbohydrates, fats, proteins, water, minerals and vitamins are essential elements of the human diet.
- Carbohydrates, fats and proteins are the energy nutrients – they are used as food fuels during metabolism.
- Carbohydrate is stored as glucose in the liver and muscles, and is the most effective source of high-intensity energy – it requires less oxygen to be burnt than either protein or fat.
- The normal body stores of carbohydrate in a typical athlete are shown in Table 1.3.

	Liver glycogen (g)	Muscle glycogen (g)
Male athlete, 70 kg	90	400
Female athlete, 60 kg	70	300

Table 1.3 Glycogen stores in a typical athlete

- During hard exercise, carbohydrate can be depleted at a rate of 3–4 g per minute.
- If this is sustained for 90 minutes or more, a very large fraction of the total body carbohydrate stores will be exhausted, and if not checked will result in reduced performance.
- Recovery of the muscle and liver glycogen stores after exercise normally requires 24–48 hours for complete recovery.

- Fats are found in the body as triglycerides, phospholipids and cholesterol.
- Triglycerides are stored in the skeletal muscles and in the fat cells, and are made up of glycerol and free fatty acids.
- Usage of carbohydrates and fats depends on the intensity and duration of exercise.

Energy source	Main functions	Used as energy fuel when:
Carbohydrates	High-intensity energy	intensity of exercise is at a level that cannot be sustained through metabolisation of fats in the aerobic energy system
Fats	Low-intensity fuel Insulation	intensity of exercise is at a medium to low level and energy requirements can be met through metabolisation of fats in the aerobic energy system
Proteins	Muscle tissue growth Muscle tissue repair Energy	the athlete has eaten a very low-carbohydrate diet or is experiencing a famine, or towards the end of an ultra-distance event

Table 1.4 The three main energy sources and their functions

MANIPULATING THE DIET

Athletic performance improves with wise nutrition and crumbles with a poor diet. So it is important, if not essential, for any serious athlete to give due consideration to their diet.

This involves ensuring that:
- adequate fuel is consumed to facilitate the intensity and duration of training
- fuel stores are full before a performance
- fuel stores are supplemented during the activity as required
- fuel stores are replenished immediately after the end of exercise
- supplementation (with vitamins such as B vitamins, zinc, etc.) is undertaken to ensure the body can utilise the nutrients required

- adequate hydration is maintained, both before and during performance
- adequate protein is consumed to enable the necessary growth and repair of muscle tissue.

And as athletes, particularly at elite level, are seeking to gain an advantage, the next question is, how can they improve on this?

CARBOHYDRATE LOADING

> ### KEY TERM
> **carbohydrate loading**
> a legal method of attempting to boost the amount of glycogen in the body before a competition or event

Fig. 1.10 *Sources of carbohydrate*

Carbohydrate loading was the strategy practised at the BBC's sponsored 'pasta party' the night before the earliest London Marathons. There is some logic in what is described – but it falls down at the point of consuming excess complex carbohydrates just before the event. Why would the body store the excess as muscle glycogen simply because you intend to run a marathon the following day? Why would your body not simply convert and store the excess as fat, as it would on any other occasion? The answer is that this is exactly what does happen.

With training adaptations, you have to force your body to adapt. The body must be 'convinced' that adapting is in its best interests because that is the easiest and most efficient way of proceeding.

Adaptations can be best appreciated when examining the supercompensation graph (see Figure 1.12, page 17).

For the body to need to increase its muscle glycogen levels, it must be stressed. That stress will not come from simply depleting the current muscle glycogen stores, as this is what happens regularly in training. The body is then usually refuelled with carbohydrates immediately after exercise. So if this refuelling does not take place, then that will cause a new stress for the body – potentially a stress great enough to encourage it to hold on to additional carbohydrates, in the form of muscle glycogen, the next time they become available.

Fig. 1.11 *The old argument in favour of carbohydrate loading*

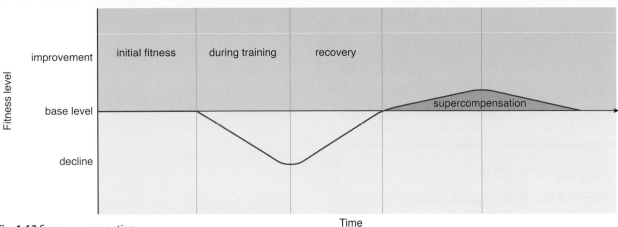

Fig. 1.12 *Supercompensation*

APPLY IT!

Complete a table similar to the one below to plan your 7-day carbohydrate-loading programme.

Day	Activity (intensity and duration)	Diet (high- or low-carb)	Objective (decrease, maintain or replenish)
1			
2			
3			
4			
5			
6			
Race day			

INGESTION AND DIGESTIVE RATES

To measure carbohydrate requirements per day, multiply your weight (in kg) by 5. This gives the amount of carbohydrate required per day in grams by a normal (or sedentary) person. Protein intake is normally at 1 g per kg of body weight.

Intake	Calories
1 g carbohydrate	4
1 g protein	4
1 g fat	10

Table 1.5 *The three main energy sources and their calorific values*

During performance, your body can digest approximately 1 g of carbohydrate per kg of body weight per hour. So a 70 kg athlete can only digest 70 g of carbs per hour (280 calories). But they could quite easily use or burn more than 600 calories per hour, which would equate to 150 g of carbs. So supplementation (with energy gels, energy bars, electrolytes, etc.) during a long-distance event will not prevent muscle glycogen and blood glucose depletion, it will just delay it. The answer is to condition your body to burn fat at a higher intensity of exercise, thus saving your muscle glycogen and blood glucose stores.

TASK

Plan the dietary intake for a 24-hour period for two contrasting athletes of your choice.

CASE STUDY
EATING FOR VICTORY

US swimmer Michael Phelps is one of the top Olympians of all time, with a record-breaking 14 gold medals. The secret behind his six-days-a-week, five-hours-a-day training regime is an extraordinary 12,000-calorie daily diet – six times the intake of a normal adult male. Calories in a typical day come from:

Morning: A bowl of grits; three fried egg sandwiches; cheese; tomatoes; lettuce; fried onions; mayonnaise; a five-egg omelette; three sugar-coated slices of egg-covered bread; three chocolate-chip pancakes; two cups of coffee

Midday: Half-kilogram (one pound) of enriched pasta; two large ham and cheese sandwiches with mayonnaise on white bread; energy drinks

Evening: Half-kilogram of pasta, with carbonara sauce; large pizza; energy drinks.

■ How does this diet work for Michael Phelps. And why would it not work for you?

▶ *Michael Phelps on 12,000-calories a day*

HYDRATION

Without doubt, water is the single most important nutrient to the athlete, as shown in Table 1.6.

Body weight lost as sweat (%)	Physiological effect	Performance effect
1		Loss of 5%
2	Impaired performance	Loss of 10%
4	Capacity for muscular work declines	Loss of 25%
5	Heat exhaustion	Potential failure to complete
7	Hallucinations	Potentially fatal
10	Circulatory collapse and heat stroke	Potentially fatal

Table 1.6 The effects of water loss

With water loss through sweat comes an additional problem of **electrolyte** loss. The most important electrolyte lost in sweat is sodium. A consequence of this is that water alone will not be sufficient to rehydrate the performer. Electrolytes are often essential minerals, they control osmosis of water between body compartments and help to maintain the acid–base balance required for normal cellular activities.

KEY TERMS

electrolytes
substances containing free ions – they play a vital role in maintaining **homeostasis** in the body, helping to regulate and manage the water and fluid levels

homeostasis
how the body regulates its internal environment to maintain a stable, constant condition

REHYDRATION

If no action is taken, the loss of body fluids and electrolytes will lead to dehydration, and eventually to circulatory collapse and heat stroke. The effect of fluid loss on the body is shown in Table 1.6.

Once you experience thirst, it is safe to assume you are already in at least the early stages of dehydration. If you experience thirst during an event, you will not be able to attain full hydration levels again unless you stop exercising. This is because the rate at which you can absorb fluids will be lower than the rate at which you lose them.

Drinking plain water causes bloating, and suppresses thirst and thus further drinking. It stimulates urine output, and so is inefficiently retained. So water might not be the best choice. Add to this the fact that water contains no carbohydrate or electrolytes, and we begin to see that there might be better alternatives available. Electrolytes in a drink, especially sodium and potassium, will reduce urine output, enable the fluid to empty quickly from the stomach, promote absorption from the intestine, and encourage fluid retention.

Two main factors affect the speed at which fluid from a drink gets into the body:

- the speed at which it is emptied from the stomach
- the rate at which it is absorbed through the walls of the small intestine.

To sustain a rapid movement of fluid into your small intestine during your exertions, if possible take three to four sips of beverage every 10 minutes, or five to six swallows every 15 minutes.

Ideally, when performing an endurance event you should plan your hydration strategy so that you lose no more than 2 per cent of your pre-race weight. This can be achieved in the following way:

- record your body weight immediately before and after a number of training sessions, along with details of distance/duration, clothing and weather conditions
- add the amount of fluid taken during the session to the amount of weight lost: 1 kg is roughly equivalent to 1 litre of fluid
- after a few weeks, you should begin to see some patterns emerging and can calculate your sweat rate per hour
- once you know what your sweat losses are likely to be in a given set of environmental conditions, you can plan your drinking strategy for specific events.

APPLY IT!

Using the list above as a guide, work out your own sweat rate per hour.

SUPPLEMENTS

There are three types of sports drink, all of which contain various levels of fluid, electrolytes and carbohydrate. These are isotonic, hypotonic and hypertonic drinks, defined by the percentage make-up, or **osmolality**, of their components.

REMEMBER

If you are exercising for an hour or less, water has been shown to perform as well as energy drinks.

KEY TERM

osmolality
a measure of the number of particles in a solution. In a drink, the particles in solution comprise carbohydrates, electrolytes, sweeteners and preservatives. In blood plasma, the particles comprise sodium, proteins and glucose. Blood has an osmolality of 280 to 330 milliosmoles (mOsm) per kg. The higher the carbohydrate levels in a drink, the more slowly the stomach will be emptied.

- Drinks with an osmolality of 270–330 mOsm per kg are said to be in balance with the body's fluid, and are called **isotonic**.
- **Hypotonic** fluids have fewer particles than blood.
- **Hypertonic** fluids have more particles than blood.

▶ *It is vital to avoid electrolyte loss*

Consuming fluids with a low osmolality (e.g. water) results in a fall in blood plasma osmolality, and reduces the drive to drink before sufficient fluid has been consumed to replace losses.

Isotonic drinks with a carbohydrate level of between 6 and 8 per cent are emptied from the stomach at a rate similar to that of water.

During exercise, there is increased uptake of blood glucose by the muscles. To prevent blood glucose levels from falling, the liver produces glucose from its stores.

Consuming carbohydrate before, during and after exercise will help prevent blood glucose levels falling too low, and will also help to maintain the body's glycogen stores.

Many athletes cannot consume food before or during exercise, so a formulated drink that will provide carbohydrate is needed.

Blood will have a typical osmotic value of 5 per cent (glucose concentration). This means that a glucose solution greater than 5 per cent (5 g in 100 ml) will empty only very slowly from the stomach. A glucose solution of a lower percentage value will enter the blood stream much more quickly, but this means taking in a lot more liquid. For example, a 100 ml drink containing 3 per cent glucose will be very quickly absorbed, but a total volume of 200 ml will only contain 6 per cent (6 g) of carbohydrate.

At this concentration, a moderately active cyclist – who would use between 500 and 750 calories per hour – would need to drink about 5 litres per hour! (600 calories = 150 g of carbohydrate: at 3 g per 100 ml, the cyclist would need to consume 50 × 100 ml drinks = 5000 ml = 5 litres in order to obtain the required 150 g of carbohydrate.)

So in order to get carbohydrates into the body quickly, a low concentration is required – but a lot of volume is necessary because of the low concentration. The example above illustrates that the trade-off of absorbing the energy quickly would be impractical for a cyclist.

In response to this problem, many sports nutrition companies use glucose polymers, which are far less osmotically active. Some drinks can be 50 per cent glucose concentration, while still being isotonic. This allows far more glucose (up to 10 times more) to be consumed in a smaller volume of drink.

Type	Content	Glucose content (volume)
Isotonic	Fluid, electrolytes and 6–8% carbohydrate	Similar to blood or the body
Hypotonic	Fluids, electrolytes and a low level of carbohydrate	Less than blood or the body
Hypertonic	High level of carbohydrate	Greater than blood/body

Table 1.7 Which type of sports drink is the best?

REMEMBER

Cold drinks are not absorbed any more quickly than warm ones.

Most commercial sports drinks fall within a carbohydrate concentration of about 5–7 per cent. But recent research, carried out at Liverpool University, indicates that cyclists who ingested a 15 per cent maltodextrin solution improved their endurance by 30 per cent, compared with individuals who took a 5 per cent glucose drink.

TASK

Using the facts provided in this chapter regarding grams of carbohydrate required per hour versus calorific expenditure, the amount of water and other supplementation required per hour, and the different forms in which these can be obtained, calculate the calories required by a 65 kg cyclist who is racing for 6 hours in the French sun.

Calculate scientifically the advantage this cyclist would have over a cyclist of similar weight, in the same race, who took only water during the race.

CREATINE LOADING

As early as 1912, it was discovered that creatine ingestion could significantly increase the creatine content within skeletal muscle. And during the 1920s it was found that ingesting larger quantities than normally required enhances muscular performance. But creatine came into public view when British Olympic athletes Linford Christie, Sally Gunnell and many of the rowing squad all used creatine in their preparation for the 1992 Olympics. In 2004 the first creatine ethyl ester supplements were launched.

While creatine is effective in treating many muscular, neuromuscular and neurodegenerative diseases, its usefulness as a performance enhancing food supplement in sports has been questioned. Despite this – and perhaps because of its popularity – some have proposed that its use as a performance enhancer should be banned.

Ingesting creatine can increase the level of phosphocreatine (PC) in the muscles by up to 20 per cent. There is scientific evidence that taking creatine supplements can marginally increase athletic performance in high-intensity anaerobic repetitive cycling sprints, but studies on swimmers and runners have been less promising, possibly due to the weight gain involved.

Creatine has no significant effect on aerobic endurance, though it will increase power during anaerobic exercise (see Figure 1.5, page 12). Creatine is often taken by athletes as a supplement for those wishing to gain muscle mass (bodybuilding).

A number of methods for ingestion exist, with powder or tablets being the most popular. Manufacturers suggest mixing the powder with high glycaemic-index carbohydrate drinks such as grape juice and some proteins, for maximum benefit.

Researchers differ regarding the value of taking creatine. Rapid weight gains have been found to occur in athletes who are taking the supplement – but the reason for this weight gain is unclear. Some researchers argue that it is due to water retention (apparently supported by the fact that much of the weight gained is lost once the athlete stops using the supplement). Other research suggests that

▶ *Creatine is popular among those aiming to gain muscle mass*

the strength gains made while taking creatine are proportional to the additional weight gained in terms of lean muscle mass. In other words, during the time of taking creatine, athletes might have experienced an increase in muscle mass. This increase in muscle mass was proportionate to the increase in strength also experienced.

So there is a lack of conclusive scientific data in support of creatine supplementation – but equally, there is a lack of information regarding the potential harm (if any) to the athlete from creatine supplementation.

Creatine use is not considered doping (see Chapter 3, page 51), and is not banned by the majority of sport governing bodies. However, in the USA the National Collegiate Athletic Association recently ruled that colleges could not provide creatine supplements to their players, although the players are still allowed to obtain and use creatine independently. In some countries, such as France, creatine use is banned.

CASE STUDY
PRE-MATCH ACTIVITIES

Thirty years ago, pre-match activity for a professional footballer would have been a meal of steak and chips at 12:00 noon with a cup of sweet tea, followed by a second cup of sweet tea at 2:30 p.m. They would leave the changing rooms at 2:50 p.m., and go through some stretches and passing before beginning the game at 3:00 p.m. Half-time would consist of segments of orange and another cup of sweet tea.

■ Attempt to justify the pre-match activities of a professional footballer of the 1970s.

STRETCH AND CHALLENGE

Research the pre-match activities of a modern-day professional sportsperson, contrasting what happens now with what used to happen 30 years ago.

▶ *Rahman defeated world heavyweight champion Lewis at altitude*

SHORT-TERM ACCLIMATISATION – ENVIRONMENTAL FACTORS

The environment can have a huge effect on performance. For example, US boxer Hasim Rahman pulled off one of the most stunning upsets in boxing history in 2001, defeating the undisputed world champion Lennox Lewis at odds of 15:1. The altitude of the fight location in South Africa was held to be partly responsible.

A realisation by athletes that being fully prepared for an event means considering every influencing factor has led to unprecedented consideration and thought being directed towards the environment.

Factors such as temperature (cold as well as heat), humidity, altitude, pollution, prevailing winds and the playing surface are all taken into account before competition.

Performing in environments that have a prevailing wind can be problematic for most sports: events such as sailing that utilise the wind would clearly be affected, but also events where the wind can be a factor, such as cycling and ball sports. Consideration of traits will allow performers to plan accordingly and enable them to adapt styles and or techniques.

Other environments that have high levels of pollution will present athletes with different issues. The higher levels of pollution will affect the respiratory functioning of the performer. If the event is of an aerobic nature, then pollution could effectively lower the VO_2 max of the performer. Prior knowledge of this not only will help the athlete to adapt, but would inform them of the need to perform at a slightly lower intensity.

HEAT ACCLIMATISATION

In hot climates, the problem is not maintaining body heat, but dissipating it.

In cold climates, the athlete needs to consider the extra clothing required, and the consequent weight and drag effects of the clothing. From a physiological perspective, extra clothing will generally lead to additional sweating, which needs to be met with additional hydration strategies.

Adaptation to hot climates is of two types: adaptation to humid heat and to dry heat (desert conditions).

Ordinarily, the body will lose excess heat by sweating. In conditions of humid heat, however, the humidity of the surrounding air prevents the evaporation of perspiration to some extent, and overheating may result.

In a drier heat, the body is better able to lose heat through sweating as the atmosphere will absorb the moisture better. The danger then becomes one of dehydration, as the athlete may not realise how much they are sweating as the sweat evaporates quickly from the skin.

The body does have the ability to adapt to its surroundings. If training and lifestyle are monitored, near-complete adaptation to heat (heat acclimatisation) can take place in up to 14 days.

Individuals will vary in their responses and adaptations to heat, but evidence supports the fact that trained athletes with a higher **VO₂ max** will adapt to heat more quickly. The main benefit of heat acclimatisation is an improved tolerance of the heat, allowing the athlete to perform as they would in more equable temperatures without incurring heat-related illnesses.

KEY TERMS

VO₂ max
(maximal oxygen consumption, **maximal oxygen uptake** or **aerobic capacity**) – the maximum capacity of an individual's body to take in, transport and utilise oxygen, per minute, per kg body weight. Often referred to as a measure of the aerobic fitness of the individual.

For technical methods of dealing with heat, see below.

PHYSIOLOGICAL RESPONSES TO HEAT

The early adaptations to heat (during the initial one to five days) involve

- expanded plasma volume (see page 25)
- improved control of cardiovascular function
- reduced heart rate
- autonomic nervous system habituation (this involves the more long-term redirection of cardiac output to skin capillary beds and active muscles that might be expected during some extreme endurance events).

During exercise in the heat, the regulation of body temperature is critical to heat acclimatisation – if the body overheats (**hyperthermia**), death becomes a serious possibility. When you exercise in the heat, adaptations occur that facilitate temperature regulation:

- increased sweat rate
- earlier onset of sweat production
- cardiovascular adjustments.

These responses together can significantly reduce central body temperature. This response is maximised after five to eight days' heat acclimatisation.

KEY TERMS

hypothermia
a condition in which the body temperature drops below that required for normal metabolism and bodily functions

hyperthermia
an acute condition that occurs when the body produces or absorbs more heat than it can dissipate (sometimes referred to as heat stroke or sunstroke)

Heat acclimatisation performed in hot-humid conditions stimulates a higher sweat rate than heat acclimatisation in a hot-dry environment. Also, the absolute rate of sweating influences thermoregulation. Another initial adaptation is the body's ability to reduce the amount of sodium chloride (essential electrolytes) lost during sweating. The sodium chloride losses in sweat and urine decrease during days three to nine of heat acclimatisation, but revert back to normal levels of loss once full heat acclimatisation has taken place.

It might seem surprising, but excess dietary water and electrolytes do not speed up the process of heat acclimatisation. Consistent daily monitoring of body weight is required to ensure that a state of dehydration does not develop. If weight levels drop by 3 per cent, then it is advised that training intensity should be reduced by up to 6 per cent.

When exercise is intense and core body temperature rises markedly, the plasma cortisol concentration increases during the initial days of heat acclimatisation, but returns to control levels after eight days of heat acclimatisation, reflecting the reduction in total body strain. During heat acclimatisation, there seems to be a clear effect on performance in submaximal activities, with oxygen uptake being reduced. The increased blood flow to the skin, which would reduce central blood volume, venous return to the heart and cardiac output, is thought to be the cause of this loss in submaximal VO_2.

The physiological adaptations to heat acclimatisation may disappear after only a few weeks of inactivity (18–28 days). The first adaptations to be lost are those that develop first: heart rate and other cardiovascular variables. The rate of loss of other adaptations is affected by the length of stay and performance in the heat, and also by the level of aerobic fitness –athletes with high VO_2 max usually lose heat acclimatisation adaptations more slowly than individuals with low VO_2 max.

GETTING IT WRONG – HEAT ILLNESS

The most common heat illnesses among athletes are heat cramps, heat syncope (fainting) and heat exhaustion.

HEAT CRAMPS

Cramps usually occur in the muscles of the legs, arms and abdomen after several hours of strenuous exercise, in individuals who have lost a large volume of sweat, have drunk a large volume of hypotonic fluid (see page 19), and who have excreted a small volume of urine. Sodium depletion probably causes heat cramps.

HEAT SYNCOPE

Heat syncope or fainting occurs most commonly during the first three to five days of heat exposure. This is due to the vascular shunting of blood to the skin in order to cool down, and the consequent reduction in venous return and subsequent drop in cardiac output, in turn leading to a drop in blood pressure.

HEAT EXHAUSTION

This is the most commonly diagnosed form of heat illness among athletes, despite the fact that its symptoms are often vague, and differ greatly from

▶ *A ball boy suffers from heat exhaustion on centre court at Wimbledon*

one situation to another. Clinical descriptions include various combinations of headache, dizziness, fatigue, hyperirritability, tachycardia, hyperventilation, diarrhoea, hypotension, nausea, vomiting, syncope, heat cramps and 'heat sensations' in the head and upper torso. This explains why heat exhaustion is defined as the inability to continue exercise in a hot environment.

INCREASED PLASMA VOLUME

An athlete undergoing heat acclimatisation may experience a temporary increase in blood plasma volume during the initial stages of acclimatisation. An increased production of plasma proteins, added to the increased concentration of electrolytes such as sodium chloride (see page 19), produces a temporary increase in blood plasma volume. This increase is likely during the first five days of exercise and heat exposure, but it is temporary, with levels reverting to normal during days 8–14 of heat acclimatisation.

HYDRATION PLANNING

Attention to hydration, and awareness of the potentially damaging effects of dehydration, are especially important in hot conditions. Hydration planning is a vital element of acclimatisation, and is covered on pages 19–20.

EFFECTS OF ALTITUDE

Aerobic performance at altitude is more difficult, so rates of performance decline when compared with those attainable at sea level. At higher altitude, the partial pressure of oxygen (ppO_2) is reduced. This leads to a reduction in the driving pressure for oxygen transport, and a corresponding fall in VO_2 max of around 5–7 per cent per 1000 metres.

An increase in altitude of as little as 600 metres has been shown to decrease the performance of many endurance athletes. The greater the altitude, the greater the severity of **hypoxia** and the more difficult the subsequent performance.

KEY TERMS

hypoxia
a shortage of oxygen in the body

hypoxemia
a deficiency in the concentration of dissolved oxygen in arterial blood. Hypoxemia is different from hypoxia, which is an abnormally low oxygen availability to the body or an individual tissue or organ. The type of hypoxia that is caused by hypoxemia is referred to as hypoxemic hypoxia.

ALTITUDE TRAINING

This information has been used by elite athletes and coaches in an attempt to boost their aerobic performance. The theory is that if it is difficult to perform at altitude, then training there will lead to adaptations that will enable athletes to perform better. Once this has happened, and the athlete returns to sea level, they will be a significantly aerobically fitter.

The effects on athletic performance of training (and, more recently, sleeping) at high altitude have been studied in the West for more than 30 years. During that time, these practices have become an almost essential aspect of the preparation of world-class competitors.

That physical training at high altitude improves performance at high altitude is not in doubt. But studies assessing performance improvements at sea level after training at higher altitudes have produced ambiguous and inconclusive results.

Training method	Result
Live High – Train High LHTH	maximum exposure to altitude – but evidence of a positive effect at sea level is controversial
Live Low – Train High LLTH	exercise in a low-oxygen environment but rest in a normal oxygen environment – some positive findings, but still no real evidence of any difference to competitive performance at sea level; training intensity is reduced so some may find they actually lose fitness with this regime
Live High – Train Low LHTL	acclimatise to altitude by living there (for more than 12 hours per day over at least 3 weeks), while maintaining training intensity at or near sea level – improvements in sea-level performance have been shown in events lasting 8–20 minutes; athletes of all abilities are thought to benefit

Table 1.8 Three different altitude training regimes

► *Pete Reed, a member of the Great Britain rowing squad, took this photo while altitude training at Silvretta Lake, Austria*

inspired, transported and made available for athletic performance.

The consequence of this is that the athlete has to significantly decrease both their training intensity and volume – not a desirable position for any elite athlete.

Because of the effects of this traditional method of altitude training, where the athlete lives high and trains high (LHTH), many coaches began to experiment with a variation on the theme – live high train low (LHTL) (see Table 1.8). Athletes either physically live at altitude, or sleep in a hypoxic (low-oxygen) chamber.

Results regarding the benefits derived from this method vary. These athletes experienced initial increases in **erythropoietin** (EPO) levels and consequent red blood cell production. After prolonged exposure, it was found that both erythropoietin and red blood cell levels returned to levels similar to those when the training began. However, gains in VO_2 max were retained.

Maintaining high red blood cell levels is dependent on high levels of erythropoietin – and both are stressful and potentially harmful to the body. The gains of LHTL must therefore be attributed to other physiological benefits that produce a more efficient use of oxygen, namely increased vascularisation of the muscles, and increased levels of myoglobin and of mitochondrial density.

> ## KEY TERM
> **erythropoietin**
> a glycoprotein hormone that controls production of red blood cells

RESPONSES AND ADAPTATIONS

On first arriving at altitude, trained subjects have no greater advantage over untrained individuals beyond that which existed at sea level. Being fit does not alter the form or rate of adaptation to altitude. On arrival at altitude, there is what can best be described as a 'detraining effect', as less oxygen is

BLOOD RESPONSES

An increased number of red blood cells and increased haemoglobin concentration are seen. This is rapid in the first few weeks at altitude, and serves to increase the oxygen content of the arterial blood. However, it might take as long as three months for the body to finally adapt and achieve the optimum level of red blood cells for the altitude.

A training period of three weeks at moderate altitudes will result in an individual increase of haemoglobin concentration of about 1–4 per cent. This is primarily due to the haematological (blood) adaptations that occur in humans in response to a hypoxic environment.

The resulting decrease in arterial oxygen saturation (**hypoxemia**), brought about by the lower partial pressure of oxygen, produces a series of physiological responses similar to those experienced after donating blood, or following periods of intense aerobic training at sea level.

The responses ultimately result in an increase in the production of red blood cells, a condition known as polycythaemia. The production of red blood cells helps to improve the oxygen-carrying capacity of the blood, and hence maximal oxygen uptake (VO$_2$ max). This increase in red blood cell level is brought about largely by increased secretion of erythropoietin by the kidney, which stimulates red blood cell production in the bone marrow (hence the illegal practice of injecting erythropoietin to boost red blood cell production). This, in turn, can lead to a loss of bone density, so extra dietary supplementation of iron is advised.

The normal difference in haemoglobin concentrations can be estimated to be about 12 per cent between permanent residents at sea level and those at 2500 metres above sea level. This difference indicates an adaptation time of about 12 weeks.

HYPERVENTILATION

The hyperventilation (or increased pulmonary ventilation) response is immediate on arrival at altitude. It is more pronounced during the first few days, and then stabilises after about a week.

OTHER RESPONSES

- Elimination of bicarbonate (HCO$_3^-$) in the urine – its main function is to maintain blood pH at near-normal levels.

- Increased muscle and tissue capillarisation – the growth of more capillaries within the muscles enables more blood to be delivered into the muscle.

- Increased myoglobin concentration – this enables the tissue to extract more oxygen from the blood, and also to remove more CO$_2$.

- Increased mitochondrial density – this enables greater and faster production of ATP through aerobic respiration.

- Enzyme changes that enhance the oxidative capacity – greater quantities and more availability of the enzymes used during respiration.

It is essential to acclimatise to altitude if your performance is to be at altitude. But if your performance is at sea level, prolonged exposure to living at altitude while training at sea level appears to offer the most physiological benefits, without the drawback of the initial detraining effect experienced when training and living at altitude.

HOTLINKS

The Stretching Institute offers the Internet's largest collection of stretching, flexibility and sports injury articles – www.thestretchinghandbook.com

The lead agency for development of the UK Coaching System – www.sportscoach.co.uk

Science in Sport provides nutritional advice and products to athletes – www.scienceinsport.com

Encyclopedia of Sports Medicine and Science, a useful resource provided by the online journal *Sportscience* – www.sportsci.org

ExamCafé
Relax, refresh, result!

Refresh your memory

SURPRISE

Revision checklist

▷ Know about the warm-up:
- o how to warm up
- o why we warm up
- o the physiological benefits of a warm-up
- o intensity and duration.

▷ Understand how to manipulate the diet
- o the energy-providers
- o different energy for different activities
- o how to supplement
- o carbohydrate loading.

▷ Understand hydration
- o what it is
- o why it is important
- o how to avoid dehydration.

▷ Know how to supplement during performance
- o with what, when and how much
- o creatine supplementation.

▷ Understand the need for short-term acclimatisation
- o acclimatising to the weather – heat acclimatisation
- o how to acclimatise
- o dangers of not acclimatising
- o acclimatising to altitude
- o effects of performing at altitude
- o strategies such as LHTH and LHTL
- o responses and adaptations that occur.

Get the result!

Sample question and answer

Exam questions

a. Identify reasons why an athlete would warm up before exercise. **(3 marks)**

b. Describe a warm-up for a named activity, identifying the different stages involved. State the aims of each stage and describe how they are achieved. **(9 marks)**

examiner's tips

When reading an examination question, first identify how many things have been asked of you. Then allocate the marks available – what, specifically, do you have to do to score the marks?

Examiner says;

The candidate has worked out that the question requires identification of three things, and has written succinctly, not wasting time writing unnecessarily.

Student answer – candidate A

a. You would warm up before exercising for lots of reasons. Warming up would increase your temperature, increase your heart rate, and increase the level of carbon dioxide in the blood.

Examiner says;

But the candidate has not really understood the question, which asks for *reasons why* an athlete would warm up – in other words, what is the athlete hoping to get from the warm-up? The three things identified in the candidate's answer are responses that would result from activities undertaken during the warm-up. These responses would contribute to providing the benefits that are sought – but you don't warm up to increase your build-up of carbon dioxide, you warm up to enjoy the benefits that an increased level of carbon dioxide can provide. This answer would score no marks.

Examiner says;

This candidate has written a lot of accurate information regarding warming up. However, they have done what a lot of candidates do – they recite information on the topic of the question, but without actually answering the question.
The candidate unfortunately only scores one mark for stating that the warm-up would reduce the risk of injury.

Student answer — candidate B

a. You would warm up to reduce the risk of injury. You would do this by stretching, firstly using static stretches and then moving on to dynamic stretches. You should not stretch cold but should do some gross motor activities first in order to raise your temperature.

model answer

Any three of the following would have scored the maximum marks available:

- to prepare physically for the activity
- to prepare mentally for the activity
- to reduce the risk of injury
- to improve performance.

CHAPTER 2 SHORT-TERM PSYCHOLOGICAL PREPARATION

LEARNING OUTCOMES

By working through this chapter, you should be able to:

■ discuss the effects of motivation and stress control in short-term preparation for sport

■ outline and suggest strategies to aid mental short-term preparation

■ explain the external influences that can affect a performer's short-term psychological preparation

In this section we take a look at how performers can prepare mentally for sport in the last few hours before competition. Sport provides considerable uncertainty – this fact alone can increase the stress levels of competitors. Stress and uncertainty may motivate some athletes, but may also induce anxiety and worry in others. Generally, the more important the contest, the greater the stress and the more likely a competitor is to be prone to anxiety.

We will look at the factors that affect mental preparation, and identify some of the training and strategies that can be used to ensure a competitor performs at their optimum level.

Sports psychology is the application of the science of behaviour to exercise and sports participation. Elite performers and their coaches use sports psychology to help them gain a competitive edge. A knowledge of sports psychology, or the intervention of a sports psychologist, can help performers manage their stress and anxiety more effectively, improving their concentration and motivation.

▶ *Performers and their coaches use psychology to gain a competitive edge*

Research into sports psychology and successful performances suggests that the best performers tend to have:

■ higher levels of self-confidence

■ more task-oriented focus

■ control over their anxiety levels

■ more determination and commitment.

APPLY IT!

How would you rate your own self-confidence, task-oriented focus, anxiety levels and commitment? Give yourself a rating out of ten.

MOTIVATION AND STRESS CONTROL

In order to perform at our best in sport, we must want to perform well and achieve. This drive to play well is referred to as motivation. In short-term preparation, coaches and players use strategies to ensure this drive is at its optimum level. There are many influences and factors that may inhibit this motivation – these stresses lead to anxiety, which we discuss in detail below.

In the short-term preparation phase, motivation can be influenced by how confident a performer feels about their role in an impending competition. Psychologists refer to this factor as self-confidence. For beginners, lack of self-confidence may relate to a general feeling that they are going to perform badly. With experienced and elite performers, it is usually related to specific situations or venues.

Bandura (1977) developed the principle of **self-efficacy**, suggesting that self-confidence is often specific to a particular situation. It can affect motivation in terms of the amount of effort a performer puts in, and how long they persist at a task.

Bandura believed that a performer's self-efficacy is influenced by four factors.

■ Performance accomplishments – possibly the most important factor. If the individual has been successful in the past, then feelings of self-confidence are likely to be high. For example, football teams often have a particular ground where they nearly always win, and this gives the team a lot of confidence.

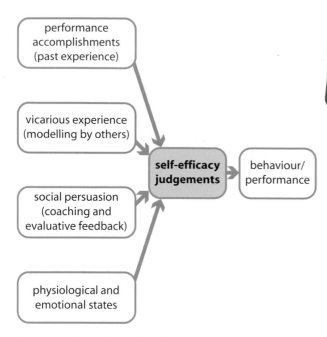

Fig. 2.1 Bandura's theory of self-efficacy

- Vicarious experience – this refers to performances we have observed before. If a performer watches others perform and achieve success, then they are likely to experience high self-efficacy. For example, many elite athletes will watch videos of previous gold medallists during their preparation for major races.

- Verbal persuasion – if **significant others** can encourage and support a performer, then self-confidence will be high. Elite rugby teams often ask ex-players to give motivational speeches and hand out shirts before international matches.

- Emotional arousal – how a performer feels about their level of arousal can affect their confidence level. If they feel they are becoming overanxious, this will have a negative impact on confidence. Being able to monitor and use strategies such as relaxation techniques to control anxiety and arousal levels is an important part of an elite athlete's short-term preparation.

KEY TERMS

self-efficacy
self-confidence in a specific situation

significant others
people who have some influence over the performer – could include parents, peer athletes and coaches

TASK

How would you help a performer with low self-confidence prepare for a competition? Use Bandura's four factors to help.

ANXIETY

The ability to deal with pressure is vital for success in sport. When a performer freezes or 'chokes' at the vital moment, **anxiety** is usually the cause.

KEY TERM

anxiety
a natural reaction to threat in the environment – part of our preparation for flight or fight

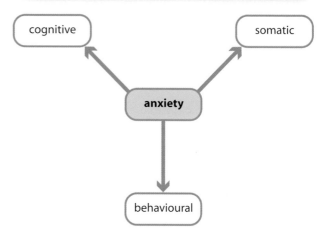

Fig. 2.2 The three dimensions of anxiety

Anxiety is said to have three dimensions:

- **cognitive** – worry and negative feelings about your own performance

- **somatic** – physiological symptoms such as raised heart rate, increased perspiration, shortness of breath

- **behavioural** – experiencing tension, agitation and restlessness.

Sports performers can suffer from two types of anxiety linked to performance:

- **state anxiety** – which is situation-specific and can be liked to a particular role (such as penalty-taking), place, or level of competition

- **trait anxiety** – which is a general and enduring feeling of apprehension.

MAIN CAUSES OF ANXIETY

The main causes of anxiety include a general predisposition to this state. If a competitor has an innate sense of anxiety, they naturally will be uneasy about competing in front of others, or in a situation of pressure.

A competitor may also suffer anxiety due to the perceived importance of the situation – the more important a match, or the more that is at stake, then the higher the level of anxiety. This is also referred to as competition-specific stress.

Some athletes may suffer anxiety through ascribing poor performance to their lack of ability – athletes at the start of their career, or making their debut for an international or professional team, may suffer from this type of anxiety. This may also be due to a fear of failure.

EFFECTS ON TECHNIQUE

The concept of anxiety is closely linked to arousal – the state of alertness. Arousal is usually displayed on a continuum of low (sleeping) to high, intense excitement. In sport, the aim is to be in a state of high arousal.

Research suggests that arousal can have either a positive or negative effect on sports performance. The type of effect depends on how the performer perceives their arousal level. Jones and Swain (1992) state that most elite athletes view pre-competition arousal as a positive feeling of alertness, rather than as anxiety, whereas novice or less-experienced athletes have negative response to this rise in arousal.

In the words of Tiger Woods, the challenge is hitting good shots when you have to, when the nerves are fluttering, the heart pounding and the palms sweating.

▶ A penalty kick could cause a player to suffer state anxiety

▶ Tiger Woods – a performer who is in control of his emotions

There are four main theories that link arousal and anxiety with performance, listed in Table 2.1.

Theory	Source	Comments
Inverted-U hypothesis	Yearkes and Dodson (1908)	A difficult theory to test, predicts a relationship between arousal and performance as inverted-U shape
Drive theory	Zajonc (1965)	Over-simplistic, fails to appreciate the different personalities of the performer and the context of the performance (see page 36)
Catastrophe model	Hardy (1996)	Suggests that arousal has different effects on sports performance depending on cognitive anxiety. Arousal will increase performance when cognitive anxiety is low, but may lead to a sudden catastrophic decline in performance when cognitive anxiety is relatively high
Processing efficiency theory	Eysenck and Calva	Anxiety may affect processing efficiency rather than task effectiveness. Anxious athletes have to work harder to maintain the same level of performance they would display If they were not anxious

Table 2.1 Four theories linking arousal, anxiety and performance

CHOKING

KEY TERM

choking
the inability to perform to an athlete's optimum performance – sudden impairment or failure of sports performance due to anxiety

Sometimes, the harder one tries, the worse the performance – this is often caused by excessive self-consciousness and concern about the mechanics of skill execution. Famous examples include Ian Woosnam in golf and Eric Bristow in darts.

An athlete's potential for **choking** depends on both the athlete and the situation. Choking usually occurs when an athlete is overly concerned about what others (teammates, coaches or an audience) think about their performance.

STRATEGIES TO PREVENT ANXIETY AND CHOKING

The following strategies can be useful:
- set your own achievable goals
- use imagery before a competition to review strategy and technique and create a sense of confidence
- use positive talk, both in preparation and in competition
- practise relaxation exercises
- use music prior to a competition to help maintain focus by controlling negative thoughts.

One method of relaxation is centring. This is used by many elite performers to produce a calming and controlling effect. Athletes may use centring when they feel they are becoming overanxious, indicated by somatic signs. Centring involves the performer focusing attention on the centre of their body.

Some of the main strategies to combat anxiety are listed in Table 2.2.

▶ *Jon Drummond of the US men's Olympic relay race team takes a deep breath at the starting block*

Technique	How to do it	Practical example
Mental rehearsal (cognitive)	Going through the competition in your mind, think about all the different situations that might occur and how you will respond to them. Identify times when you may become aggressive or anxious, and think about how you could control these feelings	A 1500-m runner might think through their tactics in a race and mentally rehearse how they will react and cope
Coping skills (behavioural)	Understand that the pressure is perception, not fact. Change your attitude so that a pressure situation becomes enjoyable. Learn to interpret signs of arousal as positive cues	A swimmer may use the physical signs of arousal as cues in their short-term warm-up before a race
Somatic and cognitive techniques	Use physical and mental relaxation methods	Somatic (physical) techniques include progressive muscular relaxation; cognitive (mental) techniques include centring
Performance-monitoring review (behavioural)	Keep a record of performances, try to match internal states (thoughts, feelings) with external states (successful performance environmental factors)	A sprinter recording their races will identify what they feel like when they produce good performances
Pre-performance routines (behavioural)	Give yourself specific, task-relevant instructions	A long-jumper will undergo a pre-planned routine in their preparation before a jump
Simulation training (behavioural)	Train to cope with anxiety by practising under conditions that mimic anticipated pressure situations	A football team might prepare for a penalty shoot-out by practising in front of their home crowd at the end of a game

Table 2.2 *Techniques and strategies to control anxiety*

There are more coping strategies outlined on page 39 in this chapter.

<blockquote>
REMEMBER

Athletes need to understand their own response to stress and be able to identify the somatic signals.
</blockquote>

AGGRESSION VERSUS ASSERTION

Aggression is a term that is used loosely in sport. Again, it can have both a positive and negative effect on performance. Aggression in this context is defined as 'intent to harm outside the laws of the game'.

But where aggression is controlled and channelled, it becomes **assertion**, and it is this approach that we should encourage in sport.

There are a number of theories that suggest causes for aggression. These tend to fall into the two categories of nature or nurture.

- The instinct (**nature**) theory suggests that aggression is an innate biological drive in all humans, and sport provides an outlet for this aggression. The frustration–aggression hypothesis is a version of this drive theory, which states that having our goals blocked can cause frustration, which then leads to aggression.

- The social learning theory developed by Bandura (1977) states that we learn to be aggressive by watching others (**nurture**).

Strategies to reduce aggression include internal control of arousal levels, punishment, and the reinforcement of non-aggressive behaviour.

▶ *There is a definite line between assertive and aggressive behaviour on the sports pitch*

EXTERNAL INFLUENCES

HOME ADVANTAGE

Studies on the concept of home advantage suggest that teams playing at home win, on average, 56–64 per cent of their matches. This advantage is especially relevant to indoor sports. This phenomenon is often seen in the success of the host nations of major global games, such as the Olympics. At the 2008 Beijing Olympics, host nation China topped the medals table with their highest-ever medal table position (51 gold medals). One suggestion is that large, supportive crowds may help the home team in terms of motivation and the amount of effort they put in.

▶ Roy Hibbert is carried by the home crowd after Georgetown University's basketball team beat Duke University

TASK

Discuss as a group whether you think the home advantage effect will be positive for Team GB in the 2012 Olympics.

Is there any evidence from previous Games to support this view?

This may also be linked to a so-called proximity effect, where crowds that are close to the action (as in basketball) are said to increase the audience's influence. There is some evidence that it takes about six to nine months for a team to regain its home advantage after moving to a new stadium. Arsenal FC, for example, suffered a drop in form when they moved from Highbury into their new Emirates Stadium.

THE CROWD EFFECT

SOCIAL FACILITATION

Social facilitation refers to the influence other people can have on performance. These other people may include:

- co-actors – other participants, teammates and opponents
- audience – spectators can have a huge impact on performance.

SOCIAL INHIBITION

Social inhibition is the negative effect of an audience on a performer. This may involve an increase in:

- arousal of the performer
- competitive drive
- speed of performance.

These may have facilitating or inhibiting effects on the performance.

One of the earliest studies on the effect of others was undertaken by Norman Triplett as long ago as 1898. He published in the *American Journal of Psychology* (9: 507–33) his finding that cyclists' performance increased by 30 per cent when they were riding in a group of other cyclists. Other research has confirmed that the presence of others tends to result in an increased level of performance.

But studies by a French professor, Max Ringelmann, published in 1913, showed that this was true only up to a certain number of co-actors. When group size gets too big, there is a tendency for some in the group to lose motivation – this is 'social loafing', sometimes called the Ringelmann effect.

Robert Zajonc was a psychologist who studied how audience influences performance. He believed that the mere presence of others was sufficient to increase the arousal levels of a performer. He developed the drive theory to explain the link between arousal and performance.

Drive theory suggests that our learned behaviours tend to be our dominant responses. Zajonc (1965) concluded that as a performer's arousal increases, they are most likely to revert to their dominant response. In relation to sport, this often results in less-experienced performers showing an incorrect response as their arousal level rises, either before or during competition.

audience + skilled performer = increased level of performance

audience + unskilled or novice performer = reduced level of performance

CASE STUDY

THE PRESENCE OF OTHERS

Zajonc identified that performance in sport could be affected by the following factors related to co-actors and audience.

☐ The presence of others increases the arousal of the performer.

☐ The presence of others is likely to promote the selection of the performer's dominant response.

☐ If the performer is an expert, or the skill being executed is simple, the dominant response is likely to be the correct one and performance will improve.

☐ If the performer is a novice, or the skill being executed is complex, the dominant response is likely to be incorrect and the performance may decline.

■ Can you identify specific skills in your chosen sport that may be affected by the presence of others? Make a list of both positive and negative effects.

HOW TO COPE WITH CROWDS

Sports psychologists suggest that performers use the following strategies to help cope with the pressure of playing in front of crowds.

■ Practise selective attention to help cut out the negative awareness of others.

■ Use cognitive visualisation techniques and strategies, such as imagery/mental rehearsal, to help focus on the task.

■ Ensure essential skills are over-learned and grooved to ensure the dominant response is successful.

■ Use evaluative practices where people are encouraged to give feedback on each other's performance.

■ Practise with simulated crowd noises, using audio recordings.

■ Incorporate stress-management and relaxation techniques into training.

The concept of being in the optimal zone of psychological preparedness is also referred to as a 'peak flow' experience. This is where the performer is in complete control – they feel that nothing can go wrong, skills and techniques are occurring automatically, and the performer has time to look around and identify space, opponents and the locations of teammates. This is normally the result of a high degree of inner drive and self-motivation.

APPLY IT!

Have you ever felt 'in the zone' when performing in a sport or competition? If so, try to write down how it feels. What was the effect on your performance?

EVALUATION APPREHENSION

A researcher called N.B. Cottrell (1972) studied the concept of social facilitation, and concluded that the key was not simply the mere presence of others influencing performance – but whether the performer felt the audience was judging or evaluating the performance. This is called evaluation apprehension, and leads to arousal and the resulting dominant response.

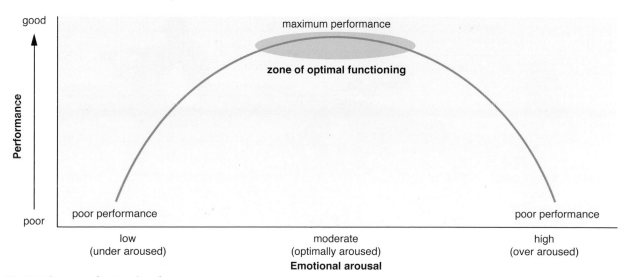

Fig. 2.3 The zone of optimal performance

THE IMPORTANCE OF COMPETITION

The more important the level of competition, generally the higher the level of state anxiety the performer will experience. Most of this pressure and anxiety will come from external sources – the bigger the competition, the more the media, audience and significant others will talk and project the result. Again, it is the way the performer perceives this extra pressure that is the key to controlling the anxiety. A cup final or international fixture will heighten the stakes, and there is a chance that the participants will feel less confident.

This concept was developed by Martens into the theory of competitive anxiety (see Martens et al., 1998). Competitive anxiety can be defined as an individual's tendency to perceive competitive situations as threatening, and to respond to these situations by experiencing state anxiety.

STRATEGIES FOR COPING

Strategies include self-talk, imagery, cue utilisation and relaxation techniques, among others.

SELF-TALK (COGNITIVE STRATEGY)

It is important that athletes practise self-talk, which may be very useful for keeping motivated during intensive training sessions.

Self-talk can also be used by athletes to enable them to link to specific skills and help them focus on correct technique. Examples might include a rugby player linking the phrases 'low' and 'drive' when they are about to execute a tackle on an opponent.

▶ *Arrow!*

During competition, an athlete may need to reassure themselves that they are well prepared and ready to compete, and self-talk can help in promoting this feeling of self-confidence. The main focus during competition should be positive reinforcement through the use of positive self-talk: 'I have trained well and I am at 100 per cent for this challenge.'

In terms of technique during competition, the key is to keep the reinforcement as simple as possible. For example, at the Winter Olympics the Great Britain luge team uses the phrase 'Arrow!' to help the riders focus and maintain the correct body shape as they progress down the course.

IMAGERY (COGNITIVE STRATEGY)

Imagery can be used by performers to improve their concentration and promote feelings of self-confidence. Imagery involves creating a series of mental pictures (also known as visualisation; see page 39). These pictures may include images of successful past performances, the flowing movements of an elite role model, or escape images where the performer imagines him or herself in a more relaxed place. All these techniques can be used to help control anxiety.

Fig. 2.4 Self-talk is useful both in training sessions and during competition

CUE UTILISATION (BEHAVIOURAL STRATEGY)

Cue utilisation helps develop the performer's attention level by getting them to concentrate on the cues that are most relevant. Often this can be combined with self-talk and the use of focus words.

Cue utilisation theory suggests that as the arousal of the performer increases, their attention narrows, and they are more able to pick up the most relevant cues. But this narrowing of attention occurs only up to a certain level of arousal – the optimum arousal level. If arousal levels are too low, then both irrelevant and relevant cues are picked up. If arousal levels are too high, then both irrelevant and relevant cues are ignored, which will lead to a drop in performance.

RELAXATION TECHNIQUES (COGNITIVE AND SOMATIC STRATEGIES)

These techniques are most commonly associated with controlling somatic anxiety, although they can also be used to control cognitive anxiety (see page 32).

Self-directed relaxation is where the performer concentrates on each of their muscle groups separately and relaxes them.

Progressive relaxation training is where a performer feels the tension in their muscles and gets rid of this tension by 'letting go'.

Other techniques include:

- visualisation – using mental mages to help create calm and control
- yoga
- listening to music and/or relaxation tapes
- toe-tensing
- deep-breathing exercises.

▶ *Yoga is a good technique for both physical and mental relaxation*

APPLY IT!

With a partner, select two of the relaxation techniques listed here, and try them out.
What can you do to assist your partner in achieving relaxation of muscles, and mental relaxation?

ENVIRONMENTAL FACTORS

In a sporting context, the effect of environment depends not so much on the playing field or physical setting, but rather on the people in that setting. These include the crowd, other competitors (including teammates and opponents), coaches, and in elite sport the media in its various forms.

Research and analysis suggest that novice performers perform best in low-arousal environments. The low-arousal environment would be where no one is watching or evaluating the performance, and where the importance of competition is low. The presence of others may have a positive impact on some performers, but may cause others to choke.

As noted above, the nature of the audience can also have an effect on performance. If the crowd is noisy and aggressive, then the performer may feel more anxious and may also become more aggressive themselves. The proximity of the crowd can also influence performance – if the crowd is very close to the court or pitch, the performer may feel threatened, which may cause their level of anxiety to increase. Conversely, some performers may feel reassured by a supportive crowd close to the action. We have also seen how other environmental factors, such as whether the performer is playing at home in familiar surroundings or away from their home base, can also have a positive or negative influence on performance.

The climatic conditions can also affect performance. Again, the better the performer, the more effective they will be at dealing with adverse conditions. Some of the key factors are discussed in Chapter 3, pages 44–45.

▶ *The presence of a hostile crowd can influence performance negatively*

Refresh your memory

Revision checklist

▷ Know about the effect anxiety can have on a performance.

▷ Know the two types of anxiety (state and trait anxiety) and the two types of response (somatic and cognitive).

▷ Explain why some performers choke.

▷ Outline strategies that can be used by performers to control their anxiety levels.

▷ Understand the theories that relate to home advantage.

▷ Discuss the theory of social facilitation and its application to sports performance.

▷ Discuss the theory of evaluation apprehension and its application to sports performance.

Get the result!

Sample question and answer

Exam question

Explain Cottrell's theory of evaluation apprehension.

(4 marks)

Student answer – candidate A

Cottrell believed that when an audience was present, an athlete's performance would decline. This is because of a fear of being judged. For example, a gymnast is more likely to make mistakes in front of a panel of judges or her family. The fear of the outcome increases the performer's arousal both somatically and cognitively. This can lead to a decline in performance because of their fear of the outcome Audience presence inhibits performance unless she is among an audience of co-actors cheering her on rather than judging.

Examiner says:

This candidate gives a good account of the negative effect of the audience and explains Cottrell's theory well.

Examiner says:

However, they don't score full marks as they don't fully explain how an audience can have a positive impact on performance – they just touch on this in the last sentence.

This candidate would have scored 3 out of the 4 marks allocated.

Examiner says:

This candidate does understand that there can be a positive or negative impact, but doesn't describe or explain in enough detail.

Student answer – candidate B

Evaluation apprehension is where a performer is influenced by the people around them who can be watching or evaluating their performance. Depending on the experience and level of the performer the presence of others can have a positive or a negative effect on performance.

Examiner says:

Again, this candidate would have scored 2 out of the 4 marks allocated.

model answer

Cottrell (1972) studied the concept of social facilitation, and concluded that the key was not whether people were watching a performer, but whether the performer felt the audience was judging or evaluating the performance.

This effect of judging performance is called evaluation apprehension. It leads to a change in the level of the performer's arousal, and results in the performer selecting the dominant response.

For elite and experienced athletes, this perception of judging can have a positive effect on performance – motivating the performer to try harder and be more focused on their task. But if a performer is less able and/or less experienced, then the presence of people judging them can have a negative effect, and this can cause them to choke or under-perform.

CHAPTER 3 SHORT-TERM TECHNICAL PREPARATION

LEARNING OUTCOMES

By working through this chapter, you should be able to:

- discuss the factors athletes need to consider in their short-term technical preparation for sport
- explain the choice of kit and equipment in relation to short-term preparation
- explain and discuss the use of ergogenic aids for short-term preparation
- explain the reasons for holding pre-match camps and for pre-performance rituals

This chapter considers the strategies and processes that elite performers go through as they prepare for global competitions.

Short-term preparation refers to the time immediately before competition. It may be hours, but normally in elite sport the build-up to a competition will begin several days before the event. Most elite teams have specialist kit managers who help performers with their technical preparation. Technical sports such as skiing, cycling and sailing often involve large teams of people and a great deal of kit and equipment, to enable adjustment to the current conditions.

KIT AND EQUIPMENT

SELECTION

There are several factors that affect the selection of playing kit and equipment, the most obvious being environmental factors. These include:

- climate – temperature, humidity and wind
- playing surface
- indoor or outdoor (also whether a stadium roof is closed or open)
- protection/reducing injury.

The climate can have a major impact on physical performance. Players need to wear kit that helps them maintain a constant core temperature. Many players now wear compression clothing underneath their playing equipment.

In some sports, where air or fluid dynamics can influence performance, athletes may use clothing or other strategies specifically designed to reduce this effect. Traditionally in swimming and cycling, performers 'shave down' in preparation for competition, but whether this has any real impact on performance is debatable – it may be more of a ritual, helping the performer to prepare mentally for competition (see page 34). In sports such as sprinting and swimming, performers may use aerodynamic suits in an attempt to reduce drag and improve their speed and power.

▶ Sports such as cycling and sailing require a lot of technical support

▷ *The Nike swift suit – aerodynamic clothing can give athletes a competitive edge*

ENVIRONMENTAL AND CULTURAL FACTORS

Performers and teams need to analyse the environmental conditions and adjust or change their playing kit and equipment in response. There are many examples, including the type of footwear that best suits the conditions underfoot in sports such as football and rugby. In sports played on artificial surfaces, such as hockey and tennis, players may need time to adjust and train on the variations in surface that may affect the speed of the ball.

Such variations may also influence the tactics a team uses. For example, it is well known for football teams facing opposition from higher leagues or teams of a higher standard to reduce the width of their pitch, to give the opposition team less space to work in.

Cultural factors may include the amount of support a performer or team receives from their home nation (or home club), particularly when competing in global competitions. Pressure from the media, and in some cases from governments and states, can affect performers as they prepare for competition.

CLIMATE

The key climatic factors that teams and performers may need to consider in their short-term preparation are:

- temperature and UV exposure
- humidity
- wind.

APPLY IT!

Think about your own sport – what factors influence the clothing and equipment you choose?

TEMPERATURE AND UV EXPOSURE

If the ambient temperature is higher than the body's normal temperature, there will be a net gain of heat from the environment to the performer. The reverse will happen in colder environments.

In many sporting environments, performers can control temperature by choosing to wear the appropriate style of playing kit. But when the ambient temperature is above 21°C, studies have shown that the body struggles to control core temperature, with a resulting negative effect on endurance, speed and power. Direct sun or high ultraviolet exposure will increase problems of convection heating and the chance of the body overheating.

HUMIDITY

Conditions of high humidity affect how much sweat can evaporate and so transfer heat away from the body. The impact of this is a rise in the core temperature, with a resulting negative effect on physical performance.

The only successful method of countering the problems of high humidity is for performers to spend time acclimatising to the conditions.

WIND

Wind can increase the rate of sweat evaporation, which can cause a direct cooling effect on the performer. Athletes will need to wear more clothing to counteract this – which could have a negative impact on performance.

Very often, a performer will be faced with two or more of the above factors, which exaggerates the effect.

As well as having direct physiological effects on individual performers, environmental factors will affect many different aspects of a sporting event.

In cricket, for example, many factors need to be considered in preparation for a test match or one-day international. Climate, specifically humidity, can have a huge effect on the way the ball moves in flight, and this will influence the selection of the team, especially which types of bowler to select. The state of the wicket – how hard, wet or green it is – can also influence both the selection of players and the tactics a team will use. The decision on whether to bat or bowl first will be affected by the environmental conditions.

▶ In cricket, environmental conditions have a big influence on tactics

CASE STUDY PITCH PERFECT

Traditional grass pitches are far less common in modern hockey, and most hockey is now played on synthetic surfaces. Since the 1970s, sand-based pitches had been favoured, as they dramatically speed up the pace of the game.

In recent years there has been a massive increase in the use of 'water-based' artificial turf. Water-based astroturf enables the ball to be transferred more quickly than the original sand-based surfaces, and it is this characteristic that has made them the surface of choice for international and national league competitions. Water-based surfaces are also less abrasive than the sand-based variety, so they reduce the level of injury to players coming into contact with the surface.

As well as affecting the speed and shape of the game, this different surface also affects the sticks used – sand pitches are very abrasive and quickly wear down wooden sticks, and on water-based astros the wooden heads soak up moisture from the pitch, which can cause cracking. Modern composite sticks go some way to withstanding these problems, but are more expensive.

Hockey players also need to consider their footwear – playing on a water-based astro can lead to very wet feet unless footwear is fully waterproofed.

■ How might the surface of a pitch affect a team's tactics?

▶ Hockey is now commonly played on a synthetic pitch

ACCLIMATISATION

To prepare for differences in environmental conditions, individuals and teams will go through a period of acclimatisation when preparing for global sports competitions. It can take between five and ten days for a performer to acclimatise (respond and adapt) to changes in heat and humidity.

As the body acclimatises, it becomes more efficient at **thermoregulation**. The sweat response starts earlier and works to a greater level. The body will begin to absorb more fluid from the performer's diet, and their blood volume will also increase. If possible, performers acclimatise best in the area where they are going to perform, but often at events such as the Olympics this may not be possible, so teams will try to find areas that have a similar climate, and use holding camps (see page 53) to help the performers prepare.

COMPRESSION CLOTHING

A recent trend in sports clothing has been the introduction of compression clothing or performance underwear, manufactured by a range of companies under a variety of brand names (such as Skins, Nike Pro, Canterbury Armourfit). The benefits the manufacturers claim can be gained from wearing these compression garments include:

- injury prevention
- performance enhancement
- speeding up of recovery.

KEY TERM

thermoregulation
the ability to maintain body temperature within certain boundaries, even when the surrounding temperature is very different

The development of these garments is based on the successes of medical therapy. Much of the early research and development on compression clothing was based on the treatment of post-operative patients. Studies found that wearing the clothing speeded up recovery, as it helped to increase blood flow to the areas covered and also had a positive impact on **venous return**.

Fig. 3.1 A range of compression underwear is available

KEY TERM

venous return
the amount of blood returning to the heart
(via the veins)

Then athletes began to identify the possible performance-enhancing properties of compression clothing. Studies in the USA have looked at the effects of compression shorts on power production in vertical jumps. The key finding was that those wearing compression shorts were able to resist fatigue longer. The benefits seem to be most beneficial for anaerobic sporting activities such as sprinting and athletic throwing events (javelin, discus, shot-put).

The key is that the compression effect creates a constant pressure on the working muscles, which in turn has a stimulatory effect on blood flow. The increased blood flow helps feed the muscle with both oxygen and energy, and also speeds up the removal of waste products, which has a positive impact on recovery. There is further evidence that compression clothing also reduces muscle vibration, which can reduce the possibility of delayed-onset muscle soreness.

The clothing also helps the body with thermoregulation – the material wicks moisture away from the skin, which keeps the muscles warm in winter and cool in summer, and also helps with reducing fluid loss.

The effect of so-called 'technical pyjamas' may be more beneficial – wearing the clothing after training or performance. The effect of maintaining a high blood flow around the working muscle and increases in **venous return** help the body remove waste products and restock its energy stores. The suggestion is that compression clothing should be worn for up to two hours after training or competition, in order to speed up the recovery process.

APPLY IT!

Is compression clothing used in your sport? What would be benefits? Are there any problems with the use of compression clothing in your sport?

CASE STUDY
POSITIVE NEGATIVITY?

Loughborough University and Canterbury (sports clothing retailer) produced a new high-tech shirt – the Ionx – for the 2007 Rugby World Cup. Loughborough University found that the shirts delivered a 2.7 per cent improvement in players' peak power when measured in short bursts of high-impact exercise on cycling machines.

The shirts produce a negative charge. This is said to help increase blood flow and the supply of oxygen to the working muscles, enabling performers to work harder, recover more quickly, and get rid of waste products such as lactic acid more easily.

The shirts were worn by World Cup champions South Africa, as well as by Australia, Ireland and Japan. Beaten finalists England did not wear the shirts, as they have a shirt deal with rivals Nike – although some England players, including captain Phil Vickery, wore Canterbury undergarments that included the formula.

■ The World Anti-Doping Agency (WADA) looked at these shirts and decided they should not be put on the list of prohibited substances and methods. But in your opinion, should this new shirt be classed as cheating?

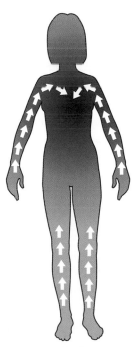

Fig. 3.2 Compression clothing helps to force blood back to the heart, and so helps the athlete recover more quickly

ICE VESTS AND THERMOREGULATION

As Olympic Games and most world cup tournaments are held in the summer months, athletes need to plan and use technology to help them control their body temperature.

When body temperature rises, the blood is diverted away from the muscle to the skin in an attempt to cool down. This means less blood flows to the muscle, which has a negative effect on performance. Companies such as Nike have developed ice vests or cooling vests that can help athletes stabilise their temperature.

Fig. 3.3 Ice vests or cooling vests come in different designs

At the Athens Olympics in 2004, many teams and performers used pre-cooling strategies – lowering or maintaining a constant core body temperature. This was done through the use of **ice vests** and hoods worn during the warm-up phase and during breaks in play, such as at half-time. The issues that arise for the use of such ergogenic aids is the cost and logistics of supplying ice and power for refrigeration on the pitch side.

The England football team also wore cooling vests during half-times at the 2002 FIFA World Cup in Japan and Korea. Nike claims that its vests allow athletes to perform for up to 19 per cent longer before temperature becomes a debilitating factor.

APPLY IT!

What would be the impact of overheating in your sport?

KEY TERM

ice vest
a vest that contains pockets in which frozen ice packs can be inserted

ERGOGENIC AIDS FOR SHORT-TERM PREPARATION

KEY TERM

ergogenic
(from the Greek *ergo*, meaning to increase work or potential for work) – in sport, ergogenic aids are substances or devices that enhance energy production, use or recovery, and provide athletes with a competitive advantage (Ahrendt, 2001)

New products making **ergogenic** claims appear on the market almost daily, most claiming to bolster strength or endurance in sports. They are not cheap – in the USA, it is estimated that the market is worth around £10 billion. Athletes need to consider such claims and try to identify if there is any evidence or research to back them up. It is also vital that athletes can be sure the product contains no substances that are banned in sport.

PURPOSE OF ERGOGENIC AIDS

Williams (1998) suggests that the purpose of most sports ergogenics is to improve sporting performance by enhancing physical power, mental strength or mechanical edge, thus preventing or delaying the onset of fatigue. This will often give the performer the winning edge. He proposed that athletes could use ergogenic aids in the following three key areas:

- to enhance physical power –
  - o increase the amount of muscle tissue used to generate energy
  - o increase the rate of metabolic processes that generate energy within the muscle
  - o increase the delivery of energy supplies to the muscle
  - o counteract the accumulation of substances in the body that interfere with optimal energy production
- to enhance mental strength –
  - o increase psychological processes that maximise energy production
  - o decrease factors that interfere with optimal psychological functioning
- to enhance mechanical edge –
  - o improve human body biomechanics to increase efficiency by decreasing body mass, especially body fat

o improve human body biomechanics to increase stability by increasing body mass, primarily muscle mass.

TYPES OF ERGOGENIC AIDS

There are generally thought to be four main types of ergogenic aids used in sport (Figure 3.4).

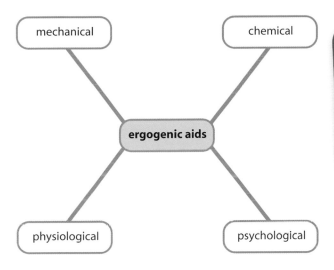

Fig. 3.4 Four types of ergogenic aids

MECHANICAL AIDS

These could include the use of simple technology such as a heart-rate monitor to identify training thresholds, or more complex systems such as **hypoxic chambers**.

Fig. 3.5 Using a treadmill in a low-oxygen (hypoxic) chamber

Many football and rugby teams now use a cycle ergometer at the side of the pitch for substitute players to warm up and prepare. The cycling action acts as a pulse-raiser, increasing blood flow to the muscles as well as raising muscle temperature. Players will combine this type of warm-up with ball work and stretching.

KEY TERM

hypoxic chamber
also known as an altitude chamber – a small, enclosed training module that uses technology to pump oxygen-reduced air (normally reduced from 21 per cent down to 15 per cent) into the module, simulating a low-oxygen altitude. The athlete can either train in this atmosphere or sleep in the module.

CHEMICAL AIDS

These may be either naturally occurring products such as **ginseng**, which has been used as a supplement; or chemical copies, such as creatine monohydrate (see page 51).

Fig. 3.6 Ginseng is one of the oldest sports supplements

KEY TERM

ginseng
a natural extract derived from the plant family Araliaceae, and one of the oldest sports supplements. It has a positive influence on glycogen synthesis in the body, allowing athletes to train and compete for longer and at higher intensity.

PHYSIOLOGICAL AIDS

These include techniques such as sports massage and acupuncture. Acupuncture is the ancient oriental technique of inserting and manipulating fine needles into specific points on the body to relieve pain and for therapeutic purposes. Its effects are not well understood, and it remains controversial among researchers and clinicians in the West.

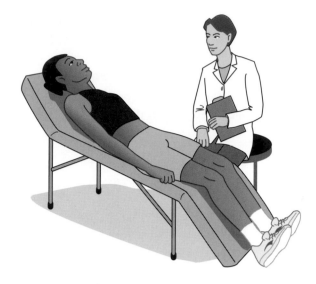

Fig. 3.8 *Some athletes use hypnosis to enhance their performance*

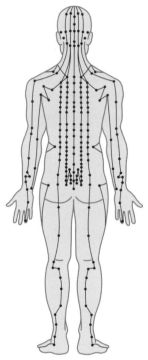

Fig. 3.7 *According to tradition, the acupuncture points lie on meridians along which* qi – *a kind of vital energy – is said to flow*

PSYCHOLOGICAL AIDS

These include the use of imagery, music and **hypnosis** (see Chapter 2).

KEY TERM

hypnosis
a wakeful state of focused attention and heightened suggestibility, with diminished peripheral awareness. Hypnosis has been used as a painkiller, for weight loss, to reduce anxiety – and to enhance sports performance.

TASK

There has been a long history of the use of hypnosis in sport. It is sometimes referred to by different names, such as mental or autogenic training. Research the use of hypnosis in sport and its benefits – use the Internet to find examples of athletes who say they benefit from hypnosis techniques.

DRUGS AND SUPPLEMENTS

Throughout the history of sport, athletes have manipulated their diets in order to improve their physical performance. The ancient Greek Olympians ate special mushrooms to give them speed and power; in medieval jousting, the knights used alcohol to help them prepare; and in the 1800s, caffeine was used by many athletes to help give them endurance. In the twenty-first century, athletes are still searching for supplements that will give them a competitive edge.

Supplements are legal additions to an athlete's diet. They are legal because the sporting bodies do not feel their use is harmful to health. As more research is done, some supplements may in time become illegal drugs.

Dietary and nutritional supplements are the most widely used in sport, and are readily available on the high street. Most elite athletes take multi-vitamins and extra minerals in order to be able to recover from heavy workouts, as well as helping to prevent illness.

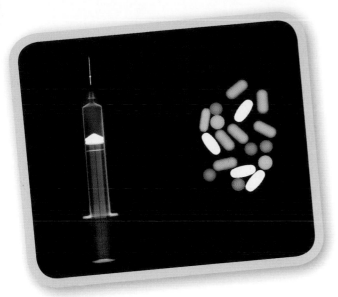

▷ *Drug-taking – the ultimate in gamesmanship?*

According to the World Anti-Doping Code, there are three main factors that influence the legality of an ergogenic substance, and at least two of these factors must be applicable in order for the substance to be illegal to use in sport and competition. The use of the substance or practice has to be proven to:

- physically enhance the performance of the athlete
- be detrimental to the athlete's health (or be potentially lethal)
- conflict with the general spirit of sport.

Drug abuse has been one of the main areas of deviance in sport during the past few years. It is not clear whether the actual level of drug taking has gone up, or whether we now know more about it because testing systems have improved. It is also very difficult to decide where the line should be drawn between illegal and legal substances – many athletes have tested positive, but claim that all they took was a cough mixture or other such product, which can be bought over the counter.

Drug-taking is the ultimate in gamesmanship – taking something to increase your performance and increase your chances of winning. There are a range of performance-enhancing drugs that athletes may take. Most originated as genuine medical treatments, but their side-effects have been used by athletes to improve their athletic performance illegally. The range and availability of these types of drugs are constantly increasing, making control very difficult.

CASE STUDY
CREATINE LOADING

Creatine is one of the most commonly used supplements in sport. You can get creatine from eating a normal, healthy diet – foods such as meat and fish are good sources. But most athletes top up their creatine levels, using up to 30 grams a day. The most common method is to consume creatine monohydrate powder with fluids.

Benefits from taking extra creatine include:

- ☐ boosts levels of amino acids in the body, which can lead to muscle growth
- ☐ helps athletes maintain energy levels for longer
- ☐ enhances the ATP–PC (alactic) energy pathway (see page 12).

- ■ What sports do you think would benefit most from creatine loading? Why?

The huge increase in rewards for winning means that the temptation to take drugs has become very great for some athletes. For Ben Johnson, for example, the risk may have been worthwhile – even though he was stripped of his 1988 gold medal and banned from competition for several years, he continued to make money from his fame.

Most media attention has been focused on the use of steroids. These artificial male hormones allow the performer to train harder and longer, and have been difficult to trace in the past as they are not actually performance-enhancing drugs. Athletes tend to take them in the closed season, when they are building up fitness. A breakthrough in detecting these drugs came with the decision to test athletes at any time during the year, meaning that illegal activity could be detected, even in the closed season.

The very fine line between what is legal and illegal causes many dilemmas for both the performer and the authorities. A sprinter can legally take ginseng, although it contains substances that have advantageous effects. An athlete can train at high altitude to try to develop the efficiency of their blood system, but **blood doping** is illegal.

KEY TERM

blood doping
the practice of boosting the number of red blood cells in the circulation in order to enhance athletic performance – because they carry oxygen from the lungs to the muscles, more red blood cells in the blood can improve an athlete's aerobic capacity (VO_2 max) and endurance

A substance is illegal only if it is on the International Olympic Committee's list of banned substances. It may be possible that athletes with access to highly qualified chemists and physiologists may be able to keep one step ahead by taking substances that have not yet been banned.

After the Atlanta Olympic Games in 1996, the American sports magazine *Sports Illustrated* undertook an 18-month investigation into drug-taking in elite sport. Their conclusion was that drug use had reached epidemic levels. 'There is a small percentage of athletes who do not use drugs. There is a small percentage that use drugs and get caught and there is a very large percentage that use drugs who don't get caught.'

At the Sydney Olympic Games in 2000, the International Olympic Committee worked hard to make the games 100 per cent free of drugs. Thirty-five athletes tested positive and were disciplined before the games started. Most of those caught were from Eastern European and underdeveloped countries. There was a suggestion by many in the international press that these athletes lack the knowledge of how to avoid detection, or cannot afford to pay out the thousands of dollars needed to buy more sophisticated drugs.

THE FUTURE

New drugs come onto the scene all the time, and this makes it very difficult for organisations such as the International Olympic Committee's Medical Commission to keep ahead. New drugs are more sophisticated and harder to detect, as they often mimic naturally occurring hormones and chemicals. One of this new wave of drugs is erythropoietin (EPO). EPO produces a hormone that stimulates bone marrow to produce more red blood cells. It is claimed by scientists to improve an athlete's aerobic performance by up to 15 per cent. Other scientists state that it can have deadly side-effects: at night the new red blood cells turn viscous, and the heart needs to work harder to move the blood around the body. Some estimates say that 25 athletes have died from taking EPO.

SHORT-TERM PREPARATION IN PRACTICE

WARMING UP

There are a number of factors that need to be planned and carried out during the warm-up phase. The length of the warm-up phase is dependent on the type of sport, but also on the level and intensity of the competition. For most amateur performers, the warm-up phase starts around an hour before the actual competition, but for elite athletes preparing for competitions, the warm-up phase may stretch over a number of days, increasing in intensity as they get nearer to the competition time.

▶ *Warming up is an essential phase of short-term preparation*

Regardless of the level of the competition and of the performer, the following areas should be included in the warm-up phase.

PHYSICAL PREPARATION

This is the traditional warm-up (see Chapter 1). The intensity and duration of training and fitness work is reduced as the athlete gets nearer to the event (a process known as tapering).

TECHNICAL PREPARATION

This includes checking, preparing and putting on playing kit and equipment. This phase also includes adjusting the kit and equipment, such as footwear, to best match the conditions, and also getting a feel for the pitch, court or route. Elite teams and athletes will often be able to train on the pitch or competition surface the day before the event, and then also spend warm-up time on the pitch in the stages immediately before competition.

MENTAL PREPARATION

This is a final mental tune-up before the game or competition (see Chapter 2). The main aims should be to focus on the task ahead and to promote self-confidence. This mental stage of the warm up should be seen as a transition from life into sport. Getting a 'game face' on means performers need to 'park' any irrelevant or external concerns and focus on the game ahead.

> ### KEY TERM
> **regeneration**
> allowing athletes to have enough rest before competition

PREPARATION

HYDRATION AND NUTRITION

Studies suggest that a drop of 2 per cent in the body's level of hydration leads to a decrease in physical performance. Keeping the body hydrated in the short-term phase of preparation is very important for the performer (see Chapter 1).

Eating a diet high in carbohydrates during the final phase of preparation should ensure that muscle glycogen stores are fully stocked before competition. However, closer to the start of competition performers need to think carefully about the food they eat and the demands and requirements of their energy systems (see Chapter 1).

THE USE OF CAMPS

Holding camps are used by international sports teams as a base for training and preparation, for use in the weeks and months before major competitions. They are used extensively by teams preparing for Olympic, Paralympic and Commonwealth Games.

In the UK, the British Olympic Association differentiates between two sorts of camp when supporting Team GB in preparing for the Olympic and Paralympic Games.

- **Holding camp** (or training camp) – a single base camp used in the weeks immediately prior to the start of the games. Here athletes can train in conditions very similar to the climate, altitude and time zone of the host city. This is the process of acclimatisation. These camps are used to help athletes improve their focus and maximise their performance at the games.

- **Preparation camp** – a training base using the facilities to be used in the holding camp phase, enabling athletes, coaches and support staff to familiarise themselves with the location. This is used up to a year before the event. It also allows the team to have a 'dry run' of procedures and transfer arrangements.

▶ *The relay team in action at the Team GB Macau Training Camp, just before the start of the 2008 Beijing Olympics*

CASE STUDY   TEAM GB

What does Team GB look for when searching for a location for a holding camp?

They need exclusive training in the facilities two to three weeks prior the event, and the facilities need to be of a high standard. The location needs to be of similar climatic conditions and time zone to the Games venue. Support facilities need to include access to a hospital with an accident and emergency department with advanced scanner technology. The camp also needs to be within half a day's direct flight from the host city, in order to avoid travel fatigue.

■ Thinking of the next major global games, where would the best holding camp be?

CASE STUDY
2007 RUGBY WORLD CUP

The semi-finals and finals were scheduled to kick off at 9 p.m. local time in France, to suit the demands of television. After successfully getting through the quarter-finals, the England team gradually introduced a new training and sleeping programme to help the players adapt to the strange kick-off times. By the final week of the tournament, the England team were training between 7 and 10 p.m. to match the timescale of the final game.

■ Can you think of other global sports competitions where the start time would require a period of adjustment?

In preparation for the Beijing Olympics in 2008, the British Olympic Association established a holding camp in Macau. This facility provided the majority of the team with elite training facilities, and was only a three hour flight from Beijing. All the team were due to fly into to Macau at least seven days before the start of the Games, in order to allow them time to recover from the jet lag of the journey and to acclimatise to the local conditions. Although the Macau base offered a multi-sports camp, some of the team had satellite camps. The equestrian team are allowed to move their horses only once, so their camp was close to the Olympic venue in Hong Kong. As the rowing and canoe teams can actually practise at the Olympic venues, their sites were close to these venues.

ADJUSTMENT TO DAY-NIGHT RHYTHM

The globalisation of elite sport has meant that the traditional afternoon fixture is now a rarity in most sports. Added to this is the increased amount of international travel that teams and athletes now have to endure. This requires careful planning to ensure athletes have time to adjust to the different competition times and time zones they travel through. Biological adaptation to a new time zone can take four to five days.

PRE-MATCH RITUALS

Many players and teams go through specific routines and programmes before they play. These routines help players prepare physically and mentally for competition. Like any other aspect of preparation, they need to be practised during the long-term training phase (see Chapter 6, page 120).

In a survey commissioned by Guinness (SportsWise, 2006), researchers found that rugby players are more obsessive about pre- and post-match rituals than footballers or cricketers. As many as 62 per cent of rugby players stated that performing rituals was critical to their performance on the field. Examples of these rituals include:

■ putting their gumshield in only when they have crossed the touchline to enter the pitch

■ touching the ceiling as they leave the players' tunnel

■ taping up old injuries, even though they have healed.

The survey also found that a quarter of all cricketers wore a lucky item when playing, and over 33 per cent had a strict ritual about dressing for the game. Footballers reported a tendency to stick to a strict pre-game dietary ritual, many eating and drinking exactly the same things before every game.

CASE STUDY

JONNY WILKINSON, NEWCASTLE FALCONS AND ENGLAND

Jonny is reported to have said that he finds the atmosphere intense before any big match. He says there's always a lot of anxiety as people are desperate to get out there and get on with the game. …'It's a nervous and aggressive atmosphere – people are psyched and very aware of what they are about to face.'

He goes on to say that just thinking about the match, by picturing the sights and the smells and hearing the sounds in his mind, can make him very nervous.

Nearly every player has their own pre-match superstition – everyone does something that's a little bit different. 'I always wear the same T-shirt under my England shirt. And I always go out to warm up, come back, put my shoulder pads on and then my England shirt. I never warm up in my England shirt.'

He claims that it is more routine than thinking 'if I don't do this, today's going to go horribly wrong.'

'People like to have their own routines to fight back the nerves to keep them sane.'

■ Describe any pre-match rituals you have developed in your own sport – or if you really don't have any, describe those of another performer you know. Is there any logic to your rituals? How did they start?

▶ *Jonny Wilkinson has a specific routine associated with warming up*

HOTLINKS

For information on swift suits go to: http://uk.youtube.com/

For information on high-tech shirts (the Ionx) go to: http://www.mcalcio.com/ionized-shirts-the-latest-in-doping-technology/

The World Anti Doping Agency's mission is to promote and coordinate at international level the fight against doping in sport in all forms: www.wada-ama.org

BBC Sports Academy carries articles on sports events and those taking part: http://news.bbc.co.uk/sport1/hi/academy/default.stm

ExamCafé
Relax, refresh, result!

Refresh your memory

SURPRISE

▷ Remember that short-term preparation refers to the time immediately before competition.

▷ Key factors include: temperature and UV exposure, humidity, wind, temperature.

▷ Know that thermoregulation is a key factor in performance – and how athletes plan and use technology to help them control their body temperature.

▷ Understand that ergogenic aids (mechanical, chemical, physiological) are substances or devices that enhance performance.

▷ Know the benefits of using holding and preparation camps in the weeks and months before major competitions.

examiner's tips

Try to use up-to-date examples in your examination answers.
Always try to explain the science behind any examples you include.

Get the result!

Sample question and answer

Exam question

Elite athletes often prepare for competition using a phase of 'carbo-loading'.
Explain the principles behind this strategy.

(4 marks)

Student answer — candidate A

Carbohydrate loading should be done at least three days prior to the competition, and definitely on each day leading up to the competition. Carbo-loading involves eating a diet that is made up of at least 70 per cent carbohydrates.

It is best to eat foods that contain complex carbohydrates such as pasta and rice as these release energy slowly over a period of time.

CHO loading also involves a reduction in the training intensity for the last few days of preparation.

Examiner says:

A sound answer: the candidate does give the basics of the principle of carbo-loading. This answer would receive 3 marks.

Examiner says:

But they fail to score full marks as they don't explain what impact carbo-loading has on performance, i.e. topping up glycogen stores and ensuring the performer has the ability to perform with the most energy possible.

Student answer – candidate B

Carbo-loading is where an athlete eats lots of carbohydrate such as pasta before they play, this will make sure they have lots of energy before the game, they will also have lots of drinks so that they are fully hydrated.

Examiner says:

This is a brief answer that doesn't really answer the question set. The student doesn't give any detail about carbo-loading, and also gives irrelevant information about hydration. This answer would receive 0 marks.

model answer

Carbohydrate loading involves an athlete eating a diet that consists of at least 70 per cent carbohydrates. Carbo-loading should involve eating complex carbohydrates such as pasta and rice for three days before competition, and also involves a reduction in training intensity and no refuelling immediately after exercise for the last few days of preparation.

Complex carbohydrates release energy slowly over a period of time, hence carbo-loading is best suited to athletes and players whose competition lasts for around an hour or over.

Carbo-loading ensures that athletes top up their glycogen stores, and thus that they will have the ability to perform with the most energy possible.

CHAPTER 4 FATIGUE AND THE RECOVERY PROCESS

LEARNING OUTCOMES

By working through this chapter you should:

- understand the concept of fatigue within the sporting context
- understand why different levels of fatigue will affect performance, including the speed and effect of the depletion of fuels, the build-up of waste products, and accumulation of lactic acid
- understand the effects of dehydration and electrolyte loss
- know about the first few hours of recovery – including cooling down, lactic acid removal, restoration of ATP/phosphocreatine, glycogen stores, and excess post-exercise oxygen consumption
- be aware of ergogenic aids such as ice baths, compression clothing and music
- appreciate and understand alternative theories to explain fatigue
- know how we recover, and what can be done by the performer in order to speed up the recovery process

In this section we will look at the concept of **fatigue** – the different terminologies used to label it, and the different theories used to explain it. We also look at its effects on performance, and how elite athletes might manipulate the stages of recovery.

KEY TERM

fatigue
a reduced capacity to complete work. In the context of exercise, usually brought about by a lack of energy, lack of oxygen, or skeletal muscle tiredness resulting from depletion and/or leaking of calcium ions from the muscle.

EFFECTS OF FATIGUE ON PERFORMANCE

DEPLETION OF FUELS

As we saw in Chapter 1, there are three main energy sources:

- fats
- carbohydrates
- proteins.

Fats provide low-intensity fuel and insulation. They are used as fuel when the intensity of exercise is at a medium to low level, and energy requirements can be met through metabolisation of fats in the aerobic energy system.

Carbohydrates provide high-intensity energy. They are used as fuel when the intensity of exercise is at a level that can't be sustained through metabolisation of fats in the aerobic energy system.

▶ This exhausted boat race crew needs to focus on recovery

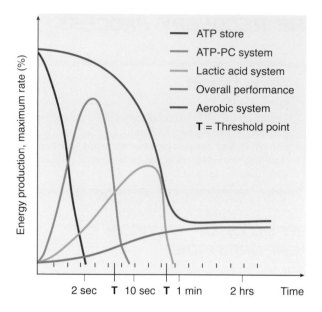

Fig. 4.1 Rates of energy production over time

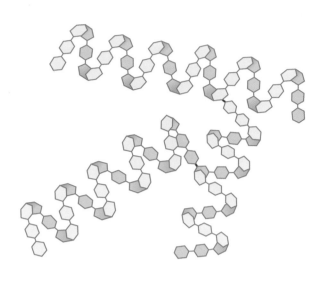

Fig. 4.2 Glycogen is a polymer molecule – each hexagon represents a glucose molecule

Proteins are for muscle tissue growth and repair, as well as providing energy. They are used as fuel when the athlete has eaten a very low-carbohydrate diet or is experiencing a famine, or towards the end of an ultra-distance event.

> ## KEY TERMS
>
> **ATP**
> adenosine triphosphate – a chemical compound which provides chemical potential energy. This is the only form of energy 'currency' that the body can spend.
>
> **PC**
> phosphocreatine (also known as creatine phosphate) – an important energy store in skeletal muscle, used to produce energy rapidly. Stores of PC are limited and will only support energy production for approximately 10 seconds.

The consequence of working at an intensity at which fats provide the primary fuel (which for most amateur athletes is somewhere below 60 per cent of the maximum heart rate) is that we have only a limited supply of the necessary fuel. This is about 8–10 seconds of **ATP** and phosphocreatine (**PC**), and up to 90 minutes of muscle glycogen – but this will be a much shorter period if the intensity of activity is cranked up.

To compensate for this, athletes may use dietary supplements during an activity to delay fatigue. But our bodies are not able to absorb carbohydrate at the same rate at which they use it during an event, so even supplementation can only delay fatigue.

DEPLETION OF MUSCLE GLYCOGEN STORES

Glycogen stores glucose in the form of a stable polymer molecule, which can be split apart when we need a rapid source of glucose for energy (see Figure 4.2). Glycogen is stored in muscle and in the liver. It is used as the primary energy source following PC depletion if intensity of exercise is high.

Glycogen is used in both the lactic acid energy pathway and the aerobic energy pathways depending on the intensity of exercise and the volume of air available.

Glycogen stores are made up in the metabolic process after the breakdown of carbohydrates, fats and proteins.

It is used up (or depleted) dependent on the body's ability to resynthesise its stores from other sources (such as fats), which in turn is affected by the intensity and duration of the activity.

REMEMBER

We have approximately 350 grams of glycogen in our body. That means approximately 90 minutes worth of glycogen-fuelled activity.

During strenuous activity, the body's blood sugar levels will go up. This is a result of both muscle and liver glycogen being broken down into glucose molecules:

- stored ATP is used up
- PC is used up
- muscle glycogen is used up
- liver glycogen is broken down, and component glucose molecules are transported in the blood, raising the blood sugar levels.

When liver glycogen levels begin to run low, or are depleted, the resulting low levels of blood sugar produce a feeling of lethargy and fatigue.

Fat could be metabolised if the intensity of the activity was low enough – but it should be noted that fat can be burned only in the presence of some glycogen. So total glycogen depletion would prevent even fat metabolisation.

REMEMBER

After an 800-metre race, glycogen levels can be restored in about two hours.

After a marathon, glycogen levels require up to 48 hours for replenishment, dependent upon diet.

▷ *Glycogen levels are low after a race, causing fatigue*

ACCUMULATION OF WASTE PRODUCTS

LACTIC ACID

There has been a great deal of research on lactic acid in recent years. Scientists have now debunked many of the myths about lactic acid impairing performance. It is now believed that lactic acid actually provides another fuel source for working muscles.

Lactic acid was previously seen as a by-product of metabolising glucose for energy, and as a waste product that causes a burning sensation in the muscles during intense exercise. Lactic acid may

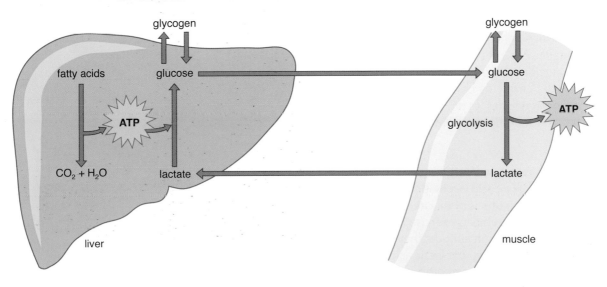

Fig. 4.3 *Glycolysis in muscle*

cause this burning sensation, but new research has confirmed that delayed-onset muscle soreness (DOMS), which was often blamed on lactic acid, is caused by microscopic tears and trauma to the muscles and inflammation, rather than by lactic acid.

Nowadays, lactic acid is seen as another important fuel source in the body. It is formed from glucose, and is used by working muscles for energy (Figure 4.3). Now it is thought that muscle cells convert glucose or glycogen to lactic acid. Then the lactic acid is absorbed and converted to a fuel by mitochondria in muscle cells.

By training at high intensity, it is thought that the body creates additional proteins that help absorb and convert lactic acid to energy.

CENTRAL GOVERNOR THEORY

'Fatigue is an emotional response that begins in your brain, not a physiological one originating in the muscles!' (St Clair Gibson et al., 2001)

Researchers Tim Noakes and Alan St Clair Gibson have developed a theory to challenge what had been accepted regarding muscle failure. The general consensus was that muscle failure set in as a result of depleted fuel, such as glycogen, and the build-up of lactic acid, which would alter the pH within the muscle, thus inhibiting the metabolic processes.

Noakes and St Clair Gibson were initially intrigued about three issues:

- the role of lactic acid in the fatiguing process
- the amount of muscle fibre recruitment during progressively maximal intensity
- muscle glycogen depletion.

They established a theory, the essence of which is the existence of a 'central governor'. They believe that your brain paces your muscles to keep them back from the brink of exhaustion. When the brain decides it's time to quit, it creates the distressing sensations you interpret as muscle fatigue.

THE ROLE OF LACTIC ACID

As noted above, lactic acid is a by-product of exercise, and its build-up is often cited as a cause of fatigue. But when subjects exercise in conditions designed to simulate high altitude, they become fatigued – despite the fact that lactic acid levels remain low. It appears that something else makes them tire well before they hit a physical limit.

MUSCLE FIBRE RECRUITMENT

During exercise, your body never uses all the available muscle fibres in a single contraction (known as a titanic contraction). Instead, it spreads the load by recruiting fresh fibres as needed. If fatigue was due to muscle fibres hitting some kind of limit, the number of fibres recruited should *increase* as the fibres tire and the body attempts to compensate by recruiting a larger fraction of the total.

But Noakes and his team found exactly the opposite. In one study, Noakes and St Clair Gibson recruited seven experienced cyclists and asked them to complete two 100-kilometre time trials on exercise bikes. On several occasions during the trial, the cyclists were also asked to sprint for 1000 or 4000 metres. Electrical sensors taped to their legs were used to measure nerve impulses traveling to their muscles. As fatigue set in, electrical activity in the cyclists' legs *dropped* – even during the sprints, when they were trying to cycle as fast as they could. To Noakes, this was strong evidence that the old theory was wrong. The cyclists may have felt as though they'd reached their physical limit. But there were actually considerable reserves they could theoretically tap into by using a greater fraction of the resting fibres.

For more information see Lindsay et al. (1996); Noakes et al. (2001); St Clair Gibson et al. (2001).

▶ *Research on muscle fibre recruitment involved experienced cyclists on exercise bikes*

MUSCLE GLYCOGEN DEPLETION

More evidence for the central governor theory comes from the fact that fatigued muscles don't actually run out of anything critical. For example, when researchers look at a slice of muscle tissue under a microscope, they can see that carbohydrate stores decline with exercise.

Carbohydrate is stored in the form of glycogen in your liver and muscles. Glycogen molecules are in the form of a linked chain (Figure 4.2), ranging in size from a few hundred to several thousand glucose molecules. But while glycogen levels might approach zero, they never quite get there. Why?

Fat could be metabolised if the intensity of activity was low enough (see page 61). But fat can be burned only in the presence of glycogen, so total glycogen depletion would prevent fat metabolisation, which would be catastrophic for the body.

So what is it that stops muscles from completely using up their stores of glycogen?

The central governor theory remains controversial. But it might help to explain why **interval training** is so effective.

> ### KEY TERM
> **interval training**
> a training technique where repeated bouts of exercise, often associated with high-intensity exercise, are separated by recovery periods and then repeated

In one study, researchers took a group of cyclists and assigned them to a four-week interval training programme. Despite the fact they completed only six interval sessions, the cyclists were able to shave an average of two minutes off their 40-kilometre time trial performance (54.4 versus 56.4 minutes). According to conventional wisdom, this improvement is down to changes in the muscles that make them better at using oxygen, or more able to fight fatigue. But Noakes believes that interval training works largely by teaching the central governor that going faster won't do your body any harm.

Noakes and St Clair Gibson argue that the central governor theory doesn't mean that what is happening in the muscles is irrelevant. Instead, the governor constantly monitors signals from the muscles, along with other information, to set the level of fatigue. In other words, physiological factors (such as the levels of glucose and oxygen in the blood) are not the direct cause of fatigue. Rather, they are signals the governor takes into account.

DEHYDRATION

Water constitutes 60 per cent of our total body mass.

Dehydration, which results from excessive water loss, will be accompanied by a loss of salt and calcium. This can lead to cramps and loss of muscle efficiency.

As more water is lost, the volume of plasma in the blood will decrease, and the concentration levels of the remaining salt will increase.

This will result in:

- decreased blood pressure
- decreased tissue fluid formation
- increased thirst
- increased heart rate
- retention of body heat
- declining performance (see Table 4.1).

So electrolyte replacement is also required if performance is to be maintained.

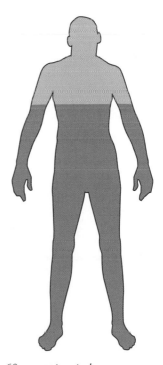

Fig. 4.4 We are 60 per cent water!

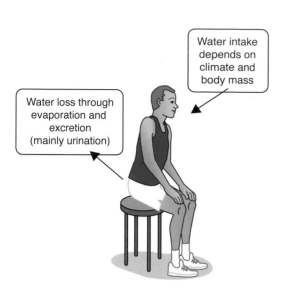

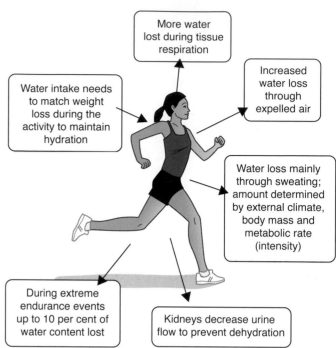

Fig. 4.5 *Water loss at rest and during exercise*

Body weight lost as sweat (%)	Performance effect
1	Loss of 5%
2	Loss of 10%
4	Loss of 25%
5	Potential failure to complete
>5	Potentially fatal

Table 4.1 *Declining performance due to dehydration*

▶ *Excess sweating has important effects on performance – and health*

TEMPERATURE REGULATION

Body temperature is maintained by balancing heat creation/input with heat loss.

Factors producing heat:

- metabolic processes
- exercise
- shivering
- sympathetic stimulation (stimulation of the sympathetic nervous system that produces an increase in heart rate)
- Q_{10} **effect**.

Factors causing heat loss:

- radiation
- conduction
- convection
- evaporation.

KEY TERM

Q_{10} effect

the Q_{10} temperature coefficient measures the rate of change of a biological or chemical system caused by increasing the temperature by 10°C. A 10°C increase in body temperature will result in a doubling of chemical reactions.

▶ *Recovering from a sprint takes a relatively short time*

RECOVERY

Recovery can take minutes, hours or days, depending on the level of stress experienced by the body. Very high-intensity activity over a few seconds is momentarily stressful, but can be recovered from fully in only three or four minutes. But running a personal best marathon or completing an iron man triathlon can take several days to recover from.

There are generally thought to be two phases of recovery: a fast component and a slow component.

FAST COMPONENT

The fast component of recovery is solely concerned with the restoration of muscle **phosphagen** stores, and takes up to four minutes.

▶ *London marathon runners after passing the finish line, wrapped in thermal foil sheets*

Recovery during the fast component represents the portion of oxygen used to resynthesise and restore muscle phosphagen stores (ATP and PC), which have been almost completely exhausted during high-intensity exercise. It is a rapid process, achieved mainly by using the aerobic energy system.

Three mechanisms contribute to the regeneration of phosphocreatine:

- energy from the aerobic conversion of carbohydrate into carbon dioxide and water is used to manufacture ATP from ADP and PC (the products of ATP consumption)

- some of this ATP is immediately utilised to create PC, using the coupled reaction –

$$ATP \rightarrow ADP + Pi + energy$$
$$\downarrow$$
$$energy + Pi + C \rightarrow PC$$

- a very small percentage of ATP, derived from lactic acid production, is made available for phosphagen replenishment.

Recovery time (seconds)	Muscle phosphagen restored (%)
10	10
30	50
60	75
90	87
120	93
150	97
180	99
210	101
240	102

Table 4.2 Approximate phosphagen recovery rates

SLOW COMPONENT

Everything else that is required to get the body back to its pre-exercise state falls within the slow component. These factors include heat dissipation, energy replenishment, rehydration, and removal of waste products.

As noted earlier, it used to be generally believed that the slow component of the oxygen debt was solely concerned with the removal of lactic acid from the muscles and the blood.

However:

- the process of removing lactic acid begins as soon as it is detected in muscle
- the majority of research into the speed of lactic acid removal suggests that 50 per cent is removed after 15 minutes, and the majority of the remainder is removed after 1 hour – so even with the most modest estimation, at least 76 per cent of the lactic acid will have been utilised, converted, or removed within the first hour after the cessation of exercise.

COOLING DOWN

After exercise, a process similar to that undertaken before exercise should be followed. This has been shown to speed up recovery dramatically.

It involves performing some kind of light, continuous exercise so that the heart rate remains elevated.

► *The final part of cooling down involves stretching exercises*

The purpose is to keep metabolic activity high, and capillaries dilated, so that oxygen can be flushed through the muscle tissue, removing and oxidising any lactic acid that remains. This will prevent blood pooling in the veins, which can cause dizziness if exercise is stopped abruptly.

This activity should last for some time (up to an hour is not classed as excessive). The heart rate can be used as an indicator of the duration required, with a varying intensity – high and low – being incorporated towards the latter stages.

The final part of the cool-down period should involve a period of stretching exercises, which should facilitate and improve the elasticity of the muscles, as they are still warm at this stage.

LACTIC ACID REMOVAL

It has been assumed that the oxygen intake following exercise is related purely to the extra oxygen that would have been consumed if the body had been able to sustain the workload through full aerobic respiration. The extra oxygen taken in after the fast component is repaid is thought to be used simply to remove lactic acid, with a significant percentage being converted/resynthesised into muscle glycogen.

More than half of exercise-induced lactic acid (exact quantities vary) is removed within 15 minutes after exercise, and the majority of the rest is removed within an hour. Even with a conservative estimate, that would mean that at least 76 per cent of the lactic acid is removed within 60 minutes of the end of exercise. So it is safe to assume that elevated heart and ventilation rates must be required for functions other than lactic acid removal. Increased temperature, growth and repair of tissue, reloading of energy stores and reloading of myoglobin all require oxygen. The respiratory and cardiac muscles will be working harder, and they also require oxygen. Heart and ventilation rates can remain elevated for some time.

As the heart also works harder, it will also require more oxygen. And tissue repair and the redistribution of calcium ions will both require energy, and thus oxygen.

Destination	Lactic acid involved (approx. %)
Oxidation into carbon dioxide and water	65
Conversion into glycogen (then stored in muscle and liver)	20
Conversion into protein	10
Conversion into glucose	15

Table 4.3 Lactic acid utilisation during recovery

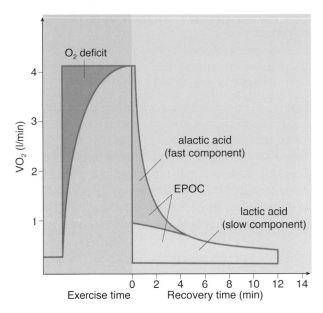

Fig. 4.6 Measuring EPOC

RESTORATION OF ATP, PC AND GLYCOGEN STORES POST-EXERCISE

There is a post-exercise 'window of opportunity' for replenishment. Fatty foods or simple sugars may be consumed during this period. They will not necessarily be stored as fat, but instead will be converted and used in the process of replenishing PC and glycogen. But the replenishment will not be as quick as it would have been if complex carbohydrates were consumed.

The better the quality of carbohydrate digested as soon as possible after exercise, the quicker the recovery.

EPOC

Excess post-exercise oxygen consumption (**EPOC**) refers to the elevation of ventilation and heart rates after exercise when compared with levels before. Previously, any form of post-activity increase in ventilation or heart rate was referred to as repaying an oxygen debt.

KEY TERM

EPOC
excess post-exercise oxygen consumption – a measurably increased rate of oxygen intake following activity

If not enough ATP can be produced aerobically, then glycolysis will take over as the predominant method of ATP supply, with its rapid depletion of muscle glycogen and production of lactic acid. (**Oxymyoglobin** stores supply a limited amount of oxygen to muscle cells to generate ATP aerobically.)

KEY TERM

oxymyoglobin
myoglobin that is loaded with oxygen (rather than with carbon dioxide, or with nothing)

Eventually, ATP production via the anaerobic energy systems will be used up and exercise must stop or the sports person will collapse!

REMEMBER

Aerobic is *with* sufficient oxygen.
Anaerobic is *without* sufficient oxygen.

DELAYED-ONSET MUSCLE SORENESS (DOMS)

Muscle soreness is often present during the latter stages of an exercise period, the day following strenuous exercise, or at both times.

Based on current evidence, it appears that DOMS is due to tissue injury caused by excessive mechanical forces that have been applied to muscle and connective tissue. DOMS is often the result of eccentric work, and may occur because of structural damage within muscle membranes. The breakdown of muscle proteins causes an inflammatory response, which is created as fluid shifts from blood plasma to damaged tissues. Local pain receptors are then stimulated by this excess fluid.

Muscle soreness can be minimised by:

- building training intensity gradually
- cross training: aerobic training increases capillarisation within the muscle, which allows greater and faster saturation of blood carrying oxygen and nutrients, and allows oxygenated blood to the lactic acid in muscle cells.

This means that the fitter sports person should suffer less from muscle soreness.

CARBOHYDRATE LOADING

Carbohydrate loading is a legal method of boosting the amount of glycogen in the body before a competition or event (see Chapter 1, page 16).

The initial view on carbohydrate loading was that if we eat a lot of complex carbohydrates the day or evening before a race, we will have more muscle glycogen and will be able to run faster.

But for the body to increase its muscle glycogen levels, rather than converting and storing the excess as fat, it must be stressed by not refuelling with carbohydrates immediately after exercise. This will encourage the body to hold onto additional carbohydrates – in the form of muscle glycogen – the next time they became available.

ERGOGENIC AIDS

Ergogenic aids are defined as any external influences that can positively affect physical or mental performance – including mechanical, pharmacological, physiological, nutritional and psychological aids. This can be as simple as taking water before and after exercising to aid hydration, to something as advanced as anabolic steroids. Other examples are ice baths and compression clothing.

ICE BATHS

Ice baths have become popular in contact sports such as rugby and American football, and with endurance athletes. For contact sports, whole-body ice baths can be considered. For sports that predominantly stress the legs, such as football, field hockey and running, immersion of the lower limbs only can be useful. Start with one-minute sessions,

► *Australian Olympic beach volleyball players endure an ice plunge bath at the Fitness First Recovery Centre at the Western Academy of Beijing*

▶ *Cathy Freeman of Australia wins the women's 400-metre final at the Sydney 2000 Olympics in an early compression suit*

progressing to a maximum of 10 minutes over a period of 10 weeks.

The use of ice baths has caught on among elite athletes. For runners, in particular, ice baths offer two distinct improvements over traditional ice techniques.

- Immersion allows controlled and even constriction around all the muscles, effectively closing microscopic damage that cannot be felt, and numbing the pain that can be felt.
- A physiological reaction is provoked by the large amount of muscle submerged. The body fights back from the shock of rapid cold immersion by sending a blood rush that flushes the damage-inflicting waste from your system, while the cold water on the outside preserves contraction.

Once you feel the blood rush, around the six-minute, mark, stay in for a couple more minutes, but don't overdo it. Muscles and tissues can tense up with too much cold, and to avoid tightness you should take a warm shower 30 to 60 minutes later.

COMPRESSION CLOTHING

Whether the reason is style, or some secret ergogenic aid, the use of compression clothing such as elastic shorts, tights and vests has become increasingly widespread among athletes and fitness enthusiasts alike (see Chapter 3, page 46). But what scientific evidence is there for its efficacy in speed training?

Compression socks gained popularity when it was found that wearing them during flying significantly reduced the risk of deep vein thrombosis, quite soon after Paula Radcliffe was seen wearing them while running. Now many leading sports teams wear full compression suits under their tracksuits to prevent flight-induced swelling, permitting them an earlier start to training and matches after intercontinental travel.

After seeing Cathy Freeman in her bullet-like one-piece suit that took her to the gold medal in the 400 metres in the 2000 Sydney Olympics, it is now the norm to see rugby players trussed up in muscle-hugging compression clothing under, or as part of, their kit.

Research in the USA and Australia, particularly at the Edith Cowan University in Western Australia, has shown several benefits from the use of performance compression sportswear (McGuigan and Newton, 2005).

The studies have confirmed benefits such as:
- better muscle alignment and structure, which
- reduces muscle damage,
- improves circulation, and
- increases awareness of muscle operation, leading to
- an increase in anaerobic threshold,
- power, and
- endurance.

Research indicates that compression clothing material can reduce the sweat rate by 30 per cent. In addition, there is evidence to suggest that compression clothing may improve exercise performance by reducing the impact of hot and/or humid conditions on the body's thermoregulatory system.

Refresh your memory

SURPRISE

Revision checklist

▷ What is meant by the term fatigue within the context of sport?

▷ What is the approximate rate of energy depletion for different activities and different intensities?

▷ What are the effects of depletion of energy on performance?

▷ How, and how quickly, do waste products build up, and what effects do they have on performance?

▷ How does lactic acid accumulate, what effect does it have on performance, and what can be done to reduce its effects?

▷ What are the effects of dehydration and electrolyte loss?

▷ What is the importance of early recovery, particularly in the first 2 hours?

▷ How and why do we cool down?

▷ At what rate is phosphagen replenished and lactic acid removed?

▷ What is EPOC? What are the two stages of recovery?

▷ What are the concepts behind carbohydrate loading?

▷ What is meant by the term ergogenic aids – can you identify appropriate ones for specific athletes?

examiner's tips

When answering questions on recovery, it is especially important to be accurate and specific.

A thorough understanding of energy, and the different mechanisms used by the body to produce it for exercise, makes it easier to work through scenarios and the likely causes/effects of fatigue.

Sample question and answer

Exam questions

Define the term flexibility, and identify the two main limiting factors. **(3 marks)**

Student answer – candidate A

Flexibility is to do with stretching and is determined by how often you stretch, the type of stretches that you do and whether you stretch before or after exercise. Static and ballistic are types of stretches, with static being the safest and most common type.

Examiner says:

The definition is not answered at all and, despite the fact that much of what the candidate has written for the next part of the answer is correct, it is not relevant to what has been asked in the question. This is not uncommon with student answers to examination questions. This student has seen the word 'flexibility' and simply written things related to flexibility, rather than analysing what the question has asked before providing the required points. So, the candidate has no marks (0) for this answer.

THINGS TO REMEMBER
1.
2.
0/6

Student answer — candidate B

Flexibility is how far you can stretch your muscles. It is affected by your age and your gender.

Examiner says:

This candidate has understood what the question has asked and provided a three-part answer.

Unfortunately, their definition is not accurate and they have identified two factors that will affect flexibility rather than two factors that will limit it.

Consequently, this candidate also scores no (0) marks.

Examiner says:

Notice how both parts of the question are answered in the model answer. Also, these have been answered accurately and an example has been given, i.e. a comparison between the shoulder and elbow joints, to clarify the answer.

model answer

Flexibility is to do with movement. The more movement you have, the greater your flexibility. Movement occurs at joints, and different types of joints allow different amounts of movement. For example, the elbow has limited movement compared with the shoulder. Also, as muscles pull on bones to create movement, the muscles need to be able to stretch. This is known as elasticity.

Exam question

Elite endurance athletes often use altitude training to improve performance. Explain why altitude training is considered to be of benefit, and describe the anatomical adaptations likely to occur.

(6 marks)

Examiner says:

A very poor answer that comes nowhere near answering the question. This candidate has a basic understanding that altitude makes exercise more difficult, and that after training at altitude there will potentially be a benefit – but the answer is too vague and is fundamentally inaccurate.

The candidate makes no attempt to answer the second part of the question, simply ignoring the requests for anatomical adaptations. Score – 0 marks.

Student answer – candidate A

Altitude training is used by athletes because at high altitude the air is thinner and so it is harder for them to work. Because of this, they will have to train harder than at sea level and so will make more benefits. When they compete after this type of training they will have improved their levels of fitness.

The candidate starts off very well, and all of what has been written is accurate. However, it does not all score marks. The first two sentences are very good and, combined, score the first available mark. But the candidate fails to explain why training at altitude will benefit the athlete, simply stating why performing at altitude is more difficult.

Although four adaptations are listed – and all four are very likely – only cardiac hypertrophy is a structural (anatomical) adaptation, the others being functional ones.

Total scored – 2 marks.

Student answer – candidate B

The partial pressure of oxygen at altitude is lower than at sea level and so it is harder for athletes to get as much oxygen into their bodies and to their working muscles per breath. As a result of this they will find it much harder to perform work than at sea level. This will lead to them having a reduced VO_2 max and so a lower performance.

The adaptations from training at altitude will be bradycardia, increased VO_2 max, cardiac hypertrophy and a quicker recovery rate after exercise.

model answer

The partial pressure of oxygen at altitude is lower than at sea level, which will reduce the amount of oxygen reaching the muscles. Altitude training enables the athlete to acclimatise and compensate for the lower oxygen saturation. (3 marks)

As a result of training at altitude, the body will be increasingly hypoxic, and so will produce more EPO, which in turn will produce more red blood cells. The increased work rate at altitude will be likely to cause cardiac hypertrophy (3 marks).

Total: 6 marks.

Exam question

Carbohydrate has long since been associated with endurance athletes. Explain what carbohydrate loading is and why it is so popular with marathon runners.

(5 marks)

Student answer – candidate A

Marathon runners are aerobic athletes and so use carbohydrates to make energy with air. If they have more carbohydrates they will be able to make more energy faster and so run quicker. They can achieve this by eating meals such as pasta and rice just before a race as both of these types of food are good sources of carbohydrates.

Examiner says:

Even before reading this question it looks unlikely to score the 5 marks available. For 5 marks you would need to make five valid points.

After reading the question it is difficult to see where the candidate would score any marks.

The first sentence is correct and might have scored a mark for the second part of the question had the answer gone a little further – there needed to be a link with marathons and the limited supply of glycogen in the body. The second sentence is inaccurate as more carbohydrate would not enable you to make energy faster.

Finally the candidate attempts to briefly explain how the athlete might carbohydrate load, which is too basic and not required for this question. Total score – 0 marks.

Student answer – candidate B

If a marathon runner was to run as fast as they were able to they would probably run out of the main energy that they use, which is carbohydrate. Most people have about 90 minutes of glycogen which is made largely from carbohydrates. As a marathon lasts longer than this the runner has to pace them selves. The idea behind carbohydrate loading is that by stressing the body and depriving it of carbohydrates just before an event, when you do allow it sufficient carbohydrates it will hold onto them and store more. That means that you should be able to exercise or run for longer or even a little faster.

model answer

Carbohydrate loading is the theory of increasing the body's stores of muscle glycogen prior to exercise. Glycogen is a long chain of glucose molecules, very similar to a complex carbohydrate, that the body uses as a source of immediate energy.

A marathon lasts for over 120 minutes and the body has approximately 90 minutes worth of muscle glycogen. If a marathon runner starts with a fast rate they will deplete their glycogen stores before the end of the race (what is known as hitting the wall). Glycogen levels can be conserved if the athlete runs more slowly but they may not win the race. To overcome this dilemma a marathon runner will increase their glycogen levels prior to the race by consuming high levels of carbohydrate (carbohydrate loading) so they will be able to run faster for longer.

UNIT 3
PREPARATION FOR OPTIMUM SPORTS PERFORMANCE

PART B
LONG-TERM PREPARATION

The term adaptation refers to a long-term and permanent change as a result of environmental factors. Training provides a stress for the body. Once this stress is experienced the body will respond in order to manage the stress more effectively. This is the purpose of long-term preparation – identifying weakness in an athlete's performance and then planning and undertaking training programmes to optimise performance. In this unit we identify the adaptations and strategies that apply to physiological, psychological and technical areas of training.

CHAPTER 5 LONG-TERM PHYSIOLOGICAL PREPARATION

LEARNING OUTCOMES

By working through this chapter, you should:

- know the key long-term adaptations linked to training methods
- understand the differences between aerobic and anaerobic training, and their physiological effects
- understand the purpose and techniques of continuous and interval training
- know the main methods of training, their applications and effects: plyometrics, circuit/weight/resistance training, speed training, fartlek training, core stability, speed, agility and quickness (SAQ) training, stretching

When referring to long-term preparation, we must first understand what we mean by 'long-term'. As noted in Chapter 1, both short- and long-term physiological preparation involve changes, but short-term refers to **responses** (changes that occur quickly, and are temporary) whereas long-term refers to **adaptations** (changes that take longer to occur, and are more permanent).

In this context, long-term preparation generally refers to the training that takes place well before a performance – training that prepares you for that performance by encouraging your body to make adaptations to the way it works. These changes produce a more efficient, and consequently less stressful, way of functioning.

TASK

Produce a plan similar to that in Figure 5.1 for your own preferred sport. Now produce a plan for a contrasting type of athlete. Explain how and why the two plans differ.

OBJECTIVE-LED PLANNING AND PERIODISATION

Elite athletes will look at their objectives and plan their training accordingly. This goes for all athletes, whether they focus on the Olympics, a World Cup match, or a regular games season.

The way in which elite athletes view the sporting calendar has changed quite significantly over recent years.

PERIODISATION

Periodisation is an organised approach to training that involves progressive cycling of various aspects of a training programme over a specific period.

KEY TERM

periodisation
splitting training into periods in order to focus better on specific objectives

- The entire period is known as the **macrocycle**. During this period, the athlete will set clear and specific objectives.
- In order to achieve these, the macrocycle is split into blocks called **mesocycles**. Each mesocycle will also have objectives that, when achieved, will contribute to the overall objective of the macrocycle.
- The mesocycles are also split into much smaller cycles called **microcycles**. These are individual or linked training sessions. Again, each training session should be objective-led, and will contribute towards the objective of that particular mesocycle.

macrocycle																				
mesocycle 1							mesocycle 2							mesocycle 3						
microcycle 1	microcycle 2	microcycle 3	microcycle 4	microcycle 5	microcycle 6	microcycle 7	microcycle 1	microcycle 2	microcycle 3	microcycle 4	microcycle 5	microcycle 6	microcycle 7	microcycle 1	microcycle 2	microcycle 3	microcycle 4	microcycle 5	microcycle 6	microcycle 7

Fig. 5.1 The cycles of periodisation

Traditionally, performers in all sports have a season that starts and finishes. The objective might have been to get fit during the pre-season, compete at their optimum level throughout the season, then have a break until it all started again the following year. There would have been variations on this within some sports, with cyclists traditionally taking part in cyclo-cross, and track athletes competing in cross-country events during the winter. But for the majority of sports, the calendar described above was quite accurate.

Nowadays, perspectives have changed quite significantly, with the season of an elite athlete being viewed almost as all their competing years of life. Athletes such as Sir Steve Redgrave and Lance Armstrong had a very clear focus during their peak performing years. Redgrave aimed to win an Olympic gold medal at rowing every four years, while Armstrong sought to win the Tour de France every July. Because of their respective objectives, they viewed their training periods very specifically. Yes, they competed at other events along the way, but this increasingly became used towards their sole goal – preparation for the ultimate event.

▶ *Lance Armstrong celebrates on the podium with his children after winning his seventh consecutive Tour de France in 2005*

▶ *Sir Steve Redgrave with his five Olympic gold medals in 2000*

It could be argued that Redgrave worked on a four-year macrocycle and Armstrong a one-year macrocycle. But it would probably be more realistic to see their training as continuing and evolving from one period to the next. Both athletes have been quoted as saying that preparation for the next one (Olympics or Tour) begins the minute the last one finishes.

Perhaps this type of planning and mindset might suit athletes such as these – but what about games players? For many games players, the season is no longer an eight- or nine-month period followed by six weeks' rest, then starting again with a traumatic pre-season.

Athletes and coaches alike still appreciate the great value of rest, but equally they now advocate active recovery periods, realising that a total break from activity will result in fitness losses that will take time to be recovered. Time will then have to be spent attempting to achieve the standards of the previous year, while competitors, who did not have the same complete break will have maintained significant fitness levels, and will be building on these as they seek to improve on last year's standards.

Being objective-led, and therefore clear about what athletes want to achieve, enables clear and precise planning. As a consequence, different athletes might periodise in slightly different ways, but the growing trend is a continuous macrocycle with an almost infinite number of mesocycles. The key is in the specific objective of each mesocycle and its role in contributing to the overall objective of the athlete.

Jun/Jul/Aug	Sep–Apr	May
70% aerobic endurance 20% strength 10% skills	30% aerobic endurance 20% speed 10% strength 40% skills	*Rest and active recovery 80–100% aerobic base training*

Table 5.1 *Extract from a football training macrocycle*

AEROBIC AND ANAEROBIC TRAINING

Aerobic and anaerobic training refer to the energy systems used by the body to provide the majority of its energy.

As noted in Chapter 1, the body has three systems that it uses to produce adenosine triphosphate (ATP), which is the energy currency that it uses to fuel muscular contraction. These three systems are:

- the aerobic energy system
- the ATP–phosphocreatine (PC) system – also known as the alactic energy system } anaerobic
- the lactic acid system.

The second and third systems can produce ATP when insufficient oxygen is available for the complete breakdown of glucose – so these are both **anaerobic** energy systems.

All three energy systems are continuously producing ATP for the working body. But only one will be the predominant energy-provider at any given time. Working intensity and duration determine which provider is dominant – the higher the intensity, the more likely the dependence will be on the anaerobic energy pathways (see Chapter 4, page 60). We all have different levels, or thresholds, at which the pathways are capable of being the dominant energy provider. Athletes will focus their training on shifting their own thresholds to suit their performance.

Duration (seconds)	Aerobic energy (%)	Anaerobic energy (%)
10	6	94
15	12	88
20	18	82
30	27	73
45	37	63
60	45	55
75	51	48
90	56	44
120	63	37
180	73	27
240	79	21

Table 5.2 *Duration of exercise against aerobic versus anaerobic energy sources*

Paul B. Gastin (2001) attempted to estimate the yield from the aerobic and anaerobic energy pathways during different durations of near-maximal intensity exercise. The intensity was based around 95 per cent of maximal effort (95 per cent of maximal effort, not of maximum heart rate).

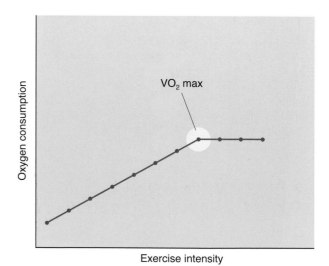

Fig. 5.2 *Oxygen consumption relative to exercise intensity*

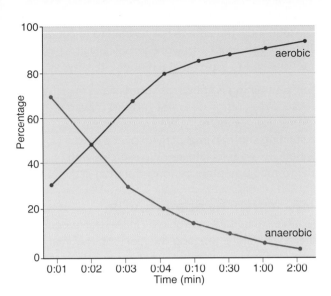

Fig. 5.3 *Percentage of aerobic and anaerobic energy used during a cross-country ski race (Source: Gastin 2001)*

▶ *Marathon runners need to run aerobically so that they can maintain activity for longer*

AEROBIC TRAINING

Aerobic training is not a method of training as such – it is a zone in which other methods of training are performed. The majority of training methods can be adapted to place stress on the way the body works either with or without oxygen.

■ If the majority of the energy required for training is made by the body, using oxygen, while the performance (or training) is taking place, then the body is working **aerobically**.

■ If the training demands energy at a faster rate than the body can produce it, then the body has to find a way to make energy without relying on oxygen – at this time the body would be working **anaerobically**.

The determining factor as to whether we are working aerobically or anaerobically is the intensity of the activity. The intensity that takes us from an aerobically dependent activity into one that is anaerobically dependent is entirely individual.

Training is undertaken to help make us more efficient when using either energy system – but also to target the intensity at which we start to become anaerobically dependent. By raising the intensity here, athletes will be able to perform faster for longer, because we can work anaerobically for only a limited period.

An example is a marathon runner who can run one mile in four minutes – 15 miles per hour. So in theory they could run a marathon (26.2 miles) in just under one and three-quarter hours. But we know that is not possible. This is because to run one mile so quickly, they must be working anaerobically, so they can run at that pace only for a limited time. Consequently, they must lower their intensity to one that is aerobically dominant and therefore one that they can maintain for longer.

But that is not the end of it for a marathon runner. As well as running aerobically, they have to think about where they will be getting the energy from to burn with the oxygen, in order to maintain running. They have two choices: from their fat stores, or from their muscle glycogen stores.

We have ample fat stores to fuel a great many marathons, but only sufficient glucose to fuel around 90 minutes of activity (see page 61).

As with aerobic or anaerobic energy, the predominant use of fat or glycogen is intensity-dependent. The greater the intensity, the greater the reliance on glycogen. The reality is that we will use energy from both our fat and our glycogen stores – we just need to try and maximise the fat use and minimise the glycogen use.

To summarise: a marathon runner needs to run aerobically and use fat as the main fuel.

To run aerobically, they must lower the intensity. Perhaps if our athlete reduces their running speed from 15 to 10 mph (two-and-a-half-hour marathon pace), then they will be working aerobically. But there is every likelihood that running at 10 mph will still be too great an intensity for the athlete to use fats – they will probably be almost completely dependent on muscle glycogen, which means they will have problems after about 15 miles.

The distance of 15–18 miles is the period when most amateur marathon runners begin to experience problems. Often called 'hitting the wall' or 'bonking', what has happened is that they have come very close to depleting their muscle glycogen stores.

So to avoid this, our runner must drop their pace still further in order to avoid depleting their glycogen stores. A speed of 8 mph would give a time of three hours and 16 minutes, but would still be too fast for the majority of athletes to run on fat-dependent fuel. A speed of 6 mph would give us a four-hour time, and possibly help us to avoid 'hitting the wall'. The only problem here is that the race was won some 110 minutes ago!

▶ If a marathon runner runs at too high an intensity they may fail to stay the course

Consequently, the athlete has to train to encourage their body to adapt – to work aerobically at a higher intensity and to burn fat at a higher intensity.

Aerobic training is known as submaximal exercise, because respiration does not support maximal contractions or intensity. We are capable of sustaining sub-maximal activity over a long period. So we associate aerobic exercise with low-to-medium-intensity, long-duration activity.

WHY TRAIN AEROBICALLY?

An athlete might train aerobically for several reasons. Their event might be a long-duration, sub-maximal event; or they might simply want to obtain the response or adaptations that this type of exercise will encourage.

WHAT ARE THE LIKELY RESPONSES OR ADAPTATIONS TO AEROBIC TRAINING?

The answer to this depends on the frequency and/or the intensity of the sub-maximal training.

But it is a little too simplistic to assume all sub-maximal training is aerobic. By definition, anything below a maximal sprint or one-rep maximum (1RM) is sub-maximal, and would therefore be aerobic. Clearly this is not the case.

Table 5.3 provides an approximate summary of the training objectives to be achieved at different sub-maximal training intensities. The percentages used could be of heart rate, Borg's rating of perceived exertion (see page 84), or similar.

Training zone	Training intensity (%)	Training objective
1	Below 60	Recovery
2	60	Critical threshold
3	60–70	Cardiovascular benefits, localised muscular endurance
4	70–80	Anaerobic threshold
5	80–85/90	Lactate tolerance
6	85–95	VO_2 max
Percentages are generic and do not take into account individual differences, which may differ by as much as 5 per cent.		

Table 5.3 Objectives at different sub-maximal training intensities

By examining Table 5.3, we can see that an athlete might perform some activity at an intensity below 60 per cent. Here the athlete is seeking not training adaptations, but responses that would aid a faster recovery.

By training regularly at or above 60 per cent, the athlete will experience a number of anatomical and physiological adaptations that will enable the body to function more effectively at these intensities. The consequence will be that the body will be able to generate the same output for a lower work rate, or alternatively a greater output for the same work rate.

Training in zone 3 (60–70 per cent) of Table 5.3 will bring about the following adaptations:

- an increase in **stroke volume** (SV)
- an increase in cardiac output when exercising (*Q*)
- increased **vascularisation** of the heart, lungs and targeted skeletal muscles
- potential to begin to increase the number of red blood cells
- potentially slight **cardiac hypertrophy**
- an increase in **end-systolic volume**
- increased **mitochondrial** number and density
- small increases in **myoglobin**
- potential increase in the thickness of **hyaline cartilage** (depending on the type of exercise being carried out)
- a decrease in body fat
- improved muscle tone and consequent improved ratio of lean muscle mass
- reduction in the resting heart rate
- improved ability to utilise fat as an energy source while exercising – this will be quicker and more effective if the intensity of training is regularly closer to the 60 per cent rather than the 70 per cent of this training zone.

HOTLINKS

www.netfit.co.uk/wkmen.htm provides training programmes and exercises for your chosen sport

www.sport-fitness-advisor.com provides advice on sports fitness and training

KEY TERMS

stroke volume
the volume of blood pumped by the right/left ventricle of the heart in one contraction

vascularisation
the formation of vessels, especially blood vessels such as capillaries

cardiac hypertrophy
an increase in the size and volume of the heart, particularly of the left ventricle (athletes may train for an increased size of heart, particularly the left ventricle; but note that cardiac myopathy, when the heart enlarges for no physiological reason, is very dangerous)

end-systolic volume
the volume of blood in the left ventricles of the heart at the end of a contraction (systole) and at the beginning of filling (diastole)

mitochondria
the muscle's energy factory – these are tiny organelles where much of the muscle's required ATP is produced

myoglobin
is located in the muscle and has a stronger affinity for oxygen than haemoglobin, which enables it to take and carry oxygen from the blood into the muscle. It also acts as an oxygen reserve for the muscle

hyaline cartilage
covers the end of bones to form the smooth articular surface of joints, preventing friction and providing smooth movement

Training in zones 4–6 (70–95 per cent) of Table 5.3 will bring about the following further adaptations:

- increased capacity for cardiac hypertrophy
- increased end-systolic volume
- increased strength of ventricular contractions
- decreased **end-diastolic volume**
- likelihood of **bradycardia**
- an increase in **VO$_2$ max** and an increased capacity to work for longer at a greater percentage of VO$_2$ max
- increased capacity to utilise, tolerate and transport lactic acid
- further decrease in body fat levels as a result of post-exercise elevated metabolic rate – at these training intensities fat is not likely to be utilised for fuel during the activity.

KEY TERMS

end-diastolic volume
the volume of blood in the heart after it has filled up, just prior to contraction

bradycardia
a resting heart rate of under 60 beats per minute. Trained athletes tend to have slow resting heart rates.

VO₂ max
(maximal oxygen consumption, **maximal oxygen uptake** or **aerobic capacity)** – the greatest volume of blood that can be taken in and used per minute per kg of body weight

BORG'S RATING OF PERCEIVED EXERTION (RPE)

Borg assigned a rating of intensity based on descriptions of how exercise feels to the individual.

Rating	Description
6	No exertion at all
7	Extremely light
8	
9	Very light exercise – for a healthy person, like walking slowly at their own pace for some minutes
10	
11	Light
12	
13	Somewhat hard (It is quite an effort; you feel tired but can continue)
14	
15	Hard (heavy)
16	
17	Very hard (healthy people can still go on, but have to push themselves and are very tired)
18	
19	Extremely hard (an extremely strenuous level – for most people, the most strenuous exercise they have ever experienced)
20	Maximal exertion

Table 5.4 Borg's RPE

Borg used a scale of 6–20 (Table 5.4), but any set of numbers could be used, with 1–10 being perhaps easier to apply:

1	Very weak	
2	Weak	
3	Moderate	
4	Somewhat strong	
5	Strong	
6		
7	Very strong	
8		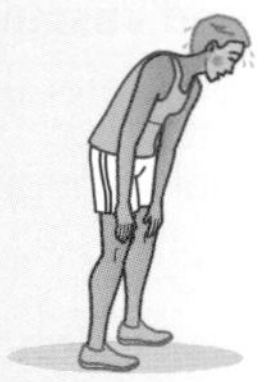
9	Extremely strong – almost maximal	
10	Maximal	

Fig. 5.4 A 1–10 scale of perceived exertion

TASK

Categorise the adaptations listed for training in zones 3 and 4–6 (page 82) under the different systems of the body – muscular, skeletal, circulatory and respiratory.

Categorise the same adaptations into structural and functional, identifying which structural adaptations lead to which functional ones.

As the body adapts to training regularly in these zones, it will perform more efficiently – hence the adaptations identified. The result will be that it will become harder to get to each zone. For example, when beginning a period of training in the aerobic zone, our marathon runner might have to run at 6 mph to get their heart rate up to 60 per cent of their maximum. But after three months' training in this zone, they might have to run at 8 mph to reach the same training intensity. This is clearly advantageous to them, as they are getting a greater output (an extra 2 mph) for the same input (a work rate of 60 per cent of their maximum).

▶ *Use the Karvonen formula to improve your output for the same input*

Unfortunately, this type of adaptation is not widely experienced, especially among amateur athletes, as a direct consequence of insufficient exposure to this level of intensity. Exercising at 60 per cent is quite low and will, initially at least, lead to exercising at a rate much lower and slower than what athletes are used to. When undertaking training at the lower end of this zone, many athletes will have to walk, where previously they would have run relatively comfortably. It is this low level of training and lack of apparent 'pain to induce gain' that deters many from training in this way.

APPLY IT!

Run, swim, row or cycle a distance that is a challenge to you, but that you know you can complete. It should take you longer than 20 minutes to do. Record the distance covered and the time taken.

Repeat the same session several days later – after full recovery – but restrict yourself to running at 60 per cent of your maximum heart rate. Use Karvonen's formula (see opposite) to calculate your desired heart rate. If you don't have a heart-rate monitor, then stop after five minutes and count your heart rate for 10 seconds (multiplying your answer by six), again after 10 minutes, and finally after 15 minutes. Adapt your speed to the results you get and the target heart rate you were working at. How much slower was the second session?

If you are able to repeat this 60 per cent training session three times for a week for a period of six weeks, you will be amazed at how much more quickly you cover the distance at the end of the six weeks, while still maintaining input at 60 per cent.

REMEMBER

The Karvonen formula allows you to determine how fast your heart should be beating for a particular zone or intensity of exercise (your desired training heart rate or THR):

$$HRR = MHR - RHR$$
$$THR = HRR \times \% \text{ intensity} + RHR$$

where:

HRR = heart rate reserve

MHR = maximum heart rate

RHR = resting heart rate.

For example:

If you have an MHR of 180 beats per minute (bpm) and an RHR of 70 bpm, to train at 60 per cent intensity:

$$180 - 70 = 110$$
$$(110 \times 0.6 = 66) + 70 = 136 \text{ bpm}$$

for 85 per cent intensity:

$$180 - 70 = 110$$
$$(110 \times 0.85 = 93.5) + 70 = 163.5 \text{ bpm}$$

ANAEROBIC TRAINING

Like aerobic training, anaerobic training is not a method of training in itself. You undertake anaerobic exercise when methods of training are undertaken at an intensity that is too high for the body to satisfy aerobically.

Anaerobic endurance is the ability to work at a high intensity repeatedly. Both the ATP–PC system and the lactic acid system should be trained, but targeted in the correct proportions for each sport. For example, tennis focuses on the ATP–PC system because of its short-burst and- frequent-rest play pattern. Squash, on the other hand, requires significant lactic acid system training as it is more continuous.

▶ *Tennis and squash both require anaerobic training – but tennis depends most on the ATP–PC system whereas squash depends more on the lactate system*

KEY TERM

anaerobic threshold
the intensity at which the anaerobic energy systems become the dominant energy-providers

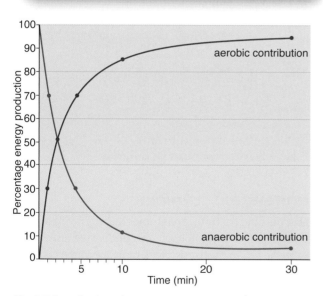

Fig. 5.5 *Contribution of energy systems to time of movement*

All exercise produces lactic acid. When we perform aerobically, the lactic acid produced is broken down and removed by the oxygen that is present. But as the intensity of exercise increases, so too does the amount of lactic acid produced. When the production of lactic acid begins to exceed the body's ability to break it down, use or remove it, then it will build up in the bloodstream. When the level of blood lactic acid reaches 4 mmol, a point of onset of blood lactate accumulation (OBLA) has been reached. The points of OBLA, lactate threshold and **anaerobic threshold** are all the same.

The anaerobic threshold varies from person to person and, within a given individual, from sport to sport. Untrained individuals are likely to have a low anaerobic threshold, while elite endurance athletes are likely to have a high anaerobic threshold.

Different exercise intensities within the body's aerobic zones produce different training adaptations. So it is safe to assume that cranking the intensity up further, into and beyond the anaerobic threshold, will mean the adaptations produced will again be different.

WHAT ARE THE LIKELY RESPONSES OR ADAPTATIONS TO ANAEROBIC TRAINING?

The fuels used by the body's anaerobic pathways to produce movement are glucose, derived from muscle glycogen stores, and phosphocreatine, (PC). When performing maximally, the body needs to make energy instantly. It does this by resynthesising ATP from ADP and the stores of PC (see Chapter 1, page 12). But there are very limited supplies of PC stored in muscle, with just about enough to fuel between 8 and 10 seconds of maximal intensity muscular activity.

If activity intensity drops slightly, then the body is able to regenerate ATP through **glycolysis**. This is not the most efficient use of the body's energy stores, as only two ATP compounds can be obtained from each glucose molecule during glycolysis, compared with up to 38 units of ATP produced through respiration.

KEY TERM

glycolysis
the sequence of reactions that converts glucose into pyruvate while producing two ATP compounds

CASE STUDY
THE BODY AS A SPORTS CAR

▶ *A sports car uses more fuel even at rest – and even more at speed*

Energy usage or depletion can be explained by looking at the fuel consumption of a very fast sports car or formula one racing car. Even when the car is idling, the sheer size of the engine means it is using quite a lot more fuel than a traditional family car would. When the car is driven towards its capacity, it will surge forward at incredible speeds, and the fuel level will visibly drop in front of you. The faster the car is driven, the faster the fuel is consumed. Anaerobic activity consumes fuel in a similar way.

- Find out how many miles to the gallon a formula one racing car might do, compared with the performance of your family car. Now compare the amount of fuel consumed by Michael Phelps (see page 18) with the amount of calories you consume in a day. What is the percentage difference in each case?

KEY TERM

lactate threshold
the exercise intensity at which lactic acid starts to accumulate in the bloodstream because it is produced more quickly than it can be removed (metabolised)

When exercising in or around your **lactate threshold**, your body's use of glucose will be far, far higher than if you were exercising comfortably within your aerobic intensities. As you increase the intensity, your body's need for fuel increases, and the usage of glucose also increases to meet the demand.

As anaerobic exercise leads to large quantities of lactic acid, continued exposure to this type of training will:

- enable the body to build up greater quantities of the enzymes used to convert lactic acid back into pyruvic acid
- increase the body's efficiency at utilising lactic acid
- increase the body's capacity to buffer lactic acid (buffering enables the body to transport, break down and convert lactic acid)
- increase the body's ability to tolerate greater levels of lactic acid (through continued exposure, the body and mind become better able to tolerate lactic acid).

Physical effects of anaerobic exercise include:

- increased thickness of the **ventricular myocardium**
- increased strength of ventricular contractions
- decreased end-systolic volume
- increased stroke volume
- **myofibrillar hypertrophy**
- increased muscle mass.

KEY TERMS

myocardium
the muscular tissue of the heart

ventricular myocardium
muscle cells of the heart ventricles that influence the force of contractions by the cardiac muscle

muscle hypertrophy
growth and increase in size of muscle cells

myofibrillar hypertrophy
the myofibrils of muscle increase in number, adding to muscular strength accompanied by a small increase in size of the muscle

METHODS AND APPROACHES TO TRAINING
CONTINUOUS TRAINING

In continuous training, the intensity of exercise is continuous or constant. It is generally associated with long-distance or duration activity that, by definition, has to be of medium-to-low intensity. It is frequently used for developing endurance and the aerobic energy system.

Continuous training is also used in recovery training, and because of the constant and relatively low intensity, it can also be used for helping to perfect technique.

Although continuous training is associated with aerobic and endurance athletes, it must not be dismissed as being suitable only for long-distance athletes. There is far more to continuous training then simply running, swimming or cycling for a long period of time.

WHAT INTENSITY AND FOR WHAT DURATION?

The intensity of exercise depends on what you are trying to achieve from your training. Referring back to Table 5.3 (page 82), we see that there are different benefits from training at different intensities. The lower the intensity, the longer it can be maintained.

Training at the lower end of these zones will:

- improve your ability to burn fat at higher intensities
- improve your cardiovascular and respiratory fitness, making you more energy-efficient
- improve your localised muscular endurance
- ultimately, improve your aerobic fitness.

Surprisingly – and unfortunately, considering that all events with a duration of more than two minutes place increasing demands on our aerobic systems – most athletes, particularly those below elite level, tend not to train at this intensity and so do not develop their aerobic fitness.

HOW DO I MEASURE THE INTENSITY?

Borg's RPE scale (see page 84) and heart rate are the most common methods of calculating training intensity. For some sports (such as cycling and rowing), power gauge meters are available. These are very accurate, but are also expensive.

REMEMBER

Training **in**tensity is the **in**put, not the outcome – which would be the speed.

CASE STUDY
OPEN WATERS

▶ *Swimming speed is very dependent on the conditions*

A swimmer swims 1500 metres in 25 minutes in a pool. He then swims the same distance in the sea or a river, where there is a current to contend with. He swims a lot harder, but it takes him longer than the 25 minutes he took in the pool.

If time or speed was the measure of intensity, we would have to assume that he did not work hard enough when swimming in the open water – when the opposite is true.

- Consider the differences between a track cyclist and a competitor in the Tour de France – what might affect the cyclist's speed on the open road?

HOW DO I OVERLOAD WITHOUT CHANGING THE BENEFITS OR ADAPTATIONS SOUGHT?

The training must be maintained at the same intensity or else the adaptations will differ. An athlete who is exercising at 65 per cent of their MHR must not overload by working harder or faster – but they can work for longer and apply progression by working more frequently. As the athlete's body adapts, they will have to exercise faster in order to achieve the same training intensity.

▶ *Cyclists benefit from continuous training – cycling events often last up to six hours*

INTERVAL TRAINING

This is a method of training where exercise (work) is interrupted (interval) by periods of rest.

The training session is split up around a work to rest (*W:R*) ratio. An example of a *W:R* ratio would be a football match with two 45-minute work periods, with a 15-minute rest interval, written as:
W:R = 45:15 or 3:1.

Training needs to be specific to the particular adaptations required for the sport in question. So the work period of the training session is calculated to a particular intensity and for a specific duration to achieve the adaptation you want.

To improve maximally, you need to work at 90–100 per cent of your maximum. You will only be able to do this for a short period of time. The rest period has to be long enough to enable the body to recover sufficiently, so that it can perform the next work period at the desired level of intensity and duration. Too little rest will prevent the training session from providing the desired effect.

The type of energy pathway used and the level of energy depletion experienced will determine the amount of rest time needed in order to fully replenish the pathway.

The rest period can be calculated in order to allow the energy pathway that has been used to replenish itself (see Table 4.2, page 65).

An example would be a games player attempting to develop their anaerobic capacity. They might seek to perform maximum sprints from a rolling start (ensuring they do not use energy on starting and acceleration) over a distance of 60 metres. As this would utilise approximate 60 per cent of their ATP–PC pathway's maximal capacity, then 60 per cent recovery time is required. So their interval training session would be described as 60 metres (maximum intensity): 2 minutes (recovery) × 4 repetitions. This would constitute one set, which would be repeated four times.

WHAT BENEFITS CAN I GET FROM THIS METHOD OF TRAINING?

The benefits are discussed at length in this section and also in the earlier section on aerobic training. Even a power athlete or anaerobic athlete would benefit from a solid aerobic base of fitness.

As well as the adaptations listed above (page 83), improved aerobic fitness will enhance your capacity to recover more quickly, both during training sessions and following them. A quicker recovery will facilitate more frequent training sessions, which will lead to a fitter athlete.

HOW WOULD AN ELITE ATHLETE UTILISE THIS TYPE OF TRAINING?

Elite athletes will look at their objectives and plan their training accordingly.

For many games players, the season is no longer separate, but is regarded as a continuous journey of improvement.

Continuous training will be used extensively during the initial mesocycles as the athlete seeks to build localised muscular endurance and baseline aerobic fitness. It will also be used during this and other mesocycles, when the athlete is seeking to 'reset' the exercise intensity at which they stop using fats as the main energy provider.

For example, a grand tour cyclist will begin their training in November or Decembers with a lot of long, relatively slow rides of up to 7 hours at a time, but ensuring that their training intensity remains between 60 and 75 per cent of maximum intensity.

Continuous training will also be used in individual microcycles, to encourage recovery after intense training or events (see Chapter 4).

Interval training is most frequently associated with anaerobic activities. But it is rapidly becoming the basis of every athlete's training programme, due to its adaptability and ability to provide **qualitative** benefits, compared with the more **quantitative** approach of, say, continuous training.

KEY TERMS

quality/qualitative training
specific training, usually of a high intensity, that an athlete carries out, designed directly to provide the results aimed for by the training programme

quantity/quantitative training
a greater volume of training, usually carried out to enable the next phase to be performed

▶ Interval training is very useful for distance runners

WHAT INTENSITY AND FOR WHAT DURATION?

As with all training, the intensity will be determined by the adaptations sought. The chosen intensity will dictate the duration of the work interval. The duration of the rest interval is determined by the energy systems used in the work interval, and the duration they were used for.

Then a knowledge of recovery needs to be applied so that the athlete can recover for the next work interval.

HOW DO I MEASURE THE INTENSITY?

If the interval training is using weights, intensity can be determined as percentages of the athlete's 1RM.

If the intervals are long, the heart rate can be used; if the sport allows, power meters could be used also. The RPE scale (page 84) is another option, which becomes the most appropriate if the intervals are very intense anaerobic ones.

HOW DO I OVERLOAD WITHOUT CHANGING THE BENEFITS OR ADAPTATIONS SOUGHT?

Increasing training frequency, number of intervals and duration will help increase the training stimulus. If the intervals are performed at a specific percentage of an athlete's maximum, then by increasing the maximum they are able to work at a harder resistance or tempo while still maintaining the same percentage intensity for training.

WHAT BENEFITS CAN I GET FROM THIS METHOD?

Interval training is such an adaptable approach that a huge number of training benefits can be targeted.

HOW WOULD AN ELITE ATHLETE UTILISE THIS TYPE OF TRAINING?

For an elite athlete, it is very important that training is specific and accurate, in order to create the environment that is most likely to encourage the adaptations needed. With this in mind, the intensity, duration and recovery time in between each repetition must be accurate. Also, sufficient repetitions and sets must be performed in order to achieve the desired effect, with careful attention not to perform too many repetitions or sets as this would have a detrimental effect.

In addition, the athlete's current individual state of fitness must be considered, as well as their age and experience, before planning intense quality exercise. The example given on page 89 – of a games player seeking to increase their anaerobic capacity – would be subject to subtle changes to each variable in order to be sufficiently specific and accurate.

For example:

- the distance might be increased or decreased, depending on their current anaerobic capacity
- with any changes in training distance, there would need to be appropriate changes in recovery time
- recovery time might also be increased if the athlete does not have sufficient or ideal aerobic fitness.

PLYOMETRIC TRAINING

For a muscle to cause movement, it must shorten. This is known as a concentric contraction. There is a maximum amount of force that a certain muscle can generate while contracting concentrically. However, if the muscle is lengthened (eccentric contraction) just prior to the contraction, it will produce greater force through the storage of elastic energy.

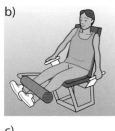
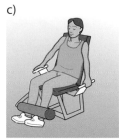

Fig. 5.6 Muscle contractions: (a) isometric, (b) concentric and (c) eccentric

This effect requires that the time between eccentric contraction and concentric contraction (known as the **amortisation phase**) should be very short, because the stored elastic energy created by the eccentric contraction is lost very quickly. This process is frequently referred to as the 'stretch-shortening cycle', and is one of the underlying mechanisms of plyometric training.

Plyometrics is a type of exercise that utilises a rapid eccentric movement, followed by a short amortisation phase, then followed by an explosive concentric movement, which enables the synergistic muscles to engage in the **myotatic (stretch) reflex** during the stretch-shortening cycle.

> ### KEY TERMS
> **myotatic reflex**
> (also called *stretch reflex*): reflex contraction of a muscle in response to stretching
>
> **amortisation phase**
> time between eccentric contraction and concentric contraction

REMEMBER

There are three main types of muscle action:
- isometric – muscle contracts but the angle at the joint remains unchanged
- concentric – muscle shortens
- eccentric – muscle lengthens.

press-ups
with claps
for pectorals,
deltoids
and triceps

Fig. 5.7 *Plyometric movements*

Plyometric exercises use explosive movements to develop muscular power and also coordination. Plyometric training will improve the neuromuscular link (between nerves and muscles). The result will be an increase in speed and force of contraction as more fibres will be recruited, and at a faster rate. This, in turn, will produce a more powerful contraction, but not necessarily an increase in maximal strength. As plyometrics involves actions performed quickly, there is a greater need for the movements involved to be linked, so coordination between the movements will improve. An indirect benefit is the need to remain balanced throughout the movement.

It should also be noted that plyometric training leaves the athlete at an increased risk of joint and soft tissue injury, and very much more susceptible to post-exercise delayed-onset muscle soreness (DOMS).

WHAT INTENSITY AND FOR WHAT DURATION?

The intensity for plyometrics should generally, by the definition of this type of exercise, be maximal.

HOW DO I MEASURE THE INTENSITY?

One of the drawbacks of this type of training is that it is difficult to gauge training intensity. Are you really working maximally, or are you saving a little for the next exercise?

It is possible with some plyometric exercises – those that produce a visible outcome, such as a horizontal jump or a vertical jump over an object – to monitor the effort exerted by comparing the outcomes. However, other exercises are not so easy to measure, and will require the athlete to be sufficiently motivated to exert the required effort.

HOW DO I OVERLOAD WITHOUT CHANGING THE BENEFITS OR ADAPTATIONS SOUGHT?

Overload will be natural if you are able to work maximally. Otherwise, increasing the number of repetitions or the duration of the session will add renewed training stimulus.

WHAT BENEFITS CAN I GET FROM THIS METHOD?

Rapid improvements in sport-specific power and speed, as well as coordination, can be obtained from plyometric training.

HOW WOULD AN ELITE ATHLETE UTILISE THIS TYPE OF TRAINING?

This method of training is used differently by different types of athlete. Runners and cyclists might undertake some plyometric training along with their aerobic training fairly early on in their cycles. This would be to increase their power in preparation for their sport-specific movements later on. Many other athletes, who naturally require significant levels of power for their events (such as field athletes or rugby players), would utilise plyometrics during their later cycles, just before competition.

CIRCUIT TRAINING

Circuit training consists of a series of exercises arranged and performed in order. The circuit will be designed to develop a specific targeted component of fitness or specific sport-related skill.

Press ups

Shuttle runs

Star jumps

Dorsal raises

Fig. 5.8 *Circuit training*

Traditionally, the athlete will move around a room performing specific exercises in different parts of the room. These areas of the room and exercises make up exercise stations. The athlete will know what component of fitness they are trying to develop, and this will be reflected in the exercise duration at each station, and also in the recovery time between stations.

For example, if an athlete is working with 12 stations and aims to improve their aerobic fitness, they would work for at least 90 seconds at each station, with a short break of 10 seconds between each station. If the circuit is arranged properly, the athlete will be exercising different body parts at each station. This enables the athlete to work at an intensity they can sustain for the 90 seconds, in the knowledge that the fatigued body part can recover while the next body part is worked.

In this way, it will take the athlete a few seconds less than 20 minutes to complete one circuit. If the athlete wished to target anaerobic fitness benefits, they could perform the same exercise stations, but working for 20 seconds at each station with

10 seconds recovery. This way they would work at a far higher tempo to last just 20 seconds, as against 90 seconds in the previous circuit.

There are two main types of circuit training.

- **Fixed load circuits**: each athlete performs a given number of repetitions at a station before moving on to the next. The time taken to complete the circuit is recorded.
- **Individual load circuits**: the athlete performs for a designated amount of time at a station and records the number of repetitions completed.

WHAT INTENSITY AND FOR WHAT DURATION?

When planning a circuit, there are several factors that need consideration. The first is the most fundamental – what do you require the circuit for? The great advantage of circuit training is that it can be used to develop a great variety of fitness components by adapting the variables available. It can be adapted further by working different body parts, or the same body part at consecutive stations, or by performing the skills of the sport.

HOW DO I MEASURE THE INTENSITY?

The intensity of any given circuit is usually determined by the duration of each individual station. Athletes often seek to work maximally for the duration of the station. For circuits that have longer at a given station, heart rate or RPE can be used.

HOW DO I OVERLOAD WITHOUT CHANGING THE BENEFITS OR ADAPTATIONS SOUGHT?

Overload is achieved in circuit training by reducing target times, increasing exercise resistance (difficulty of the exercise), and/or increasing repetition numbers.

WHAT BENEFITS CAN I GET FROM THIS METHOD?

As with all training methods that are adaptable, the adaptations will be linked to the intensity and type of circuit undertaken.

HOW WOULD AN ELITE ATHLETE UTILISE THIS TYPE OF TRAINING?

This method is perhaps not used greatly by elite athletes, unless they are seeking to relieve training monotony, or when performing skill-related drills.

APPLY IT!

Design a circuit, either fixed load or individual load, for your chosen sport. Set out clearly the objectives of the circuit training and how you arrived at your decisions regarding duration and intensity.

WEIGHT OR RESISTANCE TRAINING

Not to be confused with weightlifting, weight training involves exercising with a variable resistance. It is a predominantly anaerobic activity, although by varying the intensity and duration of training sessions, it can be manipulated to provide numerous benefits, including muscular endurance, dynamic and maximal strength, power and body composition, and improved posture.

▶ *Resistance training with fixed weights*

FIXED AND FREE WEIGHTS

Fixed weights refer to resistance machines. Each machine will be designed to work a particular muscle group, and will allow movement in the necessary planes. Resistance is offered in several ways, including hydraulics, weights and pulleys, incline/decline of the apparatus, elastic bands, etc. Machines are frequently called by the name of the exercise they offer.

Free weights are the bars and bells that are traditionally associated with weight training.

▶ *Resistance training with free weights*

SETS AND REPETITIONS

One complete range of movement of an exercise, from beginning to the end and back to the beginning again, is a repetition. A collection of repetitions makes one set.

During weight training, subjects perform a series of resistance exercises designed to develop the fitness component they require in specific sport-related muscles.

WHAT INTENSITY AND FOR WHAT DURATION?

Duration, or number of repetitions, will be directly linked to training intensity, which in turn will be related to the training objectives.

Training intensity (% of 1RM)	Training benefit
60–70	Localised muscular endurance
70–85	Dynamic strength
85–95	Power training
95+	Maximal strength gains

Table 5.5 Training intensity and benefits

HOW DO I MEASURE THE INTENSITY?

This is very easy when weight training – all weights lifted should be a percentage of the athlete's 1RM (see Table 5.5 for examples).

HOW DO I OVERLOAD WITHOUT CHANGING THE BENEFITS OR ADAPTATIONS SOUGHT?

Overload would usually be applied by working in a specific repetition range. For example, an athlete who wanted to increase his or her dynamic strength might be working at 75 per cent of their 1RM for three sets of 12–15 repetitions. That means that they would start out by performing three sets of 12 reps, and increase these until they could successfully complete three sets of 15 reps. At this stage, they would increase the resistance and drop down to three sets of 12 reps once again. By doing this, it is likely that they would also be increasing their 1RM at the same time, so their training weight will remain consistently at a specific percentage of their 1RM.

WHAT BENEFITS CAN I GET FROM THIS METHOD?

Increased musculature and improved muscle tone, increase in lean muscle mass, increased force produced, increases in strength (endurance-based, dynamic, explosive, absolute, relative and maximal), increases in power and improved body composition can all be achieved with weight or resistance training. Again, the benefits will depend on the intensity of training.

HOW WOULD AN ELITE ATHLETE UTILISE THIS TYPE OF TRAINING?

The majority of elite athletes use weight training, taking advantage of the ability to focus on specific muscles with specific training loads or intensities. Their weight training will reflect the mesocycle in which they are working and the objectives of that cycle. For example, a mesocycle with the objective of improving localised muscular endurance or baseline fitness would incorporate weight training at 60–70 per cent intensity.

SPEED TRAINING

It would be easy to assume that as strength and speed equals power then, conversely, increasing your strength and your power will improve your speed. Although there is a degree of truth in this, speed will really begin to improve only if the muscle fibres are stimulated to contract at a faster rate. The strongest muscles are not always the quickest ones!

Practising moving and accelerating more quickly helps to condition the neuromuscular system to improve the firing patterns of fast-twitch muscle fibres. This will occur as a result of faster recruitment of the contracting fibres through improved neuromuscular transmission. If the accelerations are maximal, this will encourage a greater proportion of fibres to be recruited to meet the demand.

Two variations of basic speed training are assisted and resisted speed training.

- **Assisted speed training** (also called overspeed training) helps to improve stride frequency through the use of equipment such as elasticated belts.
- **Resisted speed training** helps to improve speed-strength and stride length, again by using equipment such as sledges or parachutes that are pulled.

Fig. 5.9 Resisted speed training uses sledges or parachutes

Acceleration sprints are conducted for less than five seconds, with the athletes in a variety of starting positions – lying, sitting, kneeling or standing – depending on the sport.

Because acceleration work does not allow enough time for maximum sprinting speed to be reached, it is necessary to extend the length of the sprint. This can be done in 20-second efforts, in which maximum speed is held for five seconds, after ten seconds of gradual acceleration.

FARTLEK TRAINING

Fartlek (speed-play in Swedish) involves long-duration activity performed at varying intensities. For example, it might consist of fast, medium and slow running over a variety of distances. It is seen as ideal for games performers, as their intensity within a game is never constant. It is also equally helpful to race athletes, who might have to increase their intensity at different stages of an event in order to lose or catch opponents, race up a hill, or drive into the wind.

Fartlek training primarily takes advantage of the body temporarily being able to exceed the lactate threshold, and then recover (reduce blood lactate) while operating below the threshold but still doing physical activity. It is used extensively by elite athletes once they have built their aerobic base, with the intensity of the fartlek sessions intensifying as the mesocycles approach the competition phase.

Once into the competition phase of the macrocycle, athletes will cut down the volume of their training dramatically. During this period, they will maintain 'high-quality training' – short but intense sessions. Here fartlek and interval training are ideal.

For example, recommended fartlek training for the 800 metres includes:

■ 10 minutes warm-up jogging

■ repeat three times – maximum effort for 75 seconds, 150 seconds jogging run, maximum effort for 60 seconds, 120 seconds jogging run

■ 10-minute cool-down jogging.

For games players, the session will not involve only running, but also jogging and walking to fit in with the demands of the sport. The direction of work should not always be straight ahead, as games players have to go forwards, backwards and from side to side.

CORE STABILITY TRAINING

Core stability training is becoming increasingly popular as coaches and athletes begin to appreciate the benefits derived from strengthening this area of the body.

The core muscles are within the torso, and generally attach to the spine, pelvis and muscles that support the scapula. When these muscles contract, they stabilise the spine, pelvis and shoulders and create a solid base of support. The stronger this base, the better the platform that other muscles, particularly those of the arms and legs, have to work from. Consequently they can generate more forceful contractions. Training the body's core muscles can also correct postural imbalances and reduce the risk of injury.

Until relatively recently, the muscles of the body's core, and then really only the abdominals, would be trained only by athletes who overtly used them. Body builders would do copious numbers of sit-ups on raised platforms with 25 kg weights across their chests, because they knew they needed a visibly

Fig. 5.10 A stability ball pike – for developing core stability and upper body strength

strong stomach. Boxers would train their abdominals in preparation for taking punches to that region, but apart from that, many athletes would do a token number of sit-ups for no apparent reason.

That has now changed, as coaches and athletes have discovered that the body's core muscles are the foundation for all other movement.

Elite athletes may perform a variety of core strengthening exercises, particularly during the initial mesocycles along with their lower-intensity aerobic training. The aim is that by building a strong core early on in the cycle, the quality of effort later on will be maximised.

For example, a freestyle swimmer whose legs drop during the latter stages of a distance race will lose time and waste effort as a direct result of this now mechanically inefficient position. The reason for the dropping of their legs will be tiring of the core muscles. So by developing a strong core at the initial stages of training, all other training can be maximised.

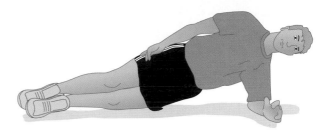

abdominal bracing for external obliques

abdominal bracing for rectus abdominis

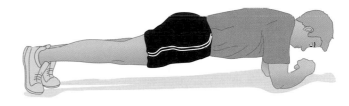

Fig. 5.11 *Core stability training*

SPEED, AGILITY AND QUICKNESS

Speed, agility and quickness (SAQ) are essential ingredients in a great many sporting activities. Athletes train to enhance these components.

'SAQ' is the title of a system patented by a company called SAQ International (see www.saqinternational.com). The system has gained national and international success, and is used by many top teams across the world, notably in the UK, USA and Australia.

The key difference between SAQ and traditional speed training is that the emphasis is on the neuromuscular system. Messages are sent to the muscles through nerves. By developing and honing the neurological firing patterns, the brain and body learn to work together much more efficiently. The theory behind this type of training is that by improving the individual's neuromuscular system, the initial movements will be more automatic and more efficient, and thus more explosive and precise.

The theory is that by getting the feet moving more quickly, the brain will have to send more frequent impulses to the muscles.

SAQ is perhaps most famous for incorporating horizontal ladder drills, and emphasising correct running technique and posture. The programme also uses explosive training, resisted running, contrast training and assisted running.

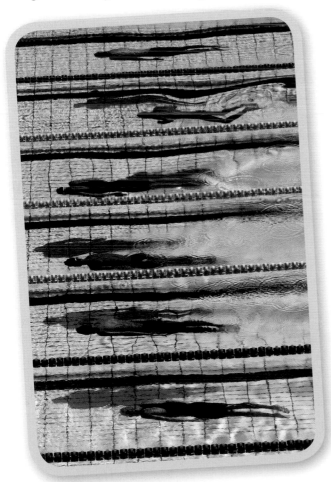

▶ *Core strength is important to swimming style, and therefore to success*

Explosive training is done using short speed bursts.

- In resisted running, the body is made to recruit more muscle fibres than normal.

- In contrast training, the resistance is removed but the body still recruits fibres as it would if the resistance was being applied.

- Increasing muscular recruitment leads to an increase in muscular power output. Assisted training increases the frequency at which the brain sends impulses. Short speed bursts can be achieved with tennis ball drops and/or reaction drills.

SAQ training is now used regularly by elite athletes to fit in with the aims of the mesocycle. It is unlikely to be used in cycles designed to develop base fitness; but in other cycles, where the aim is to build on the base and develop speed and or agility, these sessions will be used frequently.

STRETCHING

Stretching has been covered several times in the AS and A2 resources to date, but generally within the context of short-term preparation before an event or training session.

Here we are looking at a situation where an elite athlete has identified that an increase in flexibility and range of movement is a training need, and has included this as one of their mesocycle objectives.

First we need to understand what actually happens when a muscle is stretched. The stretch takes place in two places: in the **sarcomere**, and also within the connective tissue.

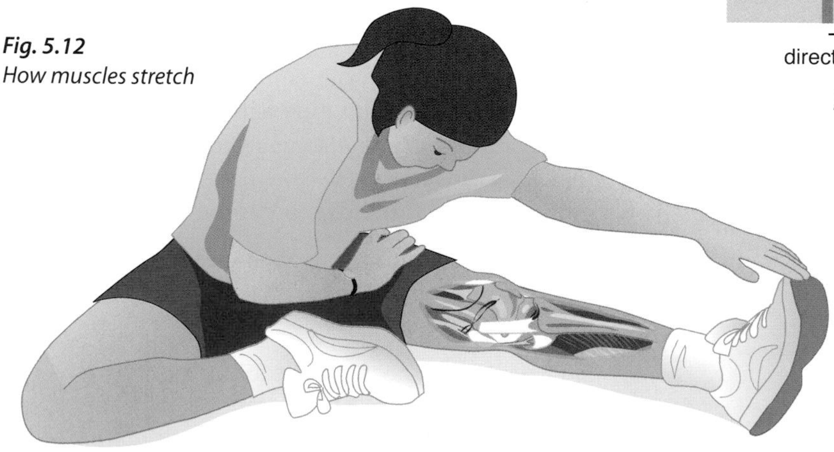

Muscle fibres that are being stretched – and it will not be all of the fibres – will experience a decrease in the overlap between the two main protein filaments within the sarcomere, the **actin** and **myosin**. As the fibres are stretched this overlap will decrease as the filaments themselves are stretched and realigned.

KEY TERMS

actin and **myosin**
the proteins that form the contractile filament in muscle **myofibrils**

myofibrils
bundles of actin and myosin filaments found within muscle cells

sarcomere
the basic unit of a muscle's cross-striated myofibril. A muscle cell, for example from a bicep, may contain 100,000 sarcomeres.

Fig. 5.12
How muscles stretch

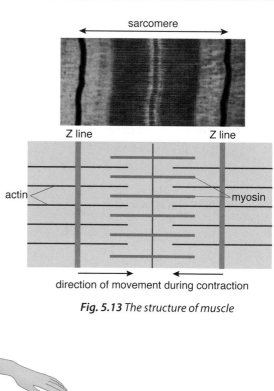

Fig. 5.13 The structure of muscle

The remainder of the force of the stretch will be absorbed within the connective tissue, namely the tendons.

Located within the muscles are different types of proprioceptors (sensory receptors – such as the muscle spindles and Golgi tendons). These send messages back to the brain via the central nervous system, which will instigate a resistance to the stretch. The degree of resistance will be matched by the degree of the stretch.

The aim of stretching is to recruit as many sarcomeres as possible and then to 'reprogram' the proprioceptors to accept a more stretched muscle as the norm.

Generally, stretching will fall into one of two main categories: static or dynamic (either stationary or moving). Each of these also falls into two categories: passive or active (done to you by someone else, or done by yourself). (For illustrations see Chapter 1, page 8.)

STATIC STRETCHING
The muscle is taken to its current elastic limit and held in position. Over time, the muscle spindles and Golgi tendons send a message to the brain that the new stretched position is not as severe as first identified. This is recognised as the safest mode of stretching, as you maintain control of the movement. But the gains are not as pronounced as they can be with other modes. It is also not particularly sport-specific, which has led many physiologists to question its role in warming up under the guise of injury prevention (see Chapter 1, page 9).

BALLISTIC STRETCHING
Ballistic stretching uses the momentum of a moving body or a limb in an attempt to force it beyond its normal range of motion. This is stretching by bouncing into (or out of) a stretched position, using the stretched muscles as a spring that pulls you out of the stretched position. An example might be bouncing down repeatedly to touch your toes. This type of stretching has often been considered dangerous. Because of the short period of time for which the sarcomeres are stretched, neither they nor the proprioceptors are able to adjust. The opposite can happen, as the muscles respond by tightening up.

DYNAMIC STRETCHING
This involves stretching the muscles through a full range of momentum and gradually increasing reach, speed of movement, or both. The major difference between dynamic and ballistic stretching is that ballistic stretching uses momentum to forcibly stretch the muscle, while dynamic stretching uses controlled movements to enhance the stretch.

ACTIVE STRETCHING
An active stretch is one where you assume a position and then hold it, with no assistance other than using the strength of your agonist muscles.

PASSIVE STRETCHING
Passive stretching is also referred to as relaxed stretching. A passive stretch is one where you assume a position and hold it with some other part of your body, or with the assistance of a partner or some other apparatus. For example, bringing your leg up high and then holding it there with your hand.

PROPRIOCEPTIVE NEUROMUSCULAR FACILITATION (PNF) STRETCHING
PNF stretching is currently the fastest and most effective way known to increase muscle elasticity and flexibility. PNF is a combination of passive stretching and isometric stretching in order to achieve maximum static flexibility (see Chapter 1, page 9).

PNF refers to a stretching technique in which a muscle group is passively stretched, then contracts isometrically against resistance while in the stretched position, and then is passively stretched again through the resulting increased range of motion. PNF stretching usually employs the use of a partner to provide resistance against the isometric contraction and then later to passively take the joint through its increased range of motion.

It is unlikely that an athlete would use ballistic stretching in a training session focusing on flexibility. It is far more likely that static and PNF stretches would be the basis of flexibility sessions, which could conceivably run through all the athlete's mesocycles.

Refresh your memory

Revision checklist

▷ The essence of long-term planning.

▷ Aerobic training:

   ○ What is it?

   ○ What adaptations does it lead to?

   ○ Why?

▷ Anaerobic training:

   ○ What is it?

   ○ What adaptations does it lead to?

   ○ Why?

▷ The methods of training:

   ○ What are they?

   ○ What are their characteristics?

   ○ How would they be used by elite athletes in their long-term planning?

   ○ What adaptations do they lead to?

examiner's tips

Questions on methods of training will require you to define the type of training, and/or demonstrate that you understand it by applying it to a suitably identified athlete. Your definitions must be accurate and specific in describing that training method. When applying the method, you must ensure that the intensity, duration, frequency and recovery are reflective of the training, the sport and the objectives sought.

Get the result!

Sample question and answer

Exam question

Periodisation is a common practice used by athletes to break their training into cycles. Identify a common structure for a periodised programme and show how an athlete might use these cycles to structure their training

(6 marks)

Student answer – candidate A

Pre-season is the first mesocycle	Enable the athlete to ease back into training post-rest period, low intensity technique work Less likely to develop injuries. Belief that it allows for base aerobic fitness to be developed
Pre-competition period	Increase in intensity/development of speed Raising of aerobic capacity. Development of lactate Increasing recovery capacity
Competition period	Maintenance work High quality but short duration Emphasis on recovery
Recovery period	Low intensity & short duration Longer rest periods/increase in rest days Greater variety of activities performed

A footballer might use periodisation to help them focus on their objectives during a season. The footballer would look at his whole year as a macrocycle, he would then split this year up into blocks that would be mesocycles. Each mesocycle would contain a number of training session, these are called microcycles. He might have three main mesocycles which would be the pre-season, the season and the off-season.

During the pre-season they would be aiming to develop their fitness levels again in preparation for the coming season. They would start off with low-intensity training and build it up as the season approached.

During the season the footballer would reduce their training because they will be playing competitive matches. The aim during this mesocycle is to maintain fitness levels.

Finally the off-season would be the recovery phase. The footballer would have a break from football and perhaps try other sports as recreation, helping them to come back fresh for the next season.

Examiner says:

This candidate has included all of the salient points that were required by the mark scheme. They clearly understand periodisation and its benefits for athletes, and have applied it well to a footballer's situation.

Examiner says:

But they have not been totally clear on what the question was asking, as they have included some points that are not necessary, e.g. 'The footballer would look at his whole year as a macrocycle, he would then split this year up into blocks that would be mesocycles. Each mesocycle would contain a number of training session, these are called microcycles.'

Examiner says:

Nevertheless, the candidate has identified three cycles and also the objectives of each to the benefit of the footballer.

Examiner says:

This answer would score the full 6 marks and would be an A grade answer.

CHAPTER 6 LONG-TERM PSYCHOLOGICAL PREPARATION

LEARNING OUTCOMES

By working through this chapter, you should:

■ appreciate the value of long-term psychological planning and interventions

■ develop applied knowledge and understanding of how to use goal-setting over time

■ experience an applied methodology in performance profiling

■ understand the concept of motivation and how to explain sports performances through attribution theory

■ learn how to develop a performance psychologically through modern psychological trends

■ develop an appreciation of the importance of the group in a successful performance, and how to build cohesion

There has always been some debate about the effect sports psychology actually has on a performance. You will have read in Part A the explanation and theories relating to how performers may use psychological strategies in the short term to prepare mentally to achieve an optimum performance.

Performers may spend many hours preparing physically during their careers, but in comparison, devote very little time to preparing psychologically. This should not be confused with the enormous amount of time we all spend thinking, dreaming and talking about our performances, or about sport in general.

Long-term psychological preparation may be ignored, or at best only paid lip service to. But it is now regarded as just as important as any long-term training programme or technical development. You will agree that if you are not mentally tuned in, if you are not 'up for the game', or if you are not fully focused, the physical performance you desire will almost certainly not be realised. This chapter aims to familiarise you with those areas of sports psychology that will aid your performance in the long term.

GOAL-SETTING AND MENTAL TRAINING

The use of psychological tools in building a performance enables individuals and teams to achieve their potential. The consistent training of the mind through the use of psychological methods is vital to a successful performer achieving their dreams and ambitions. Sports coach UK identifies four mental qualities that need to be trained in order to achieve success:

■ commitment

■ confidence

■ control

■ concentration.

Goal-setting enhances not only these mental qualities, but all aspects of a performance – psychological, physical and technical.

WHAT IS GOAL-SETTING?

A goal is an objective that we set for ourselves, or that is set for us by other influential persons. We constantly set ourselves goals in everyday life. Goal-setting is a natural human act – our dreams, hopes, fears and fantasies are all, in a way, a form of goal-oriented thinking – something we wish to come true. The goals we set may be simple and obvious ones, such as getting to lessons on time and completing our school work to a deadline, and then passing our exams with a certain grade.

In a sports or physical activity context, we may wish to gain selection for a county team, to achieve a personal best in an athletic event, or to score a century in a cricket match this season.

Such long-term goals need to be broken down into less ambitious short-term goals. This means developing a hierarchy of goals, each being the foundation for the next. Goals can be set in the short, medium and long term. This allows performers to plan more realistically for their future participation. Starting with smaller and realistic goals, while not ignoring your long-term goals, is a positive principle to follow.

There are no formal criteria for the timing of goal-setting. For short-term goals, it is reasonable to aim for a time span of approximately four weeks, which may be detailed as a day-by-day programme. Medium-term goals may be set for up to a year, while long-term goals can overlap and go beyond this, and may be the performer's single ultimate ambition. For the purposes of this chapter, we refer simply to just your short-term and long-term goals.

REMEMBER

Goals are not normally set for longer than two years – they are often adjusted with more immediate changes in performance or in the performer's lifestyle, and re-evaluation of the more immediate, short-term goals. Effective goal-setting must be time-phased – and realistic.

REMEMBER

Short-term goals are the foundation of long-term goal achievement.

Goal-setting in the sports context should not just be concerned with winning. Other areas of a performer's sports profile are equally important, and all combine to help achieve a successful performance. Technical developments, controlling stress and anxiety, and the physiological development of the performer all need to be planned for. Goal-setting reinforces a performer's strengths and helps direct attention to eliminating weaknesses.

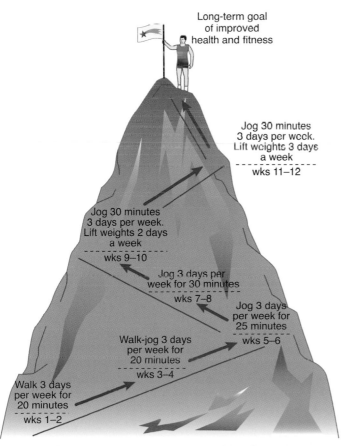

Fig. 6.1 *Short-term goals provide the groundwork for long-term goal achievement*

WHY IS GOAL-SETTING IMPORTANT?

Goal-setting is important for all people, not only those directly involved in sport and physical activities. Goals need to be agreed, which involves discussions between athletes and coaches, between team members, and between sports psychologists and performers. Effective goal-setting will provide the performer with the following benefits.

- Motivates the performer.
- Enables the performer to become more organised and efficient, which creates more time for training, performing and other responsibilities.
- Allows the performer to plan training and performance programmes.
- Provides performers with a structured pathway of development by focusing attention on the key elements of a performance.
- Helps the performer reduce anxiety and control arousal.
- Builds self-confidence and increases effectiveness.

SUBJECTIVE VERSUS OBJECTIVE GOALS

As a performer, it is vital that you distinguish between:

- **subjective goals** – general statements of intent that are not stated in measurable terms, such as 'I want to play well'
- **objective goals** – statements that focus on attaining a specific standard of proficiency, usually within a specified time.

Objective goals are easier to realise, as they have a defined intention for you, the performer, to achieve. As they are more specific, yet still personal to you, it is more productive to decide on objective rather than subjective goal-setting. For example, improving a technique or developing greater endurance will make your performance a better one – both of these can be achieved through structured training programmes that involve objective measurements. You may wish to think about those performers who have high achievement motivation and so set themselves challenging goals, as opposed to those who set relatively easy goals, knowing they can be achieved with guaranteed success.

TYPES OF GOAL

Goals are not all the same; they can be grouped into specific types, allowing your selection to be more structured. Some commonly used groups are as follows.

- **Outcome goals** – are concerned with an end product and are conditioned by specific successes, as in winning an athletics competition or a cup competition. These are often externally controlled, as luck and the strength of the opposition can influence the outcome.

- **Performance goals** – relate directly to the achievement of a performance outcome, for example achieving a personal best in swimming. These are measurable – they can be assessed through scientific means such as timekeeping, and are therefore objective.

- **Process goals** – are centred on the technical elements that underpin a performance as a focus for development. For example, a tennis player may highlight the need to improve a weak backhand technique when performing a ground stroke. These tend to be internally controlled and centre the performer's attention on their effort and ability.

- **Short-term goals** – the building blocks or stepping stones that need to be achieved consistently, leading to the successful realisation of long-term goal(s). In rugby, a lineout thrower may need to refine their technique in order to provide a successful attacking platform for their team.

- **Long-term goals** – have a larger objective and can only be achieved over time through the use and completion of short-term objectives. Long-term goals are invariably results-based and rely on the performer having a well-constructed development plan for their performances.

(Adapted from Atherton, 2003)

EXAM TIP

Ensure you learn the key terms and know them by heart – then you won't be struggling under exam conditions to understand a particular question.

GOAL-SETTING STRUCTURE

All performers need a structure to their goal-setting to guide and shape their performance pathway. This can be achieved through the application of the SMARTER principle (National Coaching Foundation). It is vital you do not focus just on the outcomes when formulating your goals.

SMARTER is an acronym that provides the performer with a pathway through which goals can be set.

- **Specific** – goals should be clear and concise. 'Playing well in a sport' is too vague, but 'improving a technique' is not. Specific and challenging goals improve performances.

- **Measurable** – goals need to be assessed through formal processes; when successful, this helps build confidence and motivation. As part of measurement, the performer must be prepared to evaluate their progress critically and adjust their goals as necessary.

- **Agreed** – goals should be discussed and agreed with others. A coach may set you a more realistic target; once agreed, this helps provide you with a sense of responsibility for your own development. Team players must all agree their objectives, such as a tactical plan.

- **Realistic** – goals must be genuine and not beyond the scope of the performer. Setting unrealistic goals can be demotivating; but goals must stretch and challenge the performer for improvements to occur.

- **Time-bound** – goals should reflect the short- and long-term objectives of the performer, and are progressive in their difficulty. Setting times within which goals should be achieved is sensible, but should not be inflexible.

- **Exciting** – goals need to provide the performer with a stimulus to progress and achieve. If the goals do not provide an exciting stimulus, performers may become demotivated, and as a consequence under-achieve in relation to their potential.

- **Recorded** – by recording their goals and creating a pathway for development, performers can see their agreed structure, time plan, and processes for evaluation and measurement. This will motivate the performer.

There are three basic strategies for goal-setting:

- **planning and preparation** – agree set goals through discussion and analysis
- **education and acquisition** – in order to research the most effective ways to set your goals
- **implementation and follow-up** – record the goals and time frame, and set in motion a process of evaluation and review.

(Adapted from Weinberg and Gould, 1999)

Plan and set your goals and agree to the commitment – long-term goals first, then short-term

↓

Put into place **strategies** that you know are realistic, that ensure your short-term goals are realised in each step and phase

↓

Evaluate regularly and **reward** success

↓

Seek the **help** of a tutor or mentor to help you, who can oversee your progress

↓

Do not be concerned if a setback occurs – always have a **plan B** at hand

↓

Never lose sight of the **long-term goal** you have set yourself

↓

Never be afraid to **rewrite** a step or phase in the process

APPLY IT!

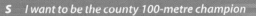

SMARTER in practice:

S   I want to be the county 100-metre champion

M   I know the time I have to run

A   My coach and I have set this as a target

R   I know I can beat the record – I have the potential

T   To go to 'All England' at the end of the season

E   I am really motivated and excited by my chances

R   I have written my goals down and will review them monthly

How will I achieve this goal of reaching the county track championships?

S   I'm going to run the 100 metres faster and beat my personal best

M   I'm going to beat my time personal best by 1.4 s

A   I will train five times a week

R   I will run 0.2 s faster each month in season

T   It will take me 28 weeks to realise my goal

E   I will train with others each session to remain motivated

R   I will meet with my coach every week to discuss and review

Now try to apply SMARTER to your own short- and long-term goals.

REMEMBER

Injury may cause you to re-evaluate your goals and performance/training programmes.

SUCCESSFUL GOAL-SETTING

There is no guarantee that a programme of goal-setting will always work. A number of associated factors will influence how you set, undertake and evaluate your goals. It is possible to see the links in the processes of goal-setting – if each link is accomplished, the goals you set can be achieved.

FACTORS AFFECTING SUCCESSFUL GOAL-SETTING

A number of factors will influence a performer's success in achieving their goals. If your goals have been planned appropriately and evaluated regularly, they should be achievable. But the following factors may influence you in achieving your goals, and are some common reasons why the process of goal-setting may fail.

- The goals you set are unrealistic and unmanageable.
- You set too many goals, and conflict occurs.
- The goals set are beyond your control.

- The time frame for completion is not appropriate to the step-by-step process working towards your long-term goal.
- No allowance is built into the programme, so there is no flexibility when goals become blocked or inappropriate.
- The review and evaluation process is *ad hoc*, and not related to the overall goal-setting process.
- Outcome goals have overtaken performance and process goals.

PERFORMANCE PROFILING

From your coursework tasks in Unit 2 (Chapter 8: Task 2.4, Performance Analysis), you will be aware of the role of performance profiling in constructing your individual development programme. Performance profiling is now a well-established, logical and functional part of elite athletic regimes – and is a methodology suitable for any performer. The long-term athlete development programmes that are now commonplace in all sports incorporate profiling as the starting point for all preparation and performance improvements.

Focusing your studies on the psychological components of your performance, and how you can construct a long-term psychological development plan, will effectively provide you with the knowledge and understanding to enhance your performance. Identifying the components of your psychological profile provides you with the tools you need to maintain your strengths and eradicate your weaknesses.

▶ *The long-term athlete development model was developed first with skiers, but is now used more widely*

WHAT DOES PERFORMANCE PROFILING ACHIEVE?

Psychological performance profiling has the following objectives:

- to identify areas that require psychological interventions
- to identify your **psychological skills training** objectives
- to aid your motivation and adherence to the programme
- to allow you to compare with and copy successful/elite performers
- to monitor changes in your profile over time.

We all have taken part in sports or physical activity when events have not gone exactly to plan. You may have lost concentration, or 'frozen' at a vital moment. Performers often resort to attributing failure in performances to mental factors – 'we were intimidated', 'I lost concentration' or 'I lacked motivation' – yet might not then consider undertaking any form of psychological intervention. The normal response when under-achieving is to undertake physical training – your coach may overtrain you as a form of punishment, or you may undertake a technical session where you hit tennis or golf balls over and over again. But the real reason for your under-achievement may be not physiological, but psychological. So what should the performer do?

Performance profiling forms the basis for the performer to build and use effectively a psychological skills training programme. Mental skills can be learned, just as physical skills can!

> ### KEY TERM
>
> **psychological skills training**
> the systematic and consistent practice of mental or psychological skills

Studies have shown that successful athletes are those who have undertaken and maintain a psychological skills training programme. But psychological factors are often unseen, and it is difficult to access what is going on inside the performer's mind. Many performers spend little time undertaking a psychological skills training programme, or do not want to undertake one because they lack the time, or the knowledge, to do so.

▶ *To help sports performance, many coaches and sport psychologists use psychological skills training programmes*

DEVELOPING A PSYCHOLOGICAL SKILLS TRAINING PROGRAMME

In designing a programme, you will move through a four-stage process.

- **Stage 1: Introduction** – learn the importance of the programme to you, undertake an honest appraisal, and agree a commitment.

- **Stage 2: Construction** – construct a performance profile, and undertake a series of strategies to enhance your desired/optimum profile goals.

- **Stage 3: Implementation** – make the psychological skills training programme an automatic daily routine and apply it to actual competitive environments.

- **Stage 4: Assessment** – review and reconstruct your profile.

Clive Woodward, England Coach to the 2003 Rugby World Cup winners, undertook an immediate performance analysis when his team won – not when his team lost, as you might expect. This was done to establish and understand exactly why the team had won, and the areas the winning performance was built on – including psychological ones.

STRETCH AND CHALLENGE

Why might 'underdogs' succeed? Sometimes we hear of a performance where an underdog has beaten those who were regarded as the better team or player. You may find it all starts with the belief that they will be successful. Suggest five factors that might contribute to the underdogs' success.

CASE STUDY

SARAH MAXIMISES HER PERFORMANCE

In order to achieve and regulate her optimum performance in competitive hockey, Sarah has identified the need to use psychological skills training to maintain concentration, enhance confidence and eliminate aggression. She achieves this through the use of imagery, progressive muscle-relaxation techniques and the use of self-talk.

- Following Sarah's example, what specific imagery, relaxation techniques and self-talk might you use to maximise your performance in your own sport?

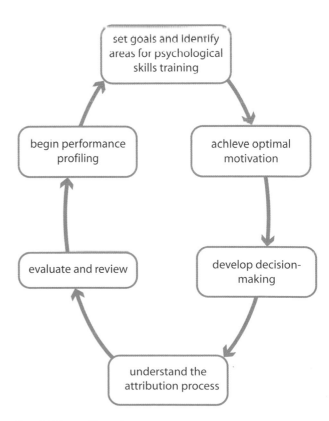

Fig. 6.2 The profile cycle

CHARACTERISTICS OF SUCCESSFUL PERFORMERS

From a psychological standpoint, there is no reason to assume elite sports performers have different components from non-elite performers in their psychological make-up. Successful performers need to develop their own strengths in sports psychology, just as they need to develop physical strengths. Research has shown that elite performers exhibit the following characteristics – so these are the most likely components for your own psychological skills training development:

- better concentration
- higher self-confidence
- more task-oriented thoughts
- more positive thoughts, determination and commitment
- lower anxiety levels.

REMEMBER

If you want to enhance and develop more successful sport or physical activity performances, you should aim to mirror the psychological profiles of successful elite performers.

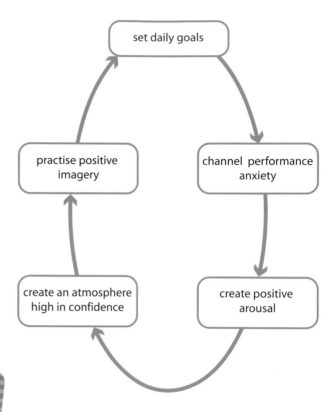

Fig. 6.3 *This simple flow chart shows the core programme of the Canadian Olympic squad*

WHAT PSYCHOLOGICAL METHODOLOGIES CAN I USE?

From your work in Part A, you will already have a core knowledge of the strategies that can be employed on a daily basis in your short-term psychological performance preparation. You may need to revisit this section to refresh your knowledge and understanding. The strategies you should include when constructing your core psychological skills training programme are:

- imagery techniques
- mental rehearsal
- self-talk
- goal-setting
- progressive muscle-relaxation techniques
- arousal regulation
- concentration/attention techniques.

WEBS AND WAGON WHEELS

A 'spiders' web' or 'wagon wheel' can be used to visualise and structure your performance components, in conjunction with your coach or centre staff. A profile is constructed that shows the areas of strength and weakness in your performance. This is the starting point for your development programme, and should be undertaken at regular intervals. The process is more straightforward for physiological aspects such as strength, speed and agility training – it is a little harder for psychological aspects.

As performers, we all have a collection of psychological components that influence our preparation and performances. The key areas that you should consider for your psychological profile are:

- concentration
- imagery/visualisation
- determination
- consistency in effort
- stress management
- motivation
- courage

- self-talk
- leadership
- confidence
- communication
- mental preparation.

You may also wish to add arousal, anxiety and cohesion. The wagon wheel will now look like the one in Figure 6.4.

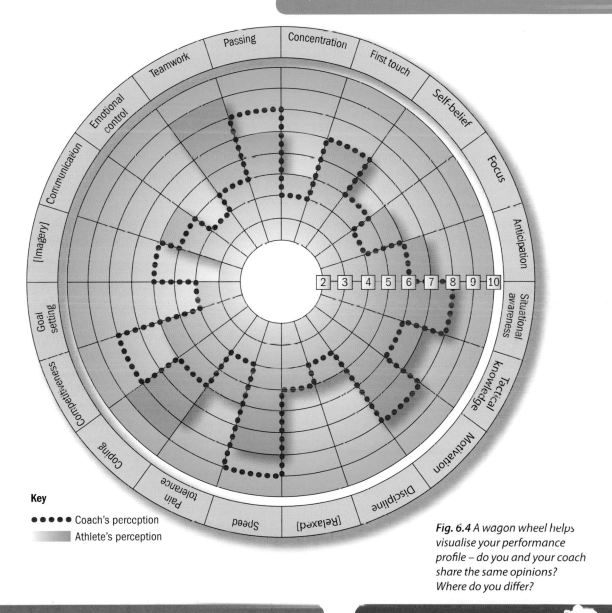

Key
●●●●● Coach's perception
▬▬▬ Athlete's perception

Fig. 6.4 A wagon wheel helps visualise your performance profile – do you and your coach share the same opinions? Where do you differ?

ISSUES WITH PERFORMANCE PROFILING

Undertaking a psychological skills training programme sounds very simple, but there are a number of reasons why this process might fail, or may not be as successful as it should. As with all developments in performance, the issues centre on the individual rather than the processes involved. Issues might include:

- lack of time
- lack of sport-specific knowledge
- failure to follow up and reassess the programme
- lack of conviction that it will make a difference to the individual performer.

MOTIVATION

Motivation is a major factor in any performer's life. Always being willing, ready and keen to perform and compete is not always as easy as it sounds. We all have 'off days', or have gone through periods when we just don't feel like playing. There are many factors that may explain this apathy and lack of motivation, from physical factors such as having no energy, through a fear of getting hurt, to being 'psyched out' by the thought of playing against superior opposition. So what is motivation, and how can I ensure I remain motivated to perform to my potential?

KEY TERM

motivation
the internal mechanisms and external stimuli that arouse and direct our behaviour

This can be very simply put as the reason, or reasons, that we feel we want to do something. Essentially, motivation is why people do what they do.

Motivation is a combination of both internal and external stimuli interacting, and varying in the influence they have on the performer at any particular time. Motivation can have either a positive or a negative effect on the performer. Winning provides a positive motive for further participation, while losing can be demotivating.

APPLY IT!

How many times have you used the following phrases?

- 'I'm up for this'
- 'I can't wait till kick-off'
- 'I don't feel ready'
- 'I'm too tired'
- 'I can't be bothered'
- 'The pitch is against us'
- 'I don't think I can do it'
- 'I don't want to train, it's too cold'
- 'I want to win, I need the money'
- 'I'm looking forward to tonight's training'
- 'The opposition are much better than us'
- 'I'm not very good, so I'm giving up'
- 'I want to be the best'
- 'There's no point, we're going to lose anyway'
- 'That referee is biased against us'

List the phrases that are the result of internal mechanisms, and those that are the result of external stimuli. Compare and discuss your results.

INTRINSIC MOTIVATION

Internal mechanisms are our 'drives', and are personal to us. These drives or needs range from our hierarchical need to seek food and shelter, to the need to seek excitement and challenges in our lives. One reason why sport and our desire for it has developed in modern society is the quest for excitement, and to feel competent and self-determining. This form of motivation comes from inside the self, and drives the individual to continue to strive for success. The performer can list such intrinsic feelings as satisfaction, joy, pleasure, pride, fun and even pain. Intrinsic motivation, also called primary motivation, is derived from the activity itself. The emotion felt in response to participating is referred to as an intangible reward. The power of intrinsic rewards over the performer is initially stronger than that of extrinsic rewards.

STRETCH AND CHALLENGE

List, in ranked order, the reasons why you take part in your major sport or physical activities. Compare your list with those of others in your group.

EXTRINSIC MOTIVATION

Extrinsic motivation is the opposite to intrinsic motivation. Sport and physical activity provide many forms of extrinsic, external rewards – also called secondary motivation. These rewards act as a force to motivate the performer. Extrinsic motivation may come from other people, as when receiving praise from your coach, and in this case it has an emotional emphasis. Or it can be from concrete things, such as trophies or money – these are tangible rewards (they can be touched).

▶ *Jamaican sprinter Usain Bolt wins the 100 metres in Beijing, 2008, showing powerful motivation*

TASK

As a group, consider what might be most important to a successful sportsman – the fame, the money, the lifestyle, the success, the personal achievement, or the trophies?

REMEMBER

If extrinsic rewards outweigh or overcome intrinsic rewards, then participation becomes work, as you could now be competing for money above all other factors.

ACHIEVEMENT MOTIVATION

In the context of sport or physical activity, performers can be categorised by their desire to be successful or to achieve. The combination of a performer's motivation to take part and desire to achieve is a very powerful one. An individual's character and personality may be seen through their thoughts and, more significantly, their actions.

As a sports psychologist, you can assess a performer's desire, drive and determination to succeed through their level of **achievement motivation**. This directs behaviour to achieve certain goals. Competition is a fundamental part of human interaction, a characteristic that is both desired and rewarded. Society places great value on performers who exhibit high achievement motivation. We like winners – but, more importantly, those who accept the greatest challenges and never give up seem to be held in even higher esteem.

KEY TERM

achievement motivation
a fundamental drive to succeed or persist with a task

Achievement motivation has been described as 'a person's efforts to master a task, achieve excellence, overcome obstacles, perform better than others and take pride in exercising talent' (Murray, 1938), or as 'a person's orientation to strive for task success, persist in the face of failure, and experience pride in accomplishments' (Gill,1986). But these are simplistic descriptions. In understanding achievement motivation, we also have to consider an individual's personality, and the context within which the performance exists.

While motivation can be instinctive, it can also be nurtured. Bound to a performer's conduct and personality is the achievement ethic that, as an established moral principle, consistently underpins the way an individual seeks out competitive situations. Some people seem to be more 'naturally competitive', and this affects their selection of sports and physical activities.

The ethic to achieve, to seek victory and avoid defeat, is the principle that runs through all sports and physical activities. Whether to win a tennis match, or to climb a particular mountain – the challenge is to overcome either an opponent, or the environment. The challenge lies with one's inner self.

TASK

The ability of an individual to exhibit consistent drive and determination to succeed – high achievement motivation – has been described as 'Redgraveness' or 'Federerness' (Barnes, 2006). Can you list the personality characteristics that both Steven Redgrave and Roger Federer have in common?

PERSONALITY FACTORS

When analysing performers' personalities through observation, we can distinguish between two groups – those who exhibit the drive or desire to **achieve success**, and those who exhibit a drive or desire to **avoid failure**. Certain individuals seek out difficult competitive situations, while others seek to avoid those situations. Atkinson (1974) defined these two individual personality types as those who:

- need to achieve – **Nach**
- need to avoid failure – **Naf**.

We see achievement motivation through the behaviour of individuals.

Nach performers:

- select challenging risks
- perform better when being evaluated
- take risks
- are not troubled by fear of failure
- seek success and pride through high-ranking victories.

Naf performers:

- seek low-risk challenges
- perform worse when being evaluated
- take easy options
- tend to concede defeat early and give up after failure
- have a drive to avoid shame and humiliation.

The difference between Nach and Naf is not always clear-cut. There will be occasions when you have high Nach in a particular sport, but Naf in another. A games player performing in their comfort zone can be characterised by Nach in team sports, while in a rackets environment they may be classified as Naf. In reality, both Nach and Naf type personalities tend to apply across all sports.

SITUATIONAL FACTORS

In addition to personality factors, the specific situation, or context, in which an individual performs will also affect their decision to accept a challenge. The two determining situational factors are:

- probability of success (**Ps**) versus probability of failure (**Pf**)
- incentive value of success (**Is**) versus incentive value of failure (**If**).

These two factors are inversely proportional to one another. The incentive value of a task to a person is how much the individual thinks he or she will gain or lose by accepting the challenge. As the probability of success increases, the incentive value decreases. Conversely, when the probability of success is low, the incentive value will be high.

By beating a higher-ranked opponent in tennis, you have matched the probability of success to the incentive value of winning – by accepting the challenge and being successful, you will have achieved a more valued victory.

ACHIEVEMENT MOTIVATION, SPORT AND COACHING

Performers tend to seek out situations that reflect their drive to succeed. The reasons why a person may accept a sporting challenge include the need to:

- succeed
- exert power
- seek out stress
- be independent
- exert aggression
- have an affiliation.

Not all performers see success as their only drive and goal. Different goals may be used to measure whether a performance was successful. Performing well while losing a match can carry as much value and esteem as actually winning.

Whether a performer shows Nach or Naf tendencies depends on a number of factors that include how important a task is, their experience, their competitiveness and their confidence. Gill and Deeter (1998) developed a sport orientation questionnaire to measure individuals' competitive orientation. The questionnaire measures three components of competitiveness:

- the feelings derived from the competition itself – being involved and competing at a certain level
- the feelings associated with winning and losing – the emotional effect on the individual
- the feelings associated with task mastery – the inner cathartic experience of knowing how good you are, and what you have achieved.

Goal perspective theory offers an alternative, and suggests two reasons why we are motivated to compete in sport:

- performers may be **task-oriented**, driven by the need to master a task, and measuring success in terms of personal improvement, focusing on performance and process goals based on technique – for example, a rock climber
- they may be **ego-oriented**, driven by the need to succeed against other people and thus show superiority, focusing on goals that emphasise their superiority – for example, a world boxing champion.

As a coach, it is desirable to engage your performers in strategies that steer them towards success and to avoid a tendency to failure. Feedback is a central feature of this process, and self-esteem is enhanced through positive reinforcement. Punishments and negative feedback serve only to direct the performer to low-risk competitions.

Performers need to be in control, and feel that their destiny is in their own hands. You can reduce Naf by focusing any negative feedback on effort rather than ability – with more effort, they can do better next time. Success should be attributed to internal factors, while failure should be attributed to external factors. The use of role models and intrinsic rewards will boost **self-efficacy**.

> ## KEY TERM
>
> **self-efficacy**
> a situation-specific form of self-confidence, related to a performer's perception of their competence in a sport

By placing a low achiever in environments where success can be achieved, and by gradually increasing the difficulty of a task, you can build a desire to seek more difficult challenges – Nach. Tasks and challenges need to motivate the individual. If a task is too easy, boredom sets in; but if a task is too difficult, apathy regarding the chance of being successful will increase. By setting a target other than just winning, a performer will become more motivated and exhibit Nach – a personal best in an athletics contest may not win the event, but is still a significant achievement for the individual. A common phrase often used by coaches is 'Focus on the performance and let the result take care of itself'.

> ## CASE STUDY
> ### CHOOSING YOUR OPPONENT
>
> For boxers, it is always difficult to decide what level of opponent to select for their next fight. Too many easy contests, and motivation decreases, as well as the esteem gained from victories. Select someone too hard to beat, and the probability of success will be low – but the incentive value will be very high.
>
> - Why do high-jumpers choose to miss a jump and enter a competition at a higher height? What factors would they need to take into account?

▶ *A pole vaulter can choose to miss a jump*

ATTRIBUTION THEORY

When performing, we have all gone through a process of explanation and analysis to explain the outcome of the event. We attribute our success and failure to a variety of factors. In explaining the outcome of a competitive performance, both **external** and **internal factors** related to the individual form the basis of performance analysis.

You will have experienced the process of attribution after every performance. This reflection after the event normally forms the basis of your future tactics, training and participation. Such self-analysis may ask the following questions:

- Why did we win or lose?
- Why did it happen?
- What were the reasons for this?
- Were the opposition better?
- Did I not try hard enough?
- Why did they have all the luck, and not us?

Weiner (1974) described two dimensions of attribution theory. The first dimension is the 'locus of causality' or locus of control, and the second is 'stability'.

The **locus of causality** seeks to attribute the reasons for success or failure of a performance to factors that are under the control of a performer, such as **ability** and **effort**, and are therefore internal to them. Factors that are external to the performer and beyond their control, for example the strength of the opposition or a 'lucky bounce' of a ball, are classed as **luck** and **task difficulty**.

The dimension of **stability** introduces a time factor, and the difference between stable and unstable factors. Stable factors do not change in the short term and may alter very little over time, so are described as relatively permanent. Your level of technical excellence in a sport will change only gradually rather than during a single performance. Conversely, unstable factors can change in the short term, and even during a performance. You may have no luck in one half of a match, or you can try harder and increase your level of effort in the second half.

APPLIED ATTRIBUTION THEORY

The dimension of stability is crucial to future expectations. Attributing success or failure to stable factors helps us predict the outcome of future events. High achievers and their coaches will gain from understanding that a successful outcome was due to ability, not simply luck. Negative feedback can often occur as a result of internal errors or mistakes, and must be avoided. If they perform well but are not successful, performers tend to seek reasons in the opposition's performance, or reasons beyond their own control – task difficulty or luck.

Weiner's model of attribution is illustrated in Figure 6.5.

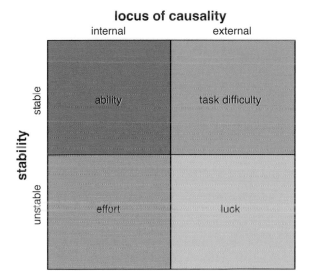

locus of causality

	internal	external
stable	ability	task difficulty
unstable	effort	luck

(left axis: **stability** — stable / unstable)

Fig. 6.5 Weiner's model of attribution

The process of attribution should follow a programmed route of analysis, as shown in Figure 6.6.

> ### REMEMBER
> Internal factors are those under the control of the performer – **effort** and **ability**, while the external factors beyond the control of the performer are the degree of **task difficulty** and **luck**.

Performers applying attribution theory tend to show a self-serving bias. They may attribute a defeat or poor performance to external and unstable factors, such as referee bias. If reflecting on a successful performance, they may seek internal and stable reasons, such as they were better than their opponents, or put in much more effort. We like to feel we are responsible for our success, and that we have control over our own destiny.

> ### KEY TERMS
> **internal factor**
> a factor we have control over
> **external factor**
> a factor normally beyond our control

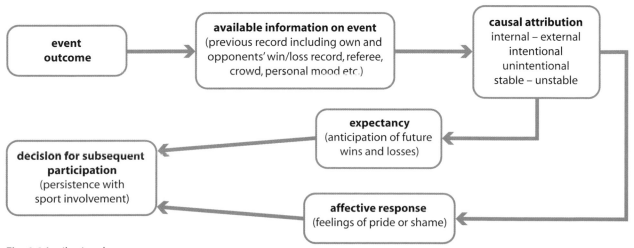

event outcome → available information on event (previous record including own and opponents' win/loss record, referee, crowd, personal mood etc.) → causal attribution (internal – external, intentional, unintentional, stable – unstable) → expectancy (anticipation of future wins and losses) → decision for subsequent participation (persistence with sport involvement); affective response (feelings of pride or shame)

Fig. 6.6 Attribution theory

LEARNED HELPLESSNESS

The process of learned helplessness occurs when an individual perceives defeat as inevitable, and as a result of stable, internal and uncontrollable events. The performer may make this decision based on their past experience, or through vicarious experiences. Performers with learned helplessness need to undertake a process of attribution retraining. Low confidence levels and feelings of poor self-esteem are common among low-achieving performers and those characterised by Naf.

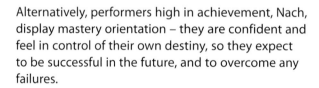

TASK

'I'm not very good at hockey, so I'm not very good at sports.' Learned helplessness can result from injury, a single defeat, a poor performance, or comments made by others. Suggest other examples of learned helplessness.

Alternatively, performers high in achievement, Nach, display mastery orientation – they are confident and feel in control of their own destiny, so they expect to be successful in the future, and to overcome any failures.

ATTRIBUTION RETRAINING

One way of helping performers avoid failure is by focusing on positive attributions and the removal of any negative feelings, such as 'I'm just not good enough'. By undertaking a reassessment, a performer can move away from internal, stable factors and from simply blaming themselves for a poor performance, and refocus on external factors, which can be changed. Success can be redefined where ability is the reason for failure – the quality of the performance may have been excellent, even if the result was not. Effort can be altered in the short term as it is unstable and so is an obvious starting point for future successes. The task difficulty facing a performer cannot be changed, but it can be placed in context to change a performer's expectations. Atherton (2003) suggested the following strategies for attribution retraining.

The coach might:

- look at a change in tactics, or blame the use of poor equipment for failure – 'change your racket!'
- use a positive approach – 'you missed the conversion because your non-striking foot was in the wrong position – next time you'll be successful'
- focus on the reasons successful performers give for their performances, and copy them
- avoid citing lack of ability as a reason for failure
- make the reasons for losing less personal – 'it's not that you're no good, it's just a change in technique'.

Figure 6.7 summarises a response pathway following a negative performance, and the place of internal and external factors in changing attributions.

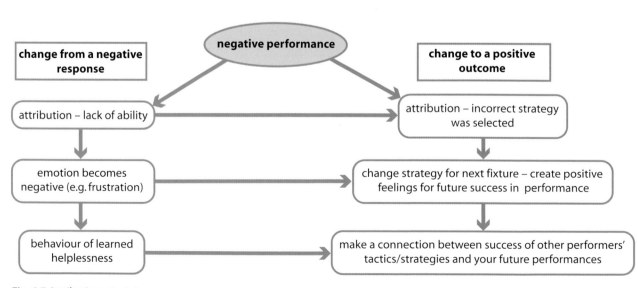

Fig. 6.7 Attribution retraining

SKILL DEVELOPMENT AND TACTICS

In this section you will look at how you can train to improve your decision-making through **visualisation**, the use of ritual in your psychological development, training for decision-making, **visual awareness training**, and finally the role and effect of group cohesion.

▶ *Visualisation is the process of creating a mental image*

KEY TERMS

visualisation
the process of creating a mental image of what you want to happen

visual awareness training
training the eyes and thought processes to control decision-making

KEY TERM

periodisation
in sports, an organised approach to training that involves progressive cycling of various aspects of the training programme over a specific period of time

THE ROLE OF VISUALISATION

The long-term psychological development of a performer involves a series of interrelated psychological components. You are now aware of the role of goal-setting, of the control of stress, and how to achieve optimum arousal. We all dream and think about what we will be doing, not only in life but also in sport. Performers visualise (create a mental picture of) future successes, winning races or achieving a personal best. Using **periodisation**, elite athletes cycle their training and plan their whole lifestyle around major competitions – this might be on a two- or even a four-year cycle of Olympics and world championships (see Chapter 5, page 78).

We have to balance the advantages of visualisation against becoming psychologically fixated on an event or goal. You will have heard many times the advice to 'take each game at a time' and to 'take one step at a time'. To be successful you will have planned your goals effectively, focusing on the short-term challenges immediately in front of you, while also building for a long-term development and keeping the bigger picture in mind.

CASE STUDY
VIRTUAL SOCCER

One type of visualisation session is that carried out by two soccer goalkeepers, who 'played out' a whole game on grass, but without the ball or other team mates. They dived, caught the ball and moved as in a game. This physical movement and psychological visualisation of what could happen in a match is very powerful, and proves to be effective in actual play.

■ Close your eyes and think of your next sports contest or activity performance – visualise what you want to happen in the first few minutes. What will you do the first time you are directly involved? Go over the scenario three or four times. Write it down. Then, after the performance, look at what you have written. Do you think it made you more focused and decisive in your actions?

CASE STUDY
RANDALL'S RESURRECTION

Derek Randall, an England test cricketer, had been out for 0 in five successive innings. He arrived early at his home ground, and with just a bat in hand he stood in the middle and imagined – visualised – playing a range of shots, then played an imaginary ball. That day he scored 100.

■ What else could Derek Randall have done?

Inherent in this process is the use of long-term goal-setting, not only through visualising successes, but also by creating a firm pathway for your development with identified milestones and evaluation at set intervals.

APPLY IT!

Define what you understand by milestones in relation to your own long-term performance development. Write down your milestones for the next 12, then 24, months.

STRETCH AND CHALLENGE

Close your eyes and create a mental picture of a significant success that you wish to achieve in the next 12 months. This may be an A-grade pass in this course – visualise the day you open the results envelope ... how does it feel?

Write those feelings down and keep the piece of paper with you – look at it and read it again and again, and visualise your goal regularly. Carry that feeling with you.

THE USE OF RITUAL

Most of our lives involve traditions and regular observances. These might relate to an annual holiday, or meeting a friend every year at a particular time, or just playing sport on a Saturday afternoon. These activities provide a richness, a comfort and a regular rhythm within our lives. **Ritual** has always been a significant psychological tool in sport and physical activities. Ritual has its roots in religious ceremonies, and is an emotive and very powerful process. Ritual by definition is simply a 'formal or ceremonial action'. In sport we see many examples of ritual, which is commonly thought of as part tradition and part superstition.

Ritual reflects culture, and serves to unite and build a common spirit with a single uniting cause. In many ways ritual provides a psychological crutch that both performers and spectators expect and come to rely on. Sports grounds are often thought of as 'cathedrals' of sport, implying an emotional, religious and ceremonial belief that unites in a cause. Belief is the crucial concept in ritual – belief in your team, belief in your ability, and belief in the cause or ideal that you follow.

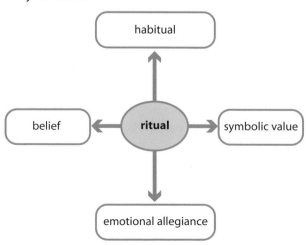

Fig. 6.8 The role of ritual

Some common rituals found in sport include:

- opening and closing ceremonies for sports events
- singing national anthems before national fixtures
- exchanging gifts before a fixture
- performing dances and songs before events
- shaking hands before and after games
- singing club songs
- wearing traditional colours
- clapping the opposition off a pitch
- playing anthems at medal ceremonies.

APPLY IT!

Working in pairs, list five specific examples of ritual in your own sport or physical activity.

TASK

Think of the New Zealand All Blacks and their use of the haka *prior to a rugby union test match. A* haka *was first performed on the New Zealand rugby tour of Britain in 1888/89. Is it used to frighten the opposition? Is it used to psychologically arouse the All Blacks team? Or is it just a ritual that has traditionally always been undertaken?*

KEY TERM

ritual
a formal or ceremonial event or action

STRETCH AND CHALLENGE

Hold a group discussion – what purpose do the opening ceremony of the Olympic Games and the swearing of the Olympic oath serve?

▶ *The Beijing 2008 opening ceremony – what did it achieve?*

CASE STUDY
WHAT IS A HAKA?

The Maori people have always excelled in the art of *haka* (a general term for any Maori dance).

The words of the All Blacks' *haka* (and there are many *haka*) are simple and hold no meaning for anyone outside New Zealand. It is the occasion when they are spoken, the ritual of delivery – the body actions, and the psychological effect of the *haka* – that makes it one of the most powerful of all rituals.

■ Hold a class debate about the value of the *haka* – does it intimidate or inspire the opposition?

▶ *New Zealand perform the* haka *before a World Cup match*

Ka mate – the All Blacks' *haka*

Ka mate! Ka mate! Ka ora! Ka ora!	I die! I die! I live! I live!
Ka mate! Ka mate! Ka ora! Ka ora!	I die! I die! I live! I live!
Tenei te tangata puhuru huru	This is the hairy man
Nana nei i tiki mai	Who fetched the Sun
Whakawhiti te ra	And caused it to shine again
A upa ... ne! ka upa ... ne!	One upward step! Another upward step!
A upane kaupane whiti te ra!	An upward step, another ... the Sun shines!
Hi!!!	

THE PURPOSE OF RITUAL

Ritual is essential in life, not just in sport. But the needs of performers are in many ways more defined and fragile than those of normal members of society. Ritual in sport provides the following psychological functions:

■ unites performers and crowd

■ generates respect and courtesy

■ strengthens social bonds, enhancing group cohesion

■ demonstrates respect for, or submission to, opponents

■ defines our affiliation to a cultural heritage

■ provides social approval from others – their respect for you

■ fulfils social and emotional needs – the outlet or avenue for channelled aggression

■ physically raises our levels of arousal – an emotional and physical tool

■ a rallying call to the cause – a bond of belief

■ reaffirmation of 'faith' – your ideological belief in team or country.

CASE STUDY
A NEW ANTHEM

Multicultural nations are keen to build a common ethos and unite their nation. Since 1997, South Africa has sung a new national anthem, reflecting the cultural roots of the nation and the building of a new country. The lyrics employ the five most populous of South Africa's 11 official languages – Xhosa (first stanza, first two lines), Zulu (first stanza, last two lines), Sesotho (second stanza), Afrikaans (third stanza) and English (final stanza).

■ We compete as four home nations. Should our international performers in the Olympics have a new GB anthem with verses in the four languages?

DECISION-MAKING AND VISUAL AWARENESS TRAINING

It is essential for all performers engaged in interactive games or competitive sports, or in physical activities involving challenge or rhythm, to interact with, and be integrated into, the performance environment. The ability to read, interpret and understand the evolving context in front of us is centred on our information-processing systems. Information processing is the ability of a performer to detect, compare and recognise cues, movements, sounds and information from **kinaesthesis**. Here you will learn about some of the mental processes involved in sports decision-making, and how to link this to visual awareness.

> ## KEY TERMS
>
> **kinaesthesis**
> the sense by which motion, weight and the position of various body parts are perceived
>
> **perception**
> the ability to interpret what is happening consciously as a result of sensory information received

Perception is the starting point for performing well. A dancer has to time their first movement to the auditory cue of the correct note, while a sprinter reacts to the starting pistol. Games players react to the stance and body actions of opponents or of an object, to anticipate subsequent movements.

Perceptual and cognitive skills (thinking skills) are dependent on, and interlinked with, encoding, retrieving and interpreting information. Unless a performer can create a psychological understanding of events, they will be unable to anticipate and make decisions on subsequent actions or movements, or to give instructions to others. Perceptual abilities are considered to be the predictor of, and the key to, becoming a more successful performer.

When training, you build scenarios of your performances. Mental and physical rehearsal enables the performer to construct plans of action – a rock climber will visualise the route to take; a dancer may write the choreography of a routine; a rugby team will have set moves to perform at scrum and line-out.

In interactive environments, where decisions are being made over and over again, second by second, the detection and recognition of relevant information is largely visually controlled. The concept of 'scanning' and the speed of a performer's thought processes require development and training, just as much as strength and speed. The ability to 'read the game' derives from our vision and perception, linked to anticipation. Performers in interactive environments need to understand what is happening in terms of the actions of other performers and their intentions, both in direct or indirect involvement.

The traditional concept of information processing still holds true in sport:

see – think – interpret – move

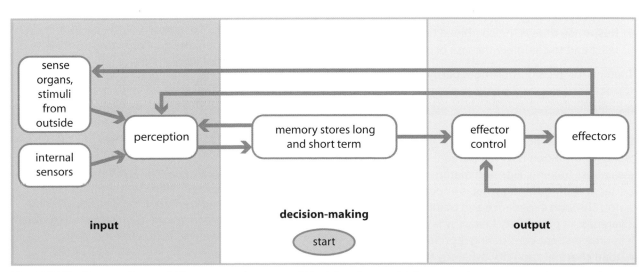

Fig. 6.9 Welford's processing model is one example – you could look for other models for comparison

Scanning, or 'gaze' as it is sometimes called, is an individual's ability to attend visually to events unfolding in front of them. Visual training to spot vital cues – when to move or stay still, when to intercept a pass or play a shot – demands that the performer focuses and narrows down the information received to just what is important – the **cue** to act or to wait. Inherent in this process is the ability to focus on what is important. This can be achieved by undertaking selective attention training and learning how to channel information. Auditory information – music, a crowd or calls from teammates, kinaesthesis and experience can all significantly influence our perceptual abilities.

cope with only so much information, means it is vital for performers to ensure the information sent to the brain is significant and important.

TASK

Select an individual and a team game. You are performing in front of large, hostile crowd. You are tired, and starting to lose control of the game. What do you need to focus on, and what should you eliminate? Make a list, then act out the next potential phases. How might your list change?

KEY TERMS

scanning
visual perception when an individual attends to many aspects in their field of vision

cue
a stimulus or signal for action – may be verbal, visual or kinaesthetic

KEY TERM

channel capacity
how information has to pass through channels of limited capacity in the brain – the brain can be trained to receive only relevant information

REACTION, MOVEMENT AND RESPONSE TIMES

Most sport is concerned not just with decision-making, but with the time it takes to make decisions. Our reaction times speed up as a result of experience and decision-making training.

- **Reaction time** is the time between a stimulus and the first movement initiated in response to it.
- **Movement time** is the time taken to complete a task once it has been initiated.
- **Response time** is the combined time taken to react and to complete the task or movement.

Training for decision-making is partly about making correct decisions, and partly about making them more quickly.

SELECTIVE ATTENTION

Selective attention is a vital element in visual awareness training. Elite and mature performers are better at distinguishing what is important from what is not. Through experience and training in visual awareness, a probability hierarchy is established, and less time is spent considering less crucial events. The natural **channel capacity**, whereby the brain can

THE HOLISTIC APPROACH

In the performance environment, if training has drilled the performer to make a particular response, individual real-time decision-making and effective skill production will be affected. When faced with the unfolding events of open play, performers cannot always perform an automatic response. Intervening variables, such as player movements, unlucky bounces of a ball, or the effects of the weather can change the response required of the performer. The performer cannot make the correct response if he or she cannot see the whole picture.

Performers can learn skills through Associationalist and Connectionist theories. However, when in the performance environment if training has only drilled or grooved a particular response then individual real-time decision-making and effective skill production becomes an issue. Cognitivists, such as Lewan, and the school more commonly known as the Gestaltists, proposed that the decision-making process in performances, the requirement to problem solve, should be viewed in an entirety.

Performers are always learning and building a bank of experiences that reflect when, where, and, crucially, why they should perform a skill in the context of that moment. Building a bank of experiences, recognising vital cues and engaging in 'insight learning' is a productive route to skills learning and application. Once this insight learning process is under way, performers become not only skilful, but also more effective decision-makers in that they can select the correct skill to fit the context.

CASE STUDY HEADS-UP

Brain Ashton, former England Rugby Football Union coach, believes in 'heads-up rugby', where decision-making about when, where and why to perform movements rests with the players on the field.

■ What are the advantages and disadvantages of this approach? Can you think of three for each?

CASE STUDY WHAT IS CTC?

Clive Woodward, England Coach for the 2003 Rugby World Cup, developed a scanning system called CTC – Cross-bar, Touchline, Communicate. Players had to look down the field towards their opposition to see what was happening, they had to look to the touchlines to see their own players and the opposition positions and their movements, and finally they had to communicate what they had perceived to their teammates – a simple but effective form of visual training.

■ Devise a form of visual training for a named sport.

TASK

In hockey, a goalkeeper facing a penalty has to anticipate the direction in which the ball will be hit. List three different factors they will take into account when deciding which way to dive.

AWARENESS

Performers need to develop awareness. When training, this involves creating opportunities to experience all the potential scenarios they may face competitively. Coaches should ensure the training environment has the following structure:

■ make practice sessions directly related to the game, and run them at full game speed

■ ensure performers are constantly addressing object and player movements

■ ensure players are constantly set decisions to make and problems to solve

■ ensure performers are reminded of what they need to be looking for – the cues of patterns and shapes, links in formations, time, space and distances

■ create challenges – what if, when and where – to engage the mental, physical and technical elements of a performance.

▶ *Developing visual awareness is important in rugby*

THE PERCEPTION DIMENSIONS

Perception, and therefore visual awareness, is dependent on four main components (Figure 6.10). Space conditions movement, so as a principle of playing, creating and denying space is the first consideration. The four dimensions of visual awareness or perception are peripheral vision, depth perception, static acuity and dynamic acuity.

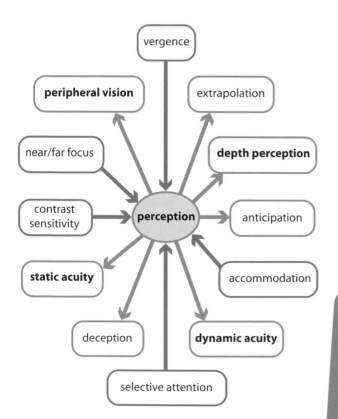

Fig. 6.10 The perception dimensions

▶ *Skills of perception are particularly important to strikers*

- **Peripheral vision** is the ability of a performer to perceive actions from the 'corner of their eye'. A developed field of peripheral vision gives the performer a wider rather than a narrower field of vision.

- **Depth perception** is the ability of a performer to see down-field and to judge how far away players, objects or targets are.

- **Acuity** is attention to fine detail, and is essentially concerned with clarity and sharpness – seeing **dynamically** the positions of players or a ball while in motion, or **statically** when there is no movement. You rely on both static and dynamic acuity when processing information.

In addition, **vergence** – the ability to fixate an oncoming or receding object; **contrast sensitivity** – the ability to determine subtle differences in black and white; and **accommodation** – the performer's ability to focus, are additional factors that build visual perceptual skills.

ANTICIPATION VERSUS DECEPTION – THE ART OF EXTRAPOLATION

We have all watched sports events and tried to guess what is going to happen next. In the interactive sports environment, two opposing processes exist. Attacking individuals and teams aim to deceive their opponents in order to gain an advantage, while defending individuals and teams try to anticipate the potential actions of their opponents. In racket sports, players build a rally to wrong-foot and out-manoeuvre their opponent, while in American football it is not only the individual who needs to read the game, but units and the whole team. The quarterback has set plays designed to fool the opposition. In turn, they weigh up the options, listen to the calls and read the cues of their opponents' line-up. If you can deceive your opponents, you will be more successful.

TASK

List five examples, in a range of sporting activities, that involve situations where one person or team uses deception to overcome the opposition. Then list examples where anticipation can overcome the opponents' deception.

Performers must also perfect the art of extrapolation – the ability of the brain to anticipate accurately what will happen next. Extrapolation when both in and out of possession of the ball, for instance in hockey or rugby league, can be the key to unlock successful

defences or to regain possession of the ball. But in an equally matched contest there may be stalemate, as individuals or teams cancel one another out.

KEY TERM

accommodation
the ability of the eye to change focus accurately from distant to near objects

STRETCH AND CHALLENGE

Give an example in sport of when vergence, contrast sensitivity and accommodation might be the most important factor in skill production.

Perceptual ability is partly inherent, but also can be trained through the following experiences and methods:

- transfer learning from past to future experiences
- distinguish between stimuli conveying explicit and implicit information
- carry out practices that stimulate the visual processes – for instance use coloured cones, bibs and other visual stimuli
- work in structured practices, at full speed, that demand decision-making
- engage in both broad scenario performance and sports activity-specific training.

MENTAL PICTURES

When we label a performer as having 'vision', this might suggest that they actually hold mental images in their mind. Visual awareness is an essential method of seeing events through mental pictures. Mental pictures that are real, as well as constructed, build up the big picture in live sporting environments that demand decision-making – often instantly. A cricket captain may have time to do this, while a mid-field player in hockey or football does not normally have that luxury.

One suggestion is for performers to create three mental pictures, constantly using, dismissing and recreating these pictures over and over, second by second, shuffling what has happened, what is happening, and what is about to happen. Scanning and visual awareness skills are built through training and playing, so the performer needs experience.

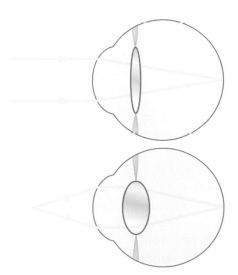

Fig. 6.11 Accommodation – light from a single point of a distant object and light from a single point of a near object being brought to a focus by changing the curvature of the lens

The three mental images are 'short stories' of events. Each story is a moving picture that leads to a range of potential outcomes, which have to be evaluated tactically in the context of the desired outcome.

TASK

Given that elite performers begin with the same visual apparatus to work with as each other, why do they make good or bad tactical decisions?

IMPROVISATION

Interactive sport requires performers to think on their feet – quickly. Events never unfold as planned, and in training for both decision-making and visual awareness, the performer constructs their awareness of the potential events that may occur. But we cannot plan for everything, such as an unlucky bounce of the ball, so those performers who can react most quickly and improvise, performing instinctively, have the edge over their opponents.

SHORT- AND LONG-TERM MEMORY

The **short-term sensory store** is the first of our three memory compartments. It can process limitless amounts of information for a very short period. The immediate information detected through the short-term sensory store from a variety of stimuli can be contained for only 20–30 seconds. We see and interpret information, then dismiss it instantly (if we did not, we would recode and record it in the long-term memory). In other words, we do not think about that moment – as Nike says, 'just do it!'. The more we think, the more our mind will throw in doubt and confusion. A driver may travel for many miles without recalling where they have been as the short-term sensory store functions – this is more evident when travelling at high speeds.

The information that is considered important or essential is then passed into the **short-term memory**. The short-term memory processes information as part of our capacity to make decisions. It acts as a link to the long-term memory store, as well as a 'work space' where immediate and stored information is mixed together and processed, ready for decision-making to take place.

The **long-term memory** is where all our experiences and movement programmes are stored.

Schema theory is just one way in which the long-term memory has been proposed to work. Before decision-making and movement, information from the long- and short-term memory, as well as the short-term sensory store, all comes together. The ability to process all this information, to decode it, and form it into understandable, recognisable and usable information on which to act often distinguishes non-elite from elite performers.

STRETCH AND CHALLENGE

Research and explain how Schema theory works. What are its limitations?

MENTAL PICTURES ON THE MOVE

Consider players in basketball, hockey and rugby having to combine their own and others' movements, pass options, personal travel options and tactical considerations, all in a split second (see Figure 12). We all create visual pictures of what is unfolding before us. We often criticise performers for not seeing the 'big picture' or for being unable to 'read the game'.

Fig. 6.12a Scanning, eyes ahead to get 'big picture'

What has just happened?
What performer movements are seen?
Where is the ball or object?
What are the external and my internal state – the task difficulty, state of the game, fitness levels?

Fig. 6.12b Recognition, eyes on ball

What is happening now?

What are the new performer movements?

How and where can I move the ball or object?

What are the new external conditions and my internal state?

Fig. 6.12c Decision-making, eyes on opposition as off-loading the ball to selected option

What is my tactical action plan?

What is going to happen now?

What are the performer movements?

Can I manipulate the ball or object to achieve my aims?

What are the new external conditions and my internal state?

Over the past decade, elite sports performers have incorporated visual awareness into their training programmes. This is not anything new – all forms of coaching in history have based their players' sporting or physical activity knowledge on the need to understand the context, scenarios and changes in events.

Performers rely on their sight as the principal stimulus in sport. While other senses, such as hearing, are important, it is our sight that principally determines our actions. The process of scanning creates a visual field before the eyes that must be as wide a possible for open environments, such as a field of play. For closed skills, such as a golf swing, a narrower and channelled focus is more productive. Vision involves many subtle and sophisticated links between the brain, muscles and eyes.

What distinguishes and justifies visual awareness training is that it is concerned with training the eyes and thought processes to control decision-making, leading to the correct response, quickly and with more consistent accuracy. By developing perceptual expertise through visual awareness training, the link between seeing events early, reading them correctly, and carrying out appropriate actions increases the performer's ability to:

- anticipate opponents' actions
- recognise typical patterns of play and interpret a game systematically – to read the game on and off the ball
- develop the use of contextual and anticipatory information through picking up advanced visual cues
- eliminate 'choking' (the inability to perform to standard)
- speed up **recycling** speeds when in possession
- increase successful performance links – passing between and through opponents, or linking movements to music or the environment.

Information sent to the brain via our eyes has to be interpreted and integrated as a three-dimensional phenomenon. This integration is known as 'fusion'. This is the brain's ability to put two images, one from the right eye and one from the left, together. While scanning, our eyes are constantly moving over a visual field. Once we see the vital cue, action or event, we 'fixate' on that object, person or group. For example, elite performers are better at grouping players together in units rather than seeing just individual players, and can link up their actions or intentions.

KEY TERM

recycling
in sport, the speed an individual takes to control, think and pass a ball – the longer you take, the more chance you will be tackled. Arsène Wenger has timed his Arsenal players to recycle at an average speed of 3.2 s.

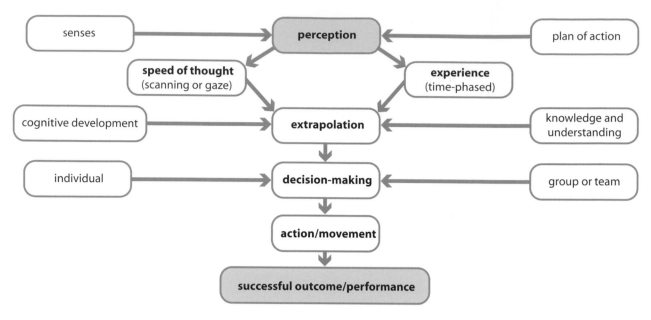

Fig. 6.13 The pathway from perception to performance

Good eyes are important for motor skills, but more importantly they contribute to the rapid succession of decisions that comprise tactical elements including player movements and shot selections. Information gathered in real-time determines the following factors, that then condition or shape a decision to act:

- defining and creating understanding of spatial awareness
- creating anticipation
- conditioning timing and reactions
- affecting both static and dynamic balance.

REMEMBER

We can learn to run set moves perfectly, but the ability to improvise is perhaps more vital than anything.

STRETCH AND CHALLENGE

Define, with examples, what you understand by improvisation.

In the context of training, coaching of visual awareness may be based on the use of coloured balls, bibs or cards to create an environment that the players will learn to see and react in. The process is designed to encourage players to start to use their eyes and react to cues that are presented to them. It teaches players to react to situations that are happening in front of them, then to take the appropriate action for a positive outcome. Changing the range of visual stimuli creates an attentional focus for rapid decision-making.

VISION – THE EYES

It has long been thought that the eyes of elite sports players, and their reactions, may be better than those of the average sportsperson. But there is no clear evidence to suggest this is true. What distinguishes elite performers from normal players is their ability to anticipate and to interpret the action in front of them through their training and performing experiences. Elite players are characterised by superior perceptual skills, not superior visual skills. This links with visual awareness training – training the eyes and working with the long-term memory are not separate from one another in developing a successful performance. Elite performers are better at **recognising patterns of play**, and at **picking up advanced cues**, so they can undertake **advanced search strategies** earlier. If your information-processing systems can be improved in these three functions, then if decision-making is correct, the outcome will be more successful.

PURSUITS AND SACCADES

The ability of our eyes to follow events in front of them cannot just be taken for granted. A netball goal-shooter can actually follow the path of a ball from her centre's hands when it is released as a chest pass to her hands. She can track the ball throughout the flight using **pursuits** – the ability of the eyes to smoothly follow an object through space.

But when an object travels at high speed, such as a cricket ball at 80 mph, its speed exceeds the ability of the eyes to follow it using pursuits. In cases where the ball cannot be followed, the eyes jump ahead, using ballistic or split-second **saccadic** eye movements, to where the individual thinks the object will be. Visual awareness training can develop this skill as a vital aspect of awareness in fast-moving sports.

EXAM TIP

Never be afraid to use a quote or reference to an author – this will demonstrate a depth of knowledge and understanding.

ATTENTIONAL FOCUS

Attentional focus is the ability to pay attention and concentrate. This is often a restricting factor in sports performances. Attentional focusing differs in width, and in whether the situation is internal or external (see Figure 6.14). The ability to maintain focus and pay attention explains how performers overcome the high speeds of certain games.

KEY TERMS

pursuit
movement of the eyes in smoothly following a moving object

saccade
a fast movement of the eye, head or other part of the body

TASK

In ice hockey, test match cricket and tennis, the object – the puck or ball – often moves more quickly than the eye can see. How do performers cope with this non-visual object stimulus?

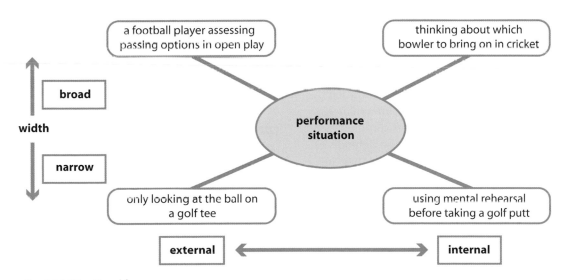

Fig. 6.14 Attentional focus

CASE STUDY

HABANA'S VISUAL AWARENESS

South African Sherylle Calder is a successful visual awareness coach. Working with teams and individuals all over the world, including England Rugby Union world cup squads, Sherylle has developed training methods that require the individual to focus on events in front of them and build hand–eye coordination.

'Visual awareness training is training the eyes to see better and process that information faster so that the mind can respond accordingly.'

Using her training methods, Brian Habana, the South African 2007 world cup winner, practises receiving a rugby ball at different angles, heights and speeds from a simple rebound net. Within three weeks, he increased a return catch ratio of 84 in 60 s to 118. This increase in fast reactions and visual awareness led him to make more interceptions in his game. Over the past two years, as result of this training, Habana has made more interceptions than in all his earlier career.

▶ Brian Habana's visual awareness training

■ Design a technical training practice that could improve your speed and visual awareness in one of your chosen performance roles.

THE PSYCHOLOGICAL REFRACTORY PERIOD

In interactive sport, players can deceive opponents with the use of fakes, dummies or mismoves. The reason this works is a simple process of 'stimulus-and-response' coordination. A player initiates an action, stimulus 1, which is recognised by an opponent, who begins response 1. Immediately this has begun, the performer initiates stimulus 2 – a change in direction, for instance, but the defending opponent cannot respond to stimulus 2 as they are committed to their response to stimulus 1. The delay, or the period when a player recognises stimulus 2 but cannot do anything about it, is known as the psychological refractory period. It is that moment when the performer realises they have been 'sold a dummy', and the recipient experiences a split second in limbo – the realisation that they have enacted an incorrect response and want to change it, but cannot. Examples such as feinting a pass in netball to wrong-foot an opponent, or a 'step-over' in football, aim to deceive the opposition.

GROUP COHESION

Performers do not exist in isolation, they form groups that have common features. Groups can vary in size, from a few individuals to large teams of players, coaches and a variety of support personnel. According to Carron (1980), these groups all exhibit the following characteristics:

■ a collective identity

■ a sense of shared purpose

■ structured patterns of communication.

A rackets player can move from singles to doubles, and interact with a trainer and coach. Team games are based on units of players combining to function as a whole team. Players and coaches often attribute a team's success or failure to how well the personnel of the team worked as a cohesive unit.

Building a group identity, providing an environment where performers feel comfortable and willing to work with and for each other, and creating a spirit of unity is all fundamental to sports success. The dynamic of the group, the energy and functioning of the members as one, is a clear aim for a successfully performing group – **cohesion** acts as a glue that binds and bonds individuals to a group identity and cause.

Carron defined cohesion as 'a dynamic process… reflected in the tendency for a group to stick together and remain united in the pursuit of its goals and objectives'.

KEY TERM

cohesion
the total field of forces that cause members to remain in a group

▶ *A successful team must develop cooperation and cohesion*

The forces that act on a group include the attractiveness of the group – 'I want to be in that team with my friends', and the means of control (Weinberg and Gould,1999). Individuals join a group as it brings them benefits, but in return the group controls their behaviour and actions so that they will perform in a certain way – 'if you want to be in our group, you must behave like this'. Boxing, for example, has had a long-established 'hold' on wayward youngsters that extends beyond the gym. But this explanation has its flaws, and it does not always follow that a team cannot be successful if it does not have group cohesion.

REMEMBER

Cohesion is the motivation that keeps the group together and inhibits the break-up of the group. Group members may be motivated to be in the group because of the success it brings them, or because they value the relationships within the group.

Cohesion comprises both task cohesion and social cohesion.

- **Task cohesion** refers to the degree to which members of a group work together to achieve common goals, for example to win a specific match or competition.
- **Social cohesion** reflects the degree to which members of a team like each other and interact accordingly.

A school team made up from players who have grown up together in the same area over a number of years can have stronger social bonds than a team of relative strangers.

BUILDING GROUP COHESION – A CONCEPTUAL MODEL

There is clear evidence that the more united a group becomes with its cause, and the more interactive group members are socially within the group, the greater the probability of success. Leaders in the sports environment should aim to develop cohesiveness within the group. The development of a group normally goes through four stages:

- forming – the group meets or is assembled
- storming – heightened tension may develop as roles are defined and tasks established
- norming – rules and standards of behaviour are agreed as cohesion is built
- performing – the group matures and works together.

REMEMBER

Task cohesion demands the creation of a cause or identity that holds value for the members of the group, and in which they believe. Social cohesion requires the creation of social bonds of interaction and development in a positive, enjoyable atmosphere.

TASK

Fabio Capello, the England football manager, has a dilemma – should he select his best players on paper and then decide a formation in which they fit, or should he have a set formation and then select the players to fit it? Give reasons for and against each approach. How much influence will the media have on his decisions?

GROUP DYNAMICS

The dynamic within the group is also an important consideration in building **group cohesion**. Group dynamics describes the processes within a group and between the members of the group. This can also be described as the energy the group exhibits. Successful groups with a dynamic have a 'chemistry'. This is difficult to guarantee – it depends on individual personalities, but can be the product of leadership and cohesion within a group. A collective motivation, a clear goal and the nurturing of personalities all contribute to the dynamic within a group. Leaders will seek out individuals to join the group who have similar social and task characteristics and a shared ethos – groups are often fashioned in the image of the leader.

CASE STUDY

TAMING THE LIONS

The British Lions Rugby Union tours occur every four years. Throwing many players together from four different countries has the potential to produce the best side in the world. But the players also have to mix, both socially and in the task of playing on tour for the Lions. The leaders of the tours devise social and task cohesion strategies to overcome old divisions, conflicts and tensions, and aim to build a group dynamic.

■ Suggest some strategies and methods the leaders might choose.

STRETCH AND CHALLENGE

List three groups that have exhibited clear task cohesion, and three groups that have shown clear social cohesion. Start by thinking outside the world of sport.

Carron identifies four factors that affect the development of cohesion:

■ environmental factors that bind players together – age, club membership, location, employment or ethos

■ personal factors – belief in the group, a desire to win, the social relationships within a community, the desire to achieve excellence

■ leadership factors – the influence of the coach or manager in building identity and affiliation through task and social cohesion factors

■ team factors – in relation to the group as a whole, its identity, targets set, the ability and role of each member of the group.

KEY TERM

group cohesion
a measure of the extent to which a group works together socially or to complete a task

TASK

How could you incorporate an isolated and demotivated player into a team?

STRATEGIES AND METHODS FOR ENHANCING GROUP COHESION

Building on Carron's four-dimensional model, there are strategies and methods for developing cohesion in a group.

Environmental factors can be enhanced through:

■ holding training camps to build unity through external changes in social circumstances

■ ensuring all members of the group have equal importance and value by avoiding star billings

■ rewarding all players equally with praise or criticism.

Personal factors can be enhanced through:

- ensuring all members of the group feel ownership of the group

- mixing young and old players together in groups, especially when staying away from home

- developing a shared responsibility for success and a belief that all members are essential to successes of the group

- creating a belief in the group and its task and social development

- avoiding the formation of cliques voicing disenchantment with the group task or the social mix – use 'sociograms' to identify positive and negative subgroups

- identifying the reasons why members individually want to be part of the group, and building on their motives

- identifying those members who exhibit 'social loafing' (make less effort than they would when alone), and introducing methods to incorporate them into the group.

Leadership factors can be enhanced through the following actions:

- unite players in their belief in you as leader through your leadership style and behaviour – mix an autocratic and democratic style

- treat players as individuals, offer both praise and criticism

- avoid criticising individuals in front of the group

- get to know your members – be aware of each person's needs and their preferred way of interacting and style of motivation.

Teams can be enhanced through:

- the appropriate use of team goals in the short, medium and long term

- clearly identifying member roles in the group as integral to the team ethic – avoid the Ringelmann effect (increased social loafing and loss of coordination as more members are added to a group)

- devise and identify a clear system of rewards and punishments that the group members have helped devise and have agreed to

- encourage social bonding through winter training camps or group social events.

ExamCafé

Relax, refresh, result!

Refresh your memory

Surprise

Revision checklist

▷ Know and be able to define the different types of goal-setting.

▷ Be able to explain the principles of SMARTER.

▷ Know the difference between intrinsic and extrinsic motivation.

▷ Define and explain what you understand by the concepts of mental rehearsal, self-talk and imagery techniques.

▷ Explain the difference between short-term and long-term goals.

▷ Understand the place of performance profiling and how to build a psychological skills training programme for your sport or physical activity.

▷ Define and explain the effect of achievement motivation.

▷ Explain the difference between static and dynamic acuity, and the concepts depth perception and peripheral vision, as applied to a sport or physical activity.

▷ Know how a simple model of information-processing works.

▷ Explain how attribution theory works.

▷ Know the components of visual awareness training, and how it works.

▷ Understand the role of ritual in a sporting performance.

▷ Understand how to build effective group cohesion.

examiner's tips

If you are struggling to understand a theory, try to apply it to specific sports examples – often you may be aware of the outcomes of actions, but not necessarily the theoretical explanations behind them.

Get the result!

Sample question and answer

Examiner says:

This answer would score
full marks because the
student has explained
the difference between
the internal and external
factors of attribution
theory, and has applied
this with reference to
the confidence of the
individual – hence
answering the question.

Examiner says:

The answer offers some
explanation of the
applied context in which
the individual may use
attribution theory both to
explain a performance
and to build confidence
for the next performance.

Examiner says:

By also including
reference to the role of
attribution retraining, a
further mark would be
awarded, but no detail
has been included –
adding a little more
information demonstrates
the breadth and depth of
your knowledge.

A total of 5 marks would
be awarded.

Student answer – candidate A

A coach could use attribution theory to help a performer gain
in confidence by focusing on the difference between external
and internal factors. By doing this the coach could remove any
negative thoughts the performer may have about themselves as
an individual, and place them in those areas that are beyond the
control of the performer. The coach might make the performer
believe that better performances are the result of internal
factors such as skill and effort, things they can control, and
when a bad performance or result occurs, place the reasons for
this on external factors such as luck and the difficulty of the
task. Sometimes the coach may need to tell a performer that they
are good enough in terms of ability and that they tried hard when
they won, so this makes them feel good, but blame the opposition
when they lose, telling him that opposition were just lucky in that
they had the referee on their side or that the opposition were
of a higher standard, but they did well against them anyway. A
coach might tell a performer they lost because they did not try
hard enough, so if they try harder next time they might win.
Some performers may need to undertake 'attribution retraining'
in order to build confidence.

Examiner says:

The answer could have been extended further by dealing with the
stability factor. Ability and task difficulty are both stable factors and are
not likely to change in immediately, while effort and luck are unstable
factors as they can change during a performance. This affects the
short- and long-term application and use of attribution theory.

Examiner says:

The student has failed to understand attribution theory, and confused this with personal attributes. The student has not mentioned the four key terms in this theory or the two dimensions. No constructive strategies were offered for confidence-building other than 'talk'. This answer would score no marks.

Student answer — candidate B

A coach may use attribution to explain the result of a match. Players often blame one another for the result. Players never take responsibility for themselves and are never wrong but blame others. The attributes of a good player are strength, determination and never letting your friends down. If a coach feels a player has let him down he could punish them or drop them from team. Confidence is a personal thing and the coach could talk to the player when he is not playing.

CHAPTER 7 LONG-TERM TECHNICAL PREPARATION

LEARNING OUTCOMES

By working through this chapter, you should:

- understand the mechanical aspects of long-term preparation
- be able to discuss refinement of technique, the perfect model, and use of feedback for example through video and computer software
- know about ergogenic aids, including force plates, pedometry, heart-rate monitoring and the use of GPS technology

MECHANICAL ASPECTS OF LONG-TERM PREPARATION

As with long-term physiological preparation (Chapter 5), we must first understand what we actually mean by 'long-term'. In this context, long-term generally refers to the training that takes place well before a performance. This is training that prepares you for performance by encouraging your body to make changes, or adaptations, to the way it works, which, in turn, produce a more efficient and consequently less stressful way of functioning.

We often assume that this preparation is solely concerned with the athlete's physiology. And for many amateur athletes, this is often the case. The beginning of a season approaches and the athlete begins to exert huge amounts of effort and energy on improving their performance by running, swimming, cycling or rowing further and further. By doing this, they are compounding the technique they used last season – and the one before that. That would be fine if their technique was perfect, or close to perfect. But unfortunately that is rarely the case. The consequence of this for the amateur athlete is twofold:

- learning or compounding bad technique
- wasting a significant amount of effort and energy.

To avoid this, a considerable amount of time and effort is spent by elite athletes, mainly in the early stages of training, in refining their efficiency of movement. The aim is that any effort expended on physiological training will be maximised with the optimum performance – the least effort for the most gain.

CASE STUDY
'CAN HE SWIM?' 'WITH A NAME LIKE "ROCK"!'

▶ *Sylvester Stallone as Rocky*

In the film *Rocky 2*, there is a sequence where Rocky is swimming to improve his fitness still further. We have seen that he can sprint upstairs, punch cattle carcasses, lift weights, chase and catch cockerels, sprint along the beach …. but put him in a pool and he struggles to complete one length. Why? It is not a lack of general fitness, but a lack of sporting efficiency, which results in the need to expend a huge amount of effort for a small return.

- How could an athlete use technology in order to improve their swimming efficiency?

APPLY IT!

Recruit two people who are relatively fit in different sports – for example one runner and one swimmer. Ask them both to run 1000 metres together at a comfortable pace, while wearing heart-rate monitors. Then, ask them both to swim 100 metres freestyle, again together and at the same pace.

Predict the differences in heart-rate averages for the two athletes.

Account for the differences in heart rate for the swimming – swimming requires greater technique.

▶ Rebecca Adlington of Team GB swimming to a gold medal and a new world record in the women's 800 metres freestyle at the Beijing Olympics

▶ A researcher analysing a swimmer's stroke at an Olympic training centre in Colorado Springs, USA

REFINING TECHNIQUE

The greater the efficiency of movement, the greater the impact of any physical effort, and therefore the greater the result.

For example, a swimmer who has an efficient body position and who catches and pulls water efficiently may swim 25 metres comfortably in only 16 strokes. Compare that with an inefficient swimmer who thrashes and splashes their way through almost 30 strokes over the same distance, takes more time to get there, and is clearly panting as a result of the extra effort.

OBSERVATIONAL FEEDBACK

This need to improve and refine performance was traditionally met through observation and feedback from a coach. But this method has limitations and drawbacks:

- it presupposes that the coach has a very clear understanding of what the 'perfect model' would or should look like
- it assumes the coach is proficient in observation – although this may seem obvious, in some cases, particularly when an elite performer is being observed, adjustments, misalignments or timings might be out to an extremely small degree
- it assumes the coach is able to explain the necessary amendments to the athlete … and
- that the athlete will be able to understand what is required and, more importantly, implement the changes.

THE PERFECT MODEL

Two elite performers might have achieved their status by virtue of their ability to perform the required skills successfully and consistently. But they may perform the same skills in very different ways. A detailed examination of the swing of a dozen professional golfers would probably produce at least four distinct variations on the theme. Compare the very upright running style of Michael Johnson with that of other, more traditional sprinters.

That does not mean one of the athletes is wrong – simply that, for the individual, a different technique has proved more effective. This does not mean the concept of the **perfect model** is redundant. The perfect model is the generally accepted way of performing the skill.

When analysing a performer, you should compare them with the perfect model. To break this down it is easier to think in terms of either:

- start position, transition, execution and recovery
- or head position, body position, arm action, leg action and total body efficiency

depending on the type of skill being performed. For example, if you are analysing a sprinter, it is easier to use the second style; whereas analysing a skill such as a tennis serve lends itself better to the use of the first.

TASK

Identify five sporting skills that would be categorised by each of the two styles.

▶ *Once the use of video cameras had become accepted practice, it was only a matter of time before this (now basic) form of technology was developed further.*

KEY TERM

perfect model
the recognised and accepted way of executing a given skill or sequence

VIDEO AND COMPUTER SOFTWARE

To combat the potential obstacles in relying on a coach's analysis, video analysis is now increasingly used. The power of sight is greater than that of sound for many individuals, so actually being able to see what they might be doing wrong at a given time can be of far greater assistance.

The two best-known software programs in this area are Dartfish and ProZone.

Dartfish software (www.dartfish.co.uk) was developed and became accessible during the 1990s. It took analysis and feedback to a new level. With the use of a computer, video camera and Dartfish software, teachers and coaches were now able to:

- record and show delayed playback while another performer is being recorded
- observe several performers on the same screen at the same time
- when observing multiple performers executing the same skill, synchronise the start of a move to compare timings
- overlap and superimpose performers on top of each other so that direct comparisons can be made
- strobe and track images
- obtain graphical data by converting the performer into a moving stick object, to view and compare the biomechanical efficiencies of a performance.

These capabilities open up the scope for both coach and athletes to communicate far more effectively, and to take the execution of skills to a higher level.

▶ Dartfish software

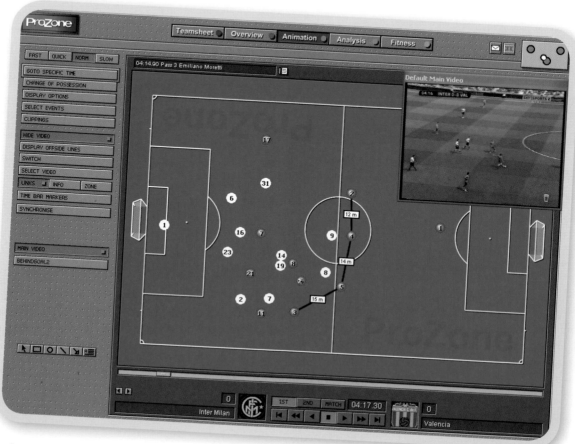

▶ ProZone software

CASE STUDY
TRACKING WITH PROZONE

The following report relates to the success of a competitor to Dartfish – ProZone (www.prozonesports.com).

We have developed a system of game-tracking software that is revolutionising the work of leading sports club coaches up and down the country.

ProZone is a unique technology that tracks every movement of every player on the field throughout the game. The ensuing images captured by up to 12 sensors placed around the stadium are fed into a database every tenth of a second to provide an interactive and aerial replay of each game. This precision tracking tool allows football and rugby coaches to analyse each play in detail and enhance the performance of their team.

The sophisticated match analysis system has already been adopted by the majority of the Premiership clubs as well as many of the Championship clubs across the country.

Developed in association with Leeds Computing School, the ProZone sports performance analysis system is now attracting interest from overseas sports clubs and ProZone has already been adopted by three clubs in the United Arab Emirates.

At our busy HQ in Roundhay north Leeds, ProZone employs some 40 full-time workers many of whom are qualified sports scientists.

The feelings of those in the company is:

'A TV camera can only focus on that small area of the pitch where the ball is in play, but ProZone covers the pitch from every angle so that each player's movements can be carefully tracked. It's a fantastic coaching tool and some of the best teams in the country are reaping the benefits of using the system to pinpoint their strengths and weaknesses.'

'Game analysis has become much more technical and the number of coaching staff per sports club has increased to reflect the more scientific approach to sport. We know there is a lot of interest overseas in ProZone, however we want to adopt a strategic approach in mapping out our plans for overseas trade.'

- Identify the advantages and any possible disadvantages that could be gained from using software such as ProZone.

TECHNICAL ERGOGENIC AIDS

Ergogenic aids are any external influences that positively affect performance (see page 68).

As winning margins decrease, and athletes apply similar training methods and have access to similar data, any sort of edge can give a potential advantage that will produce the winning margin. Due to the huge commercial nature of many elite sports, the benefit of being associated with the winner, let alone being credited with assisting or even producing the win, brings huge commercial value.

One example was the 2004 Tour de France. Lance Armstrong had won the previous five Tours before 2003, which he lost by the smallest margin. If he won the race in 2004, he would become the first man ever to win the race on six occasions. His bike of choice was always manufactured by Trek, who had certainly benefited from their association with a five-times Tour winner. Between the 2003 and 2004 races, Trek invested several million dollars in designing a new bike. The end result had a bulge or 'fin' on the frame that was supposed to enhance aerodynamics to the extent that it would save 2 minutes on a 200 km race.

FORCE PLATES

According to Newton's Third Law of Motion (Law of Reaction), for every action there is an equal and opposite reaction. Due to gravity, there will be interactions between the body and the ground. The reaction force supplied by the ground is specifically called the ground reaction force (GRF), which is the reaction to the force the body exerts on the ground. For example, the reaction of a falling ball to the ground is seen when the ball bounces upwards after making contact with the ground.

Ground reaction force can be measured with the aid of a force plate, which can either be portable or fixed.

When fixed, it will usually be situated in an area of a sports hall, or on a long jump run, or similar. The force plate has sensors built into it that constantly measure the take-off force and relay this to the computer up to 500 times per second. The height of the jump, jump power and other parameters are automatically calculated from the take-off force. This information can be used in a variety of ways, with athletes in a range of sports, but basically it can tell us the amount of force an athlete can impart in a certain amount of time.

ground reaction force

driving action

Fig. 7.1 *Ground reaction force*

Fig. 7.2 *Force plate training*

Force plates are ideally suited to athletes whose sport demands high levels of power and endurance. By performing differently on the force plate, information can be obtained regarding power output, power generated, and efficiency of movement.

For example, if an athlete was to perform continuous jumps with bent legs for up to 60 seconds, information can be obtained about the athlete's endurance, consistency of contact time, and how they accelerate their own body mass over that time.

Alternatively if an athlete was to perform a squat jump, data on their strength and power can be examined with feedback to the coach providing information on whether the athlete should work more on force (load) or speed (velocity).

PEDOMETRY

A pedometer or stepometer is a device that calculates the distance you have walked or run. It senses your movements and counts your steps. You do a basic calibration to tell it the length of your stride, then the pedometer converts your steps into distance.

CLEAR

Fig. 7.3 *A simple pedometer*

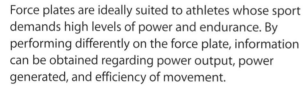

HOTLINKS

For more information on force plates see the English Institute of Sport's website, www.eis2win.co.uk

STRETCH AND CHALLENGE

Look at some force plate manufacturers' websites to find out (a) how they work, and (b) what their main recommended uses in different sports might be.

Although a pedometer can be useful to calculate distance travelled when running or walking, it is perhaps most useful worn throughout a day. The distance travelled during the day can then be used to help predict calorific expenditure so that weight-loss strategies can be applied more accurately.

▶ *Pedometers are used by amateurs and professionals alike*

APPLY IT!

Use a pedometer to calculate the distance you cover during a normal day. Then, using the information provided and the time taken, calculate your average speed. As a result, you should be able to calculate your energy expenditure and therefore your required energy intake for a given day.

How many calories do you need to consume in order to:

- *maintain current body mass?*
- *lose 5 kg of body mass?*

Fig. 7.4 *Portable display of a heart-rate monitor*

HEART-RATE MONITORING

Heart-rate monitors are now accessible to most athletes, and as a result are the most popular method of measuring exercise intensity, particularly among amateur athletes. Sensitive monitors can be set to record changes in heart rate every second, with the data being displayed immediately on a wristwatch worn by the athlete, or on a central display held by the coach.

These monitors allow the athlete to predetermine the intensity at which they will train and then maintain that intensity level throughout the session.

Heart-rate monitors are not totally accurate in terms of training intensity, so they are not necessarily used by all elite athletes, who may prefer to use power-measuring units if they are available. However, they do provide a wealth of information that can help an athlete to be more objective-led in their training.

POWER GAUGES

A variety of devices exist to measure power accurately. This mode of measuring intensity can be manipulated for a variety of activities, but seems to lend itself most naturally to cycling. An accurate reading can be provided instantly on a cycling computer, providing

▶ *Testing an Olympic bicycle in the wind tunnel of the Dresden University of Technology in Germany*

the athlete with up-to-date and very accurate data. Companies such as Polar, SRM and Garmin all produce power-measuring equipment that is accurate and easily accessible to any serious athlete, not just elite performers.

WIND TUNNELS AND AERODYNAMICS

Wind tunnels allow coaches, athletes and manufacturers the opportunity to make finite adjustments in the hope of making a performance more efficient.

The image of a cyclist in a wind tunnel illustrates the benefits of many hours of testing. Data from the tests enable the coach to analyse the effects that different equipment, clothing, shapes, body position, etc. can have on performance.

There are a great many variables that can be analysed, including:

- depth of wheel rims
- size and number of spokes in wheels – or lack of them
- width of handlebars
- position of rider's back and forearms
- amount of clothing worn, and material it is made from
- width of bottom bracket
- position of the rider's thumbs – by moving their thumbs up during a race, a rider can add 20 seconds to a 30-mile time trial!

TASK

Research what other sports can benefit from the use of wind tunnels or improved aerodynamics.

GPS TECHNOLOGY

For certain athletes, such as sailors, GPS is considered an essential item of kit. For wilderness sports such as mountain-bike riding, trekking and skiing, which are enjoying significant growth in participation, GPS is becoming more valuable.

CASE STUDY
GLOBAL POSITIONING SYSTEM

'The GPS is a satellite-based navigation system made up of a network of 24 satellites placed into orbit by the US Department of Defense. GPS was originally intended for military applications, but in the 1980s the government made the system available for civilian use. GPS works in any weather conditions, anywhere in the world, 24 hours a day.'

(Source: Garmin, www.garmin.com)

- Some examples are given above of how this type of information can be used in sport. But can you suggest three other contexts in which GPS might be useful to athletes?

▶ *GPS has obvious uses in sailing*

But what about more traditional sports? One example might be a runner who wants to be scientific and in control of their training, but without being tied to the gym treadmill – the new GPS allows them to run without getting lost, while receiving information such as distance covered, average and maximum speeds, leg cadence, stride length, altitude covered, and also heart rate.

TASK

Can you think of three more examples of how GPS could be useful in giving technical information, either in practising a sport or in training?

ExamCafé
Relax, refresh, result!

SURPRISE

Refresh your memory

Revision checklist

▷ Know what we mean by the refinement of technique and its importance to athletes.

▷ Understand when technique refinements might become the focus of training.

▷ Know how technology has developed to aid analysis and feedback, including:

○ video analysis

○ Dartfish and ProZone

○ wind tunnels and aerodynamics

○ force plate technology

○ pedometers and heart-rate monitors.

○ GPS.

examiner's tips

Be specific when answering any examination question. Identify the number of points you need to make, and the facts required to score for each point. Then write accurately and without waffle. If you are struggling to express yourself as well as you would like, provide an example to support or illustrate your point.

Get the result!

Sample question and answer

Exam question

Identify examples of the types of technology used by elite athletes in order to monitor their training intensity. Select one example, and highlight any advantages or potential disadvantages for the athlete as a result of this type of technology.

Examiner says:

The question asks the candidate to do three things – identify, state advantages, and state potential disadvantages. The student's answer is generally very good, but they do not do all three, so could not hope to score the maximum marks available.

Examiner says:

In total this candidate would score 2 out of the 4 marks.

Student answer

Elite athletes might use heart-rate monitors, pedometers, GPS or power monitors to help them measure their training intensity.

By using heart-rate monitors the athlete can always see how hard they are working as measured against their heart rate. This is helpful for the athlete because it is very accurate and can guide them as to how hard they should train.

Examiner says:

The candidate scores the first mark for identifying the types of technology. They then focus on heart-rate monitors and their advantages. The next two sentences are both on the right lines, but are a little vague. The first is close enough to score a mark, but the last sentence should be qualified a little more – how does it guide future training?

model answer

Converting the student answer into a model answer is not too difficult.

Elite athletes might use heart-rate monitors, pedometers, GPS or power monitors to help them measure their training intensity.

By using heart-rate monitors the athlete can always see how hard they are working as measured against their heart rate, which is more accurate than measuring how fast they are travelling. This is because running downhill is easier than running uphill. That means you will be running faster, but for less effort, when going down.

This is helpful for the athlete because it is very accurate and can guide them as to how hard they should train: by training at 60 per cent of their maximum heart rate, they would know that their training is improving their baseline aerobic fitness.

One disadvantage of using heart-rate monitors is that you need to know how to calculate your heart-rate zones, and also to know what benefit accompanies each zone.

model answer

Below is the same answer, but split into four sections, which informs the candidate that they have provided four points and so hopefully will score the four marks available.

- Elite athletes might use heart-rate monitors, pedometers, GPS or power monitors to help them measure their training intensity.

- By using heart-rate monitors the athlete can always see how hard they are working as measured against their heart rate, which is more accurate than measuring how fast they are travelling. This is because running downhill is easier than running uphill. That means you will be running faster, but for less effort, when going down.

- This is helpful for the athlete because it is very accurate and can guide them as to how hard they should train: by training at 60 per cent of their maximum heart rate, they would know that their training is improving their baseline aerobic fitness.

- One disadvantage of using heart-rate monitors is that you need to know how to calculate your heart-rate zones, and also to know what benefit accompanies each zone.

UNIT 3
PREPARATION FOR OPTIMUM SPORTS PERFORMANCE

PART C
MANAGING ELITE PERFORMANCE

Elite performers and teams now spend vast amounts of time and resources preparing for global competitions. In this section we investigate the various systems used around the globe to nurture and support elite athletes. This involves an in-depth investigation into the elite sports programmes of the former East Germany, Australia, the USA and the UK.

Chapter 8 investigates the needs of elite athletes in the twenty-first century and includes sections on training and preparation needs, as well as funding requirements and sports science support. The chapter also includes an overview of elite sports systems from a range of global cultures.

Chapter 9 looks at the way technology now plays a fundamental role in the preparation of elite athletes, the chapter investigates how the various sports science disciplines harness technology in their drive to help athletes and teams achieve optimum sporting performance.

CHAPTER 8 CENTRES OF EXCELLENCE

▶ *Prizefighters of the eighteenth century were some of the first athletes to train for their sport – Daniel Mendoza (1764–1836) was the acknowledged English heavyweight champion and operated a successful boxing school in London*

This chapter investigates how elite athletes are supported throughout the world. We look at the history of support for elite sports, identifying the key stages of development and discussing the different types of support that different countries use. We also discuss the benefits and issues relating to the use of sports institutes and academies.

HISTORY AND DEVELOPMENT OF ELITE SPORT

The concept of sporting excellence in the UK really began with the development of professional sportsmen during the seventeenth and early eighteenth centuries. They were mainly the paid retainers employed by the upper classes. These men represented their patrons in foot races, prize fights and horse racing. This practice was also common in cricket – some estate workers were employed mainly because of their sporting ability, usually their bowling skills, so that they could represent their master's team. In all these activities, the driving force was wagering and the quest for sporting excellence was fuelled by the patrons' desire to increase their chances of winning and therefore the size of their purse.

By the late nineteenth century, there had been a social shift in terms of sporting excellence – the best performers were by now almost exclusively drawn from the middle and upper classes, products of the expanding public schools and their philosophy of 'muscular Christianity' and the games ethic.

Sporting prowess, both as an individual and in representing the house or school, became highly valued. In an educational system before exam results and league tables, sporting success became an important marketing tool used to attract scholars – and in particular parents to pay for their sons and daughters to be educated at a particular school.

To help facilitate this sporting success, schools began to take sporting pursuits seriously, giving pupils ample time to practise and compete in their chosen sports. They also began to build increasingly extravagant facilities that included sporting pavilions, practice grounds, gymnasiums and swimming pools.

Several schools also began to employ a 'professional', whose role was to coach and provide the pupils with skilful opponents. In sports such as cricket and racket sports, these became commonplace. This was the first attempt in the UK at systematic sports preparation.

This enthusiasm for sport was also taken up by the two main universities of the time, Oxford and Cambridge. Their sporting rivalry developed into a series of sporting events, which at the end of the nineteenth century became the very pinnacle of elite sport. For the rest of the nineteenth and much of the first part of the twentieth century, Oxbridge athletes figured largely in the formation of rules, national associations and international and domestic amateur sports teams.

The university boat race, together with corresponding fixtures in athletics, cricket, football and rugby, formed major features of the British sporting calendar.

Students who competed in the annual university (or varsity) match in their chosen sport were awarded a 'blue' (after a blue ribbon attached to the Cambridge boat in one of the first boat races). These sporting blues became the first elite band of sportsmen in the UK. Their influence on the development of sport was huge – not only in the way they dominated the early international teams, but also through their role in diffusing sport throughout the rest of society and overseas.

As sport began to diffuse via the British Empire and the trading routes spreading out from the UK, other countries took up these new activities and very quickly international fixtures began to develop. It was quickly recognised by many that sport offered an opportunity to test oneself against other nations. The term 'test match' was coined by the Australian cricket team in the late nineteenth century as they prepared for a series of matches against England. They clearly saw victory at cricket as reflecting the wider progress the colony had made.

The benefits attached to international sports success meant that teams and athletes began to look more closely at training and preparation.

The other main focus for the early development of sports excellence was the founding of the International Olympic Committee in 1894, on the initiative of a French nobleman, the Baron de Coubertin. He blamed the French defeat in the Franco-Prussian War of 1870–71 on a lack of proper physical education, and aimed to improve this. He became interested in reviving the Olympics (originally ancient Greek games, held between 776 BC and 393 AD) as an international event, and the first modern IOC Olympic Games took place in 1896 in Athens. There were only 250 competitors, but at that time the games were the largest international sporting event ever held.

▶ *Oxford and Cambridge crews in the nineteenth century*

Although de Coubertin's ideal was that this global competition would allow athletes to test themselves against others in a spirit of friendship, again countries soon recognised the kudos a good performance could bring, and from the first modern games in Athens to the present-day Olympics, the unofficial medal table remains the main focus. It is interesting to note that the US team 'won' the first games in 1896 – they were already involved in systematic training, with a process that has remained in place to the present-day universities.

CASE STUDY
US COLLEGE SPORT

College sport, and the support it gives to elite athletes in the USA, first began in the 1850s with a series of rowing matches between Harvard and Yale universities. Although college sport in the USA was initially organised, funded and conducted by interested students, its popularity was such that, before long, university administrators took control of sport, hiring coaches, building programmes, and generally treating intercollegiate sport as a phenomenon that could increase an institution's prestige and attract more new students. The athletic scholarship became a vehicle to encourage the most able students to attend a particular university and at the same time help produce a 'conveyor belt' of talent for the US national teams and professional leagues.

■ How does the US approach differ from the role of university sport in the UK?

As the twentieth century progressed, a new world order began to develop in sport. The Americans and southern hemisphere nations, as well as other European nations, began to view sport in a different light and were not constrained by the very British concept of amateurism. This originally developed to accommodate a rigid class system on the playing field – but the new world nations did not have such an entrenched class system.

After the Second World War, another force in international sport emerged – one whose approach to the achievement of excellence would shape programmes across the world over the next century. The alignment of states in Eastern Europe and the dominance of the Soviet Union created a so-called 'Eastern Bloc'. Since the disintegration of the communist system in the early 1990s, this is now only a historical grouping. But its culture, originally dominated by the Soviet Union, is worth study because of the phenomenal sporting success Eastern Bloc countries achieved in a short timescale.

In the twentieth century, sport in the (then) Soviet Union and German Democratic Republic (East Germany) was completely state-controlled. Every aspect of sporting excellence, from selection to training and diet, was coordinated by the central government. Success in international sport, the so called 'shop window' of the nation, was the objective. It provided an opportunity for the Eastern Bloc to show off its political system. The philosophy was that a win for an Eastern Bloc country was a win for the communist system, and undisputable proof that this system was superior to the capitalist system of the West.

▶ In the USA college football is popular among the general public, not just among students

In all Eastern Bloc countries, sport played a very important role. Success came as a result of a carefully structured system that fitness-tested the entire population and fed talented individuals through to sports schools and training centres, and ultimately to national sports academies and national teams.

Although much of their success has been put down to the widespread use of drugs, this alone does not account for the level and rate of success. Performers in these countries had the best facilities, coaches and support available. Centres such as the Neubrandenburg Institute in East Germany have became the blueprint on which most modern sports institutes are based.

Sport in the Eastern Bloc societies reflected the egalitarian ideology of the communist system, which fostered the idea that everyone was equal in status. Although in practice this was not strictly true, in sport everybody had an equal chance of success. If you were identified as having talent in a sport, you were selected, no matter what your race or background. This ensured that the state had the widest possible base from which to select.

By the turn of the twenty-first century, the globalisation of sport and the continued development of emergent cultures have meant that virtually all countries now have a planned elite sports programme. Most nations competing in global games have developed central training bases for their top athletes, usually a national institute of sport, and have also developed support mechanisms to help fund and develop the performance of their elite sports squads.

OVERVIEW – ELITE SPORT IN DIFFERENT COUNTRIES

THE FORMER EAST GERMANY

A HISTORICAL PERSPECTIVE

After the Second World War, Germany was divided into two separate states along the lines of Allied occupation in 1949. The German Democratic Republic (East Germany) existed from 1949 until 1990, when East and West Germany were reunified after the fall of the Berlin Wall.

During its brief 41-year history, East Germany's approach to the achievement of excellence shaped programmes across the world for the next century. Despite having a population of only 16 million, East Germany reached the dizzy heights of second in the Olympic medal table of 1976 (second only to the Soviet Union).

The East German elite sports programme started early – every primary school child was put through a battery of tests that included biometric measurements, fitness and skill tests, and medical examinations. Full-time specialist PE teachers would take the children through daily sports lessons, and coaches and medical staff would observe these sessions, recording the progress of each individual child – what they were doing was spotting talent.

If a child showed potential in one of the state's list of programme sports (mostly Olympic disciplines), they would be sent to one of the country's 25 Child and Youth Sport Schools.

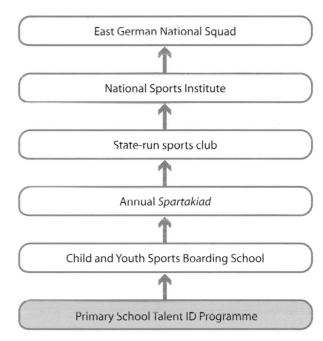

Fig. 8.1 *The East German sports model*

Here children would train for over 50 hours a week in their specific sports, and also fit in some academic study. These were boarding schools run according to a strict regime. Scientists and coaches planned virtually every minute of the young athletes' lives.

Each year, a series of *Spartakiads* (mini-Olympics) were held between the different age groups. This was meant to replicate the pressure of the real thing, but was also an important stage in evaluating the progress of individual athletes.

▶ The gymnastics teams of the Soviet Union, Romania and East Germany winning gold, silver and bronze at the 1988 Seoul Olympics

Those who failed to progress in school, or failed to deliver at the annual games, were released from the schools.

A more sinister side to the work of these sports schools was the fact that, as well as being appointed a full-time coach, each athlete also had their own doctor. Their role was to ensure each athlete was in top physical condition and to provide supportive medicine. In the drive to ensure the system won medals, the East German Government launched a programme called State Plan 1425, which resulted in the systematic doping of all East German athletes.

STRETCH AND CHALLENGE

In 2005, 190 East German competitors launched a legal case against the German pharmaceutical giant Jenapharm. They claim that the East German firm knowingly supplied the steroids that were given to them by trainers and coaches from the 1960s onwards until East Germany's demise in 1990. Jenapharm, now owned by Schering, argues it was not responsible for the doping scandal, and blames the communist system.

Find out more about this case, and consider the arguments for and against.

TASK

Would drugs alone account for the success of the East German athletes during the 1970s? Can you suggest other reasons for this success?

Each sports school was linked to state-run sports clubs, often associated with a particular trade union. Certain names (still evident in the current UEFA Champions League) were common across the Eastern Bloc countries – Dynamo clubs were linked to the police; Spartak to the electricians' union; Lokomotiv the railway union; and CSKA the army. This allowed sportsmen and women to train and perform full-time without jeopardising their Olympic amateur status. Those at the sports school who were still making progress would start playing for their club senior teams after the age of 16.

The final piece of the East German elite sports jigsaw was the work of several national institutes of sport that were used for the final stage of preparation in the run-up to the Olympic Games and other major championships. These institutes had state-of-the-art facilities for athletes to be trained and monitored. The most famous was the German College of Physical Culture in Leipzig, which also housed the Research Institute for Physical Culture and Sport, where most of the 'supportive medicine' was researched and developed. The East Germans were at the forefront of sports science development. They were the first to develop treadmills and swimming flumes, and also put athletes into **hypoxic chambers** in order to reproduce the training effects of altitude. If you visit any contemporary sports institute or sports academy, you will see evidence of the East German legacy.

KEY TERM

hypoxic chamber
training module in which the pressure of oxygen can be altered to mimic the affects of altitude

There is evidence that both France in the 1960s and Australia in the 1980s adopted many of the elite sports practices the East Germans had developed. In turn, countries such as the UK have also adopted talent identification and sport institute models.

MODERN-DAY GERMANY

After the reunification of Germany there was some initial success, but allegations of doping and widespread drug abuse in the former East Germany meant that there was some reluctance simply to develop the East German system across the new state. This did not stop many of the former national coaches being headhunted by other nations and given leading roles in their elite sports systems.

Germany still has several national Olympic training centres, and support is offered through educational centres including the German Sport University Cologne.

HOTLINKS
The German Sport University Cologne (in German):
www.dshs-koeln.de/wps/porta

AUSTRALIA

The Australian Institute of Sport (AIS) has led the development of elite sport in Australia for two decades, and its success is widely acknowledged by the Australian public. It is now highly regarded internationally as a world best practice model for elite athlete development. Many countries, including the UK, are now actively setting up similar programmes in a bid to emulate Australia's sporting success.

The AIS was born out of Australia's disappointing performance at the 1976 Olympics in Montreal, in which they won just one silver medal and four bronze medals. The federal government conducted a review of the nation's elite sport system, and the outcome was that Australia needed a centre of excellence that would prepare athletes for international competition. Its role in developing sports excellence can be judged by the fact that at the 1992 Barcelona Olympics, Australia won 27 medals including seven golds.

But the key was the wider public displeasure about the poor performance of Australia's athletes. This gave the Australian federal government a mandate to spend large amounts of public money on creating an elite sports system that would ensure success at future international sports events.

The AIS was opened on Australia Day 1981, just outside Canberra. The first intake of 150 athletes in eight sports – basketball, swimming, weightlifting, track and field, gymnastics, netball, soccer and tennis – was based in Canberra. Now the AIS offers scholarships every year to almost 600 athletes in 32 separate programmes covering 25 sports, and employs around 75 full-time coaches in a range of sports. Although the focus has been mainly on the Olympics, there are now plans to expand the role of the Institute to accommodate a wider range of sports.

The AIS provides Australian athletes with world-class training facilities, high-performance coaching, state-of-the-art equipment, a world-class sports medicine and sports science facility, travel, accommodation for 350 residents on site, and reimbursement of education expenses.

One of the most successful sports science experiments developed by the AIS was 'Sports Search' or the National Talent Identification and Development programme. The rising cost of preparing elite athletes (2006 AIS budget of Australian $12 million) has meant that Australia has had to be more economical in targeting this potential. This need is further exaggerated by Australia's relatively small population of only 20.7 million (compared with the 60.5 million living in the UK), which means they must target their resources the best way they can.

Back in 1988, a small group of sports scientists based at the AIS analysed all the rowers taking part in the Australian National Championships. Rowing had been identified as a sport that was relatively weak at international level, would fit well into the AIS model, and should bring Australia success. The scientists were interested in the differences between those who won and lost in the various categories. What they discovered was that the rowers who won the races tended to share similar physical characteristics.

They concluded that the ideal rower should be tall, longer in the legs than in the back, have longer forearms and narrower hips than average, and show a higher level of endurance. From this information, they put together a bank of fitness tests and anatomical measurements that would identify this body type, and visited a number of high schools. They decided to concentrate on female rowers, as they felt that it would be easier to win in women's events due to the minority participation in female rowing across the world.

In the run-up to the 2000 Sydney Olympics, Australian schools were asked to participate in a national sports talent search scheme, with pupils subjected to a series of speed, strength and flexibility trials to pinpoint those with speed, anatomical and physiological characteristics. The tests were designed by sports scientists at the AIS, specifically to measure suitability for Olympic sports. Scientists had looked at muscle structure and aerobic capacity, and predicted the combinations most likely to produce future champions.

Another support service to Australian scholarship holders is the Athlete Career and Education (ACE) programme. It was set up to enhance the personal development and performance of Australia's elite athletes through a number of career and education services. A national network of advisers throughout

▶ *Rowing was one of the sports targeted by Australia's Sports Search programme*

Australia help athletes with educational guidance, career planning, job searching and personal development, to make sure they plan for life after sport.

The AIS also provides administrative, sports science and coaching services, and funding assistance to state and territory institutes and academies of sport and national sporting organisations.

The AIS is at the leading edge of sport science and research developments. The Sports Science and Sports Medicine division is credited with revolutionary breakthroughs such as the ice jacket used at the Atlanta Olympics, the 'super roo bike', and the use of the altitude house as an important facility in helping athletes prepare for competition. The division comprises some of the world's leading authorities in physiology, biomechanics, psychology, nutrition and sports medicine.

HOTLINKS

Australian Institute of Sport – www.ausport.gov.au

National Coach and Athlete Career and Education – www.ausport.gov.au/participating/athletes/career_ and_education

National Talent Identification and Development programme –www.ausport.gov.au/participating/ got_talent

eTID – an online electronic talent identification tool that allows anyone (aged 12–29) to assess their sporting potential –www.ausport.gov.au/participating/ got_talent/test

CASE STUDY

THE SUPER ROO BIKE

Australian track cyclists won impressive victories at the 1995, 1996 and 1997 World Track Championships and the 15th Commonwealth Games. The Australian team trained and competed using a new state-of-the-art bike built using carbon fibre. The Super Roo cycle was designed and built by a project team from the Royal Melbourne Institute of Technology and the AIS.

- Discuss whether you think it is fair that improved equipment can have such a major effect in sporting competition.

STRETCH AND CHALLENGE

Team GB's track cyclists were very successful at the Beijing 2008 Olympics. Was this due to their skill, or their bikes? How did they compare with the bikes used by other competitors?

Since 1998, the AIS has moved away from its centralised model, and in addition to its centre in Canberra, now offers support through a network of coaches and support staff based in institutes in each of the Australian states. This evolution from a centralised to a decentralised system now fits more easily with the federal/state political administration of Australia. But it is also the result of the other key factor in Australia's success – that they are continually looking to review and improve their sports systems. It was found that athletes often preferred to stay in their local area, and that residence at an institute was not always beneficial both in performance and social terms. These state institutes are non-residential and provide a central location for management, coaches, athlete support, and sports science and medical support.

USA

A distinctive feature of sport in the USA is the way sporting talent is nurtured through the high school and college system. Although unique to the USA, it is a system that a number of other cultures are now experimenting with.

The development of elite sport in the USA is focused almost exclusively on the school and college system – this is completely different from the club-based approach in most European countries. High school and college sport in the USA is a mirror of the professional sports system. Most high schools have lavish facilities for both players and spectators. The other key feature is the support that school and college teams receive from their local community – in many towns, school sport is almost akin to

► *Sport is taken seriously at all levels in the US system*

► *Basketball is one US sport where the colleges play a lead role in nurturing future elite performers*

a religion, with huge crowds attending games and practices. Often this support also includes considerable financial input, which goes some way towards explaining the high standards of both performing and coaching.

The basic connection between high school, college sport and the professional leagues is due to the unique system of athletic recruitment practised in the USA. This is the selection process whereby students move first from high school onto scholarship programmes for the various sports teams at college level, and then, if they are good enough, enter the annual 'draft'. Although this is the dream of all aspiring school athletes, it must be noted that this is a very elitist and competitive selection process, with fewer than 4 per cent of high school first team players progressing to the draft stage of recruitment.

HIGH SCHOOL SPORT AND NURTURING TALENT

High school sport is the starting point for athletes wishing to make a career in sport, and there is only one route to the top in most US sports. Schools belong to their state's High School Athletic Association, which in turn belongs to the National Federation of State High School Associations. These two organisations coordinate and regulate contests in sport and other physical activities.

Interschool sport reaches its greatest intensity in grades 11 and 12 (ages 16–18), when students represent their school first team in the various sports. Although larger schools play a range of sports, most tend to specialise in football or basketball. This often follows a geographical pattern, with city schools concentrating on basketball and those in smaller towns on football.

Those selected to play in the school basketball and football teams have their timetables altered so they can train for a number of hours on most schooldays. Most games take place on a Friday night, attracting a large community following. Schools initially play in local conferences or leagues, where rivalry is intense. The team with the best result at the end of a round robin tournament then progresses through to district and then state championships.

Coaches are members of the high school faculty, and occasionally they will be teachers, although larger schools employ a number of specialist coaches for their teams. Teams have a large budget to ensure they have the best possible equipment and preparation. This funding comes from the gate money from home games, and from fundraising from the school's booster club.

Booster clubs are another unique feature of school sport in the USA. Made up of local businessmen and former players and pupils, these clubs raise money that helps support their school team.

College scouts follow every game, and from early in the season will be targeting key players.

It is accepted that successful high school performers will be the recipients of athletic scholarship grants-in-aid to cover tuition fees and board. A skilful high school player may be offered 30–40 scholarships from different universities, so once again this is a very competitive process, and a number of abuses do arise.

COLLEGE AND UNIVERSITY SPORT

Up to the 1960s, college football developed and grew in popularity more than the professional game. Although it still receives a disproportionate amount of attention in terms of the media and community support, it now acts as a 'middleman' to the professional game. Its role is to groom the best talent recruited from high school, toughen them up through a gruelling four years of training, playing and completing some study, and then filter them into the professional clubs via the annual draft.

The elite college football and basketball teams generate huge revenues from gate receipts, commercial sponsorship and media fees for their institutions. But due to old rules linked to the nineteenth-century concept of amateurism, they are forbidden from receiving anything but free tuition, meals and accommodation – which is generally

referred to as the scholarship. What the athletes do receive is the chance to fulfil an 'American dream' and have a go at making the pros – although this is a reality for only very few college athletes.

The National Collegiate Athletic Association (NCAA) controls college sport in the USA. It was established in 1906 (as the Intercollegiate Athletic Association), primarily to bring order to American football, and by 1920 had taken over control of all sports at college level. Its philosophy was (and to some extent still remains) the Corinthian ideal of producing 'scholar athletes'.

STRETCH AND CHALLENGE

The 'Corinthian ideal' in sport is used to describe the 'amateur' value system that elevates sport practised with self-interest above that done for pay (professionalism). It was believed that in ancient Greece, the athletes of Corinth competed for no reward other than a laurel wreath.

■ Name some sports that still distinguish between amateur and professional players. How realistic is this in the modern world?

It should be remembered that, alongside the high-profile sports, thousands of US college athletes train and compete in a huge variety of amateur sports. They, too, add to the development of excellence in the USA, as they often make up the teams in the Olympic disciplines that are not large enough to have a professional arm. Benefiting from the excellent facilities at most universities, and the more limited demands on their time, these athletes can train and prepare for competition on campus.

Before the 1990s, this was also a means of side-stepping the amateur rules of the Olympics and international athletics. These so-called **'shamateurs'** could receive financial aid from commercial companies as long as they were labelled 'academic'. In the 1990s the International Olympic Committee withdrew the rules, stating that performers at the Olympic Games had to be amateurs, and many other sports governing bodies followed.

Coaches also use the college as a stepladder to success, and, like the players, will have already cut their teeth in high school games. Most of the professional coaches in both the National Football League and National Basketball Association have worked their way up through the school and college sports system.

CASE STUDY

THE AMERICAN DREAM

American football's most famous coach, Vince Lombardi (1913–70), is a good example of how coaching follows the high school–college–professional route.

1940s	Assistant and then Head Coach	St Cecilia Catholic High School, Englewood, New Jersey
1948–53	Head Coach	US Military Academy, West Point
1954–58	Assistant Head Coach	New York Giants
1959–67	Head Coach	Green Bay Packers
1969	Head Coach	Washington Redskins

■ How does Lombard's career reflect the 'American dream'?

THE ANNUAL DRAFT

With the professionalisation of football from the 1920s onwards, players who had developed their skills at university could now make a career out of sport. Cashmore (2000) states that this seamless transition from university to professional club has been a feature of American football ever since, with the draft being brought into play in 1936 as a mechanism for equalising the league and avoiding the imbalance of power.

The annual **draft** in US football and basketball now attracts national attention, and is followed closely by both the media and sports fans. Just as the colleges select and 'cream off' the best sporting talent from high schools, so the professional clubs select and recruit the best college players. Every college game is recorded and analysed by a national office, which then scores and ranks every college player across the states, identifying the best athletes, who go forward into the draft. For the major professional sports, this is the only route into the professional ranks, and is very elitist – only a very small percentage of college players get this far.

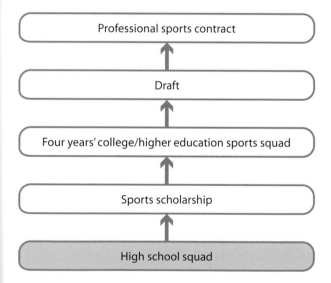

Fig. 8.2 *The flow of elite sports talent in the USA*

In order to retain as much equality as possible between the professional teams, the draft works in reverse order, with the weakest team from the previous season getting the first pick of the best college athletes. There are a number of rounds to the draft, and there is much trading and competition between teams. If a player successfully makes the draft, this still does not ensure they have made the grade – the majority of draftees will be placed in a team's minor or feeder teams, and could spend another five years making their way up through these reserve teams. Of those who reach the draft stage, only around 5 per cent will eventually play in the club's first team.

HOTLINKS

UK Sport – www.uksport.gov.uk

Sport England – www.sportengland.org

Sport Scotland – www.sportscotland.org.uk

Sports Council Wales – www.sports-council-wales.org.uk

Sport Northern Ireland – www.sportni.net

World Class Performance Pathway – www.ukathletics.net/world-class

Sports Coach UK – www.sportscoachuk.org

KEY TERM

draft
the US system whereby the top college players are recruited into the professional leagues; the worst club from the previous season gets first pick

UNITED KINGDOM

UK Sport is the United Kingdom's organisation for directing the development of sport within the home countries. Formerly the Sports Council, UK Sport was initiated in spring 1996. It is answerable to the Department for Culture, Media and Sport.

The four home country sports councils are:

- Sport England
- Sport Scotland
- Sports Council Wales
- Sport Northern Ireland.

There are a number of supporting structures.

WORLD CLASS PERFORMANCE PATHWAY

The World Class Pathway funds performance and subsistence costs of UK elite athletes. The funding comes from the Lottery Sports Fund via the athlete's home sports council.

The programme aims to invest world-class funds to achieve consistent success in top-level international competitions such as the Olympic Games, Paralympics and World Deaf Games.

Teams and individuals on the World Class programme must pass agreed selection criteria before they are nominated by their respective governing bodies. The programme has three stages, with the amount of support and funding available increasing as athletes move towards the World Class Performance (Podium) level. But all athletes on the programme will have access to the network centres.

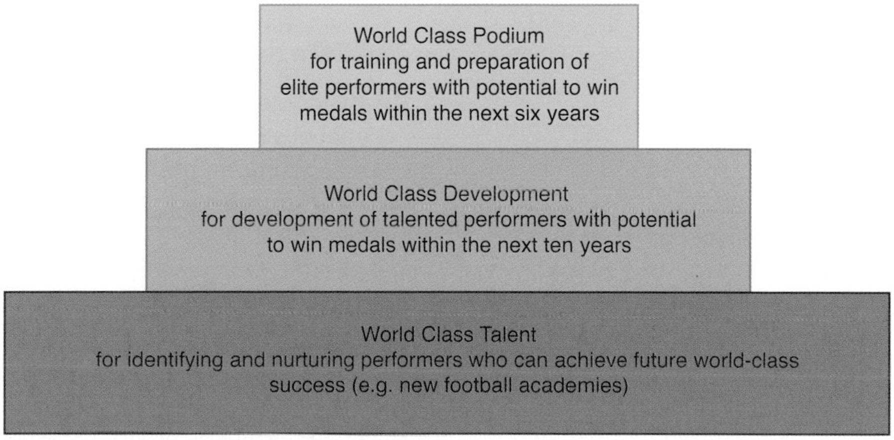

World Class Podium
for training and preparation of elite performers with potential to win medals within the next six years

World Class Development
for development of talented performers with potential to win medals within the next ten years

World Class Talent
for identifying and nurturing performers who can achieve future world-class success (e.g. new football academies)

Fig. 8.3 The World Class system as a pyramid

The funding of elite athletes in the UK is made up of two parts:

- programme funding – awarded to governing bodies to cover support services to athletes, such as coaching and medical staff, warm-weather training and sports science
- athlete personal awards – awarded to athletes to support their living costs and sporting costs; the average grant is £10,000–12,000.

Currently, the UK Sport World Class Performance programme supports 24 sports and 730 athletes, with a budget of around £20 million a year. But this funding still relies wholly on the public's purchase of tickets for the Wednesday and Saturday night National Lottery draws.

TASK

What is the elite pathway for your sport?

UNITED KINGDOM SPORTS INSTITUTE (UKSI) NETWORK

This is a network of elite training and research centres to assist governing bodies and their top performers to prepare for international and global championships. These centres provide state-of-the-art facilities, as well as support from sports scientists, medical professionals, coaches and support personnel.

From a comparative study of successful sporting nations, UK Sport has identified that a system needs to invest in young, talented performers from an early age. Only if the system supports the most talented individuals can it help them reach their potential and excel on the world stage.

The United Kingdom Sports Institute headquarters is in London, and this office coordinates all the excellence programmes across the UK. Its main role is to monitor and assess the quality of the service and facilities offered to sports and athletes across the network. It also coordinates research and development, focusing on the priorities identified by participating sports, monitoring developments around the world, and devising programmes to apply them in the UK.

The UKSI headquarters also coordinates and manages the following programmes.

NATIONAL NETWORK CENTRES

There are four devolved Institutes of Sport for the UK comprising the English Institute of Sport (EIS), Scottish Institute of Sport (SIS), Sports Institute Northern Ireland (SIN) and Welsh Institute of Sport (WIS), which form the National Institutes of Sport (and these organise the networks of elite training and research in their parts of the UK, some of which are referred to as High Performance Centres).

- Sport England Centres
  - East of England – Bedford
  - East Midlands – Loughborough University/ Holme Pierrepont National Sports Centre
  - North – Gateshead International Stadium
  - North West – Manchester Sports City
  - South – Bisham Abbey National Sports Centre
  - South coast – Southampton University
  - South East – Crystal Palace National Sports Centre
  - South West – University of Bath
  - West Midlands – Lilleshall National Sports Centre
  - Yorkshire – Don Valley Stadium
- UKSI Scotland – University of Stirling
- UKSI Wales – University College of Wales
- UKSI Northern Ireland – University of Ulster, Jordanstown Campus

In practice, the network centres act as a coordinating mechanism to harness the services in each region of the country. There will also be a number of smaller, specialised centres in each region.

The main role of each network centre is to assist national governing bodies and their top performers, identified through the World Class programme, to reach their targets in terms of championships and medals. This is achieved by providing both athletes and coaches with a comprehensive network of services and facilities based at each centre. They will bring together the best sports scientists, medical professionals and support personnel, and provide them with a base from which to work. The centres will also act as a vehicle for accessing an international network of facilities and services, including warm-weather training, acclimatisation, altitude and winter sport venues.

NATIONAL GOVERNING BODIES

The sports national governing bodies are still continuing to develop their excellence and talent identification programmes. The English Hockey Association, for example, is currently introducing at World Class Talent Level a programme of player assessment at ages under-15, 16, 17 and 18, after which players would be invited to attend national assessment camps, followed by blocked training periods at the regional academies throughout the year. Once players reach the top level, they then become eligible for nomination for England Hockey Affiliated School for World Class Performance funding, which in 2007 supported 48 elite-level players (24 men and 24 women) with £15,000 per year, and a further 48 players with a smaller amount of £2000–3000.

ELITE COACH EDUCATION PROGRAMME

This initiative, jointly developed with Sports Coach UK and the British Olympic Association, aims to meet the needs of coaches in the world class environment. Coaches identified by each sport's performance director are offered a range of training and resources to aid in their coaching education.

In June 2008, the UK government announced the creation of a UK Centre for Coaching Excellence to be based at Leeds Carnegie University. The aim is to develop a coaching faculty that will pass on expertise to coaches in line with international best practice. A UK-wide network of coaching experts, sports science and medical experts will also be established to support training and coach education throughout the country.

ATHLETE CAREER AND EDUCATION PROGRAMME (ACE UK)

Based on the Australian model, and currently headed by the AIS's former ACE Director, this programme (now renamed Performance Lifestyle) aims to enhance an athlete's personal development and sporting performance through access to individualised support, to help them cope with their life as an elite athlete and also to help prepare them for life after sport. Athletes can access services such as career advice, educational support, personal finance training, media and presentation skills training.

SUPPORT ROLES AND FINANCE

The increasing standard of elite sports competition makes it extremely difficult for athletes to compete for medals unless they commit themselves full-time to training. In the past, countries such as the USA and the Soviet Union funded athletes indirectly through the armed forces or student grants. Increasingly, over the past few decades, more and more countries are now funding their athletes directly. But in most cases this is not enough, and athletes need to seek part-time work or try to secure sponsorships and other commercial support.

The funding of elite athletes differs around the world. There are four main methods of financially supporting elite performers:

- funding directly from the state
- funding from charities and private institutions (lotteries, pools, sports institutes)
- sponsorship (e.g. Nike Running Camps, www.ussportscamps.com/running)
- salaried sports (the traditional professional sports such as soccer and rugby league).

Funding may be paid directly to the athlete, or more usually, they receive funding through a development programme on which they are enrolled. Funding for elite performers can be allocated on a needs basis, to cover the costs of training and living, or athletes may be paid by result.

Elite performers will use this personal funding to cover the costs of travelling to training and competition, entry fees, training and medical support, as well as taking a basic salary to live on. Without this funding, athletes would need to work and/or borrow money, and this would disrupt training and their mental preparation.

CASE STUDY
DIY ATHLETICS?

In 2005, the DIY chain B&Q launched a support programme for young elite athletes, in partnership with the British Olympic Association. Team B&Q is an initiative whereby elite athletes are employed by their local B&Q store. They are offered flexible working hours to allow them to train virtually full-time, and are also given time off to compete.

- This programme must cost B&Q a great deal of money. What's in it for them?

HOTLINK
www.uksport.gov.uk/pages/athlete_zone

STATE FUNDING – FOR AND AGAINST

The main argument against direct state funding is that the money may be better spent at the base of the pyramid, where it could have an impact on many more individuals. State funding also makes sport a political tool, and there may be pressure on athletes to compete and travel to particular countries and competitions to suit the government; equally, they may not be allowed to compete in or travel to countries that the government has issues with.

Another argument against state funding is the fact that the most successful nation in Olympic history, the USA, does not publicly fund any of its Olympic teams or individual athletes. The US Government believes that funding sport is a private and community affair. Most financing of US athletes is provided by the US Olympic Committee, which raises most of its funds from corporate sponsorship.

Research by PricewaterhouseCoopers (2008) found a direct link between state funding and the number of medals a nation wins. This was particularly important to nations with small populations, such as East Germany and Australia, which have a smaller pool of talent from which to select. This Australian research suggested that each gold medal cost on average US$37 million worth of funding.

▶ The Go For Gold scratchcard supports the 2012 Olympic Games and Team GB's training

CHARITY FUNDING

THE NATIONAL LOTTERY

Since 1994, the UK National Lottery has raised more than £3 billion to support sport at all levels in the UK. About £200 million of this was used to support elite sport in preparation for the 2004 Olympic games in Athens.

In 2005, an additional 'Go For Gold' lottery scratchcard was launched, with two aims:

- funding the costs of organising and staging the 2012 London Olympics
- supporting Team GB in their preparation for 2012.

It is estimated that the total cost of the 2012 Games and the regeneration of the East London area will be over £9 billion. Up to £2 billion will be raised through private funding from sales of tickets, merchandise and domestic sponsorship. London council tax payers will contribute around £500 million. The rest of the budget will come from Lottery funds, some from the Go for Gold Lottery and the remainder from the general Lotto fund.

PRIVATE SECTOR ACADEMIES

There are an increasing number of private companies and professional sports clubs that are establishing sports academies. These tend to charge participants a fee for the services provided – and in return they supply top-class facilities and high-level coaching, often from former top-class performers.

Most of these private sector academies offer short, intensive courses that often coincide with school holidays, rather than full-time residential support, as in the case of the publicly funded sports institutes.

CASE STUDY

CANADA – THE CARDING SYSTEM

In Canada, the government has set up the Athlete Assistance Program (also called the carding system). The sports arm of the Canadian Federal Government, Sport Canada (www.pch.gc.ca/progs/sc), provides direct funding to elite performers. Those who receive funding are referred to as 'carded' athletes.

To qualify for the funding, athletes need to be in the top 16 for their sport in world rankings, or have the potential to achieve a top 16 place. Athletes are nominated by their national sporting organisation, and if successful are paid a monthly salary of £450–740, as well as having any education costs covered. This funding is not intended to cover living expenses, but does help with some of the additional expenses that elite performers incur from training and competing.

- How do these figures compare with average wages in the UK – and with those of professional sports performers?

One example of such private sector provision is Dubai Sports City (www.dubaisportscity.ae), a purpose-built sport, leisure and hotel complex. Dubai Sports City is home to a range of world-class sporting academies, which offer customised training programmes in a range of sports.

Established academies within Dubai Sports City include:

- Manchester United Soccer School
- International Cricket Council Global Cricket Academy
- David Lloyd Tennis Academy
- Butch Harmon School of Golf
- International Hockey Federation World Hockey Academy.

The effectiveness of the academy model is still open to some discussion. It appears to work best with more closed-style sports, such as cycling, rowing and gymnastics. One criticism of the academy approach is that there is often an overemphasis on physical preparation and fitness. This can lead to problems such as burnout, especially in younger athletes. Some claim that selection of young athletes focuses on fitness levels as opposed to skill.

Although they are an effective means of preparing elite athletes, academies are very costly, and cater only for a small number of athletes. Many argue that the money would be better spent on supporting a wider range of athletes and performers lower down the participation pyramid. The lure of short-term results attracts support from states and governments, but again, a more effective approach may be a longer-term investment in the foundation level of the sports pyramid.

TRAINING FOR THE OLYMPIC GAMES

Team GB state the following requirements in order to prepare for a global sports competition:

- exclusive training in the facilities 2–3 weeks prior the event
- high standard of training and living facilities
- location with similar climatic conditions to host venue
- location in a similar time zone as the host venue
- support facilities with access to a hospital with an Accident and Emergency Department and advanced scanner technology
- within half a day's direct flight from the host venue (in order to avoid travel fatigue).

Training camps are used by international sports teams as a base for training and preparation in the weeks and months before major competitions.

▶ *Private sector academies provide intensive training – for those who can afford it*

They are extensively used by teams preparing for Olympic, Paralympic and Commonwealth Games. In the UK, the British Olympic Association differentiate between two sorts of camp when they are supporting Team GB:

- holding camps
- preparation camps.

Holding camps are single-base camps used in the weeks immediately prior to the start of the Games. The location of the holding camps must relate to the venue of the Games.

Here athletes can train in conditions which are very similar to climate, altitude and time zone of the host city, this process is called acclimatisation.

These camps are used to help athletes improve focus and maximise their performance at the Games

Preparation camps are training bases using the facilities offered in the holding camps. These enable athletes, coaches and support staff to familiarise themselves with equipment and procedures.

These are used up to a year before the event. They also allow the teams to have a 'dry run' of procedures and transfer arrangements.

TASK

Reading back through this chapter, can you summarise what the needs of elite athletes in the twenty-first century are?

Refresh your memory

SURPRISE

Revision checklist

▷ The concept of sporting excellence in the UK began with the development of professional sportsmen during the seventeenth and early eighteenth centuries.

▷ The increasing globalisation of sport in the twentieth century and the Cold War created a 'sports war' where nations developed elite sports systems in an attempt to gain shop window success.

▷ East Germany (which is no longer a separate country) was one of the first nations to develop a state-run elite sports system with screening of potential talent at primary school, sports schools and specialist sports institutes.

▷ The Australians revamped their elite sports systems after an embarrassing performance at the 1976 Olympics. The Australian Institute of Sport is the core, with satellite centres in all major cities.

▷ In the USA, elite athletes are supported through the education system. The best athletes are offered a scholarship, which enables them to train full-time; the best athletes are then drafted into the professional leagues.

▷ In the UK, elite sport is managed by UK Sport through the World Class Performance Pathway, funded mainly by the Lottery.

▷ The World Class programme provides elite athletes with personal funding and access to elite training facilities and sports science support through the United Kingdom Sports Institute (UKSI) network.

▷ Elite athletes need financial support so they can train full-time. This can be provided through state support or decentralised sources such as sponsorship and educational scholarships.

examiner's tips

Try to keep your examples up to date – keep checking out the UK Sport website (www.uksport.gov.uk) to keep up with what's going on in elite sport in the UK.

Try to find some local examples of performers who are following (or have followed) one of the talent pathways discussed in this chapter. Is there anyone at your school or college? You are encouraged to use local examples in your examination answers.

Get the result!

Sample question and answer

Exam question

Explain why most countries have adopted a sports academy as the most effective means of supporting elite athletes.

(6 marks)

Examiner says:

The candidate makes some good points, but starts off by being too descriptive: they are not explaining why an academy is an effective model.

Examiner says:

They do begin to explain their points in the later part of the answer, and this is where they pick up most of their points. This answer scores 4 marks.

Student answer – candidate A

Academies have been adopted by countries such as Australia and France as the most effective way of supporting their elite performers. Academies are central bases that provide top-class facilities for training.

Performers can also access top-class coaching as this is where they will also be based.

Most academies also offer sports science services such as access to sports psychologists and nutritionists. This means that the performers don't have to travel to get to these people and that makes this an effective model.

Academies allow performers to focus on their training, some will also offer accommodation so that the athletes can stay at the academy all the time.

Student answer – candidate B

An academy is where elite performers can train and prepare for major competitions, they are often funded by the government of the country. Some cater for younger athletes, some cater for the best athletes in the country.

These athletes will have access to top-class facilities, these will often have been developed to match the types of facilities they will compete in at the global championships.

The academy will also provide top-class coaches and sports science support such as physiotherapists and sports psychologists, who will help the athletes prepare and recover from international competition.

model answer

There are several types of academy model used around the world that help elite athletes prepare for global competition. The former East Germany was one of the first nations to develop an academy, and their success in global sport has meant that this model has been a popular one, adopted by many other nations.

The basic idea of the academy is to put the best performers together with top-class facilities and support, such as coaching and sports science. This is an effective method, as it cuts out the need to travel in order to train with support from sports science. Therefore this model also has some economic benefits.

The philosophy of putting elite athletes together has other benefits. An atmosphere of excellence is created, and peer pressure to train hard and win is fostered. The system also allows the transfer of skills and knowledge between athletes and coaches, and also between different sports.

The continued success of nations, such as Australia, that have adopted this approach means that many nations see this as an effective way of supporting elite athletes.

CHAPTER 9 TECHNICAL SUPPORT

LEARNING OUTCOMES

By working through this chapter, you should be able to:

- Understand the role of technology in training analysis
- Discuss how technology and sports science can be used for the enhancement and evaluation of sporting performance
- Understand and identify how national agencies support the preparation of elite athletes

KEY TERM

biomechanics
study of the forces, and the effects of those forces, on and within the human body and other living organisms

THE ROLE OF TECHNOLOGY IN TRAINING ANALYSIS

The continual improvement in athletic performance is a result of the complex interaction of support from a range of sports science disciplines – primarily physiology, **biomechanics**, nutrition and sports psychology. Institutes working in these fields provide up-to-date feedback that enables athletes and their coaches to modify and optimise their training programmes.

Sports institutes and academies provide elite athletes with the optimum conditions in which to maximise their performance, and ensure that accommodation, training facilities and support are all available in the same place.

The idea of modern global games was developed during the late nineteenth century (see Chapter 8, page 151). The philosophy of games such as the first modern Olympics in 1896 was that international sport would help improve health and education, promote world peace, and celebrate human performance.

There has been much discussion about a 'recreational ethic' – whether taking part is the main motivation in sport, or whether from these early games to the present day, the main focus for the vast majority of competing athletes has always been to win.

▶ *From triumphant ancient Olympic heroes to Portsmouth FC, winners have been feted in their home town*

Haake (2000) argues that winning gold in 1896 was just as important as it had been in the ancient Olympic games. Wining athletes were – and still are – treated like heroes, given extrinsic rewards and instant fame.

With so much at stake, elite performers have always looked for a competitive edge – something that will allow them to perform slightly better than their opponents. It is in finding this edge that technology has played an increasingly important role in elite sport.

The key role of technology in sport is in the enhancement and evaluation of sporting performance.

Sports technology can be used to improve performance in two main ways:

- helping the performer to perfect technique through the use of analysis
- refining the playing kit and equipment used to give the performer a competitive edge.

APPLY IT!

How is technology used in your own sport? Think about both performance and training.

In some sports, technological advances have had such an impact that the rules of the sport have had to be altered and adapted to keep up with these developments. There is some debate concerning whether technology in sport fits with the concept of fair play and the spirit of sport. If it is available only to an exclusive group of athletes – those who can afford to access it – technology could be seen as cheating. Only if athletes have equal access to the technology will their success be solely dependent on the ability and skill of the individual athlete.

CASE STUDY

ASTON VILLA FC – STATE-OF-THE-ART TRAINING

In 2008, Premiership side Aston Villa spent £13 million updating its training complex at Bodymoor Heath near Birmingham. As part of the update, all players at the club are now given an individual conditioning programme as well as a nutritional and dietary plan. The complex includes HydroWorx® hydrotherapy pools, a series of hot and cold pools that help the players recover after training and playing. Some of the pools include underwater treadmills that allow players to train without placing stress on their joints. The pools also have underwater cameras, which can provide instant analysis of leg strains and injuries.

An 18-metre swimming pool is used for rehabilitation. All players have to do a 15-minute recovery session in the pool after training. Players wear weighted belts, and jog and walk up and down the pool to aid recovery. The players have to eat at the complex after training, and the club has also developed a 'recovery shake' with a company called Science in Sport, which provides players with a blend of liquid protein, carbohydrate and vitamins to aid recovery.

Other facilities at the complex include a range of outdoor pitches, which are the same dimensions and texture of the pitch at Villa Park, an indoor three-quarter size pitch, and an indoor running track that also includes a force platform to measure players' jumps and acceleration. There is also a sports laboratory that includes machines to measure the players' body fat – the average at Aston Villa is 8 per cent body fat.

- Can you summarise the support players receive from the Aston Villa training complex?

▷ *An underwater treadmill allows training without stressing joints, and aids rehabilitation*

Sports manufacturers such as Nike and Speedo spend millions of dollars each year on research to develop the footwear and swimsuits that could help shave vital milliseconds off world records. But research and analysis of results suggests that in many of these sports, the impact has been minimal.

In sports involving **gross motor skills**, like sprinting, technology has less impact than in sports where more techniques and **fine motor skills** are required. In elite sprinting there has been a downward trend in improvement, and the gains that were seen in the late twentieth century were down to improvements in diet, fitness and training methods rather than technology.

KEY TERMS

motor skills
actions that involve the movement of muscles in your body

gross motor skills
larger muscle movements involving the arm, leg, or feet muscles, or the entire body (e.g. running, and jumping)

fine motor skills
smaller muscle actions (e.g. picking things up between the thumb and finger)

CASE STUDY   THE JAVELIN'S TRAJECTORY

In 1908, the wining throw in the men's Olympic javelin final was a mere 50 metres – and by 1976, the winning throw was over 95 metres.

What had changed over nearly 70 years was undoubtedly the fitness and physique of the athletes – but also, importantly, the design of the javelin. In 1984, Uwe Hohn from the former East Germany threw a staggering 104.8 metres in an athletics meeting in Berlin. This was virtually the full length of the stadium. This raised safety fears for both fellow athletes and spectators, and the International Amateur Athletic Federation had to redesign the javelin to 'underperform' so that it would have a steeper flight path and fall to the ground more quickly. This was achieved by moving the centre of the javelin's mass 4 cm nearer to the point. The impact on performance is that athletes now are throwing distances 15 metres below Hohn's world record throw. The record statistics had to be restarted, and the record of Uwe Hohn thus became an 'eternal world record'.

■ Are there any technology rules in your sport?

▶ *Javelin – a sport that has had to change its rules to reflect the impact of technology*

PERFORMANCE ANALYSIS

Performance analysis is an area of sports science that informs the coaching process through the provision of statistical and video information. This often represents the core work of the institutes and academies of sport (see Chapter 8, page 164).

> ### KEY TERMS
>
> **performance analysis**
> the combination of biomechanical and notational analysis techniques to study how movements relate to sports performance
>
> **notational analysis**
> an emerging technology used in professional sports for competitive advantage, primarily concerned with strategy and tactics

In terms of developing performance, the following two disciplines work in combination.

- **Biomechanics** works on the fine detail of movement technique, identifying the link between mechanics and anatomy – for example, an analysis of a cricket fast bowler's ball release speed or run-up speed.

- **Notational analysis** focuses on gross movements or movement patterns within a team. This can be used to analyse the effectiveness of tactics and strategy. For example, in football, notational analysis could provide feedback on:

  o match indicators – shots on target, shots off target, number of corners, crosses, fouls committed

  o technical indicators – number of passes, dribbles, lost control, tackles won, tackles lost

  o tactical indicators – time in possession, passing distribution, possession linked to pitch position.

Research has shown that providing athletes with accurate feedback, based on systematic and objective analysis, is a key factor in improving sporting performance. This feedback can help coaches and performers highlight good and bad techniques, and also compare the performance of individuals with elite 'perfect models'. It can also be used to identify techniques and faults that may lead to injury. Notational analysis can also help to assess the physiological and psychological demands of a sport or a role within a sport.

The basic analysis programme developed by biomechanics specialists involves comparing the movement patterns of a performer using video and computer analysis. Each segment or subroutine of a skill can be isolated and assessed in turn. Performers and their coaches can then use this information to optimise their performance, and also to highlight any weaknesses in technique that may lead to injury. There is a range of commercial sports video analysis software programmes available, including Dartfish (www.dartfish.co.uk) and Siliconcoach (www.siliconcoach.com) (see page 139).

To achieve the desired improvement, specialists combine a detailed knowledge of performance analysis with a range of computer software and video technology customised to individual needs. This approach ensures the provision of accurate, precise and reliable feedback tailored to each sport or individual athlete. Feedback is presented to the coach and athletes during planned interventions, with permanent records created through reports, compilation DVDs and archiving. Two popular systems of team analysis used by many sports are ProZone (www.prozonesports.com) and Amisco (www.amisco.eu).

ProZone is an analysis system used by most leading football and rugby teams (see page 141). It uses a network of eight to 12 cameras around the stadium, which plot each player's movement every tenth of a second. The feed from the cameras is sent to the ProZone headquarters in Leeds, where a team of sports scientists put a wide range of performance data into a very accessible format. Clubs and teams pay around £13,000 a year for a subscription. Within 48 hours of a game, they are sent a DVD containing statistical and fitness data for every player on the pitch.

Coaches and managers of clubs can use the information to give feedback to players and teams. The system can also be used to check out the upcoming opposition. The tactical data provided include passing patterns, individual player movements, subteam movements (such as a football back four), and analysis of set-piece moves.

CASE STUDY

ANALYSE THIS!

ProZone has identified that in a game, Wayne Rooney covers on average 11.82 km.

This includes the following:

- ☐ walking   4 km
- ☐ jogging   4.8 km
- ☐ light sprinting   1 km
- ☐ full sprinting   500 m

He touches the ball on average 105 times:

- ☐ feet   90 times
- ☐ chest   13 times
- ☐ head   2 times

He spends 10 per cent of the game in defence and 33 per cent in the opposition penalty box.

- ■ How could this type of information be used to plan a player's training programme?

▶ *Each match, Wayne Rooney covers an average 11.82 km*

MOTION ANALYSIS

Motion analysis is an analysis technique used in the science of biomechanics. The performer moves through, or executes their skill on, a force plate (which measures the forces exerted on it electronically) at the centre of four video cameras. The basic motion of the performer is then analysed by computer. For example, the system could be used to track a golfer's swing or a tennis player's serve. A biomechanist will be able to analyse the data produced and advise the athlete whether energy is being wasted in any direction, and whether a change in technique might remedy this.

SPORTS SCIENCE AND SUPPORT

Traditionally, the three main areas of sports science were as shown in Figure 9.1 below.

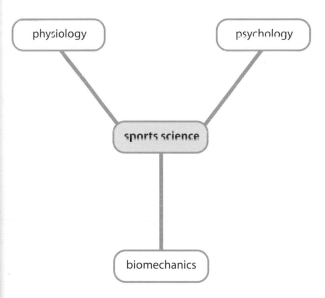

Fig. 9.1 The three traditional areas of sports science

Now, in the twenty-first century, sports science includes a vast array of support services and experts, including areas as diverse as **podiatry** and sports vision.

KEY TERM

podiatry
(or chiropody) – the study and treatment of disorders of the foot, ankle, knee, leg and hip

Sports science alone cannot make a performer into a world-beater – but it now plays an essential role in the preparation of elite teams and individuals. Sports science needs to offer support alongside quality coaching, top-class facilities and medical support if its impact is to be maximised.

ELITE PERFORMERS IN THE TWENTY-FIRST CENTURY

Houlihan and Green (2005) suggest that the early development of sports science in elite sport tended to focus on equipment rather than performers. This was primarily because of the potential profits that can be made from the sale of new equipment, as opposed to essentially non-profit-making research into nutrition, psychological preparation and training regimes.

The influence of sports science is now found in every aspect of a performer's training, preparation and performance analysis.

■ Elite performers have their training schedule prepared by sports science experts, to ensure they are doing the right kinds of training to match the specific demands of their sport and position, so that they will be in a peak physical and mental state for their competitions.

■ Their diet and fluid intake is measured, monitored and adjusted by sports scientists.

■ Their clothing and equipment has been designed by sports scientists to ensure they can perform at their optimum level.

■ Once they have completed their performance, statisticians, video reviewers and coaches will analyse their performance, giving detailed feedback and advice about what went right and wrong, and how they can improve future performance.

The main support roles of sports scientists, and how they affect training and performance, are detailed below.

EXERCISE PHYSIOLOGIST

The role of **exercise physiology** is to optimise training objectives, ensuring the performer follows prescribed training that is specific to the demands of their sport and position.

The physiologist should also work with the nutritionist, ensuring the athlete has the correct balance of nutrients to meet the demands of training, competition and recovery.

CASE STUDY THE SPEEDO LZR RACER SWIMSUIT

In February 2008, Speedo® launched its revolutionary new swimsuit, the LZR Racer (www.speedo80.com/lzr-racer).

By April 2008, swimmers wearing the new suit had set 35 new world records, leading to questions about the validity of the suit. One journalist called it 'doping on a hanger'; other swimsuit manufacturers asked the international swimming federation (Fédération Internationale de Natation, FINA) to investigate the legality of the suit.

Speedo designed the new suit in conjunction with NASA (the US National Aeronautics and Space Administration) and the Australian Institute of Sport. It has a tight, corset-like mid-section, which is said to reduce fatigue at the end of a race. The suit is seamless and uses a water-repellent material that reduces drag in the water. Analysis of the swimming times of those using the new suit suggest an improvement of 2 per cent in performance. The suit costs around £350 and lasts for about eight swims.

Speedo responded to the criticisms by stating that while they had spent millions researching the new suit, other manufacturers had focused on developing suits to keep up with fashion trends.

■ How could the swimsuit be against the spirit of sport?

▶ The exercise physiologist works out a training programme for the athlete

KEY TERM

exercise physiology
a discipline involving the study of how exercise alters
the structure and function of the human body

SPORTS PSYCHOLOGIST

Sports psychology helps the athlete develop the
mental preparation for competition (see Chapters 2
and 6). This may involve helping to develop coping
strategies so that the performer can deal with
feelings of arousal. Sports psychologists can also
play a central role in promoting team-building and
helping performers cope with injury.

KEY TERM

sports psychology
the study of performers' behaviour in sport, seeking
to understand the mental factors that affect
performance in sports, physical activity and exercise,
and to apply these to enhance individual and team
performance

NUTRITIONIST

The key role of the nutritionist is to assist the athlete
in choosing the right food and fluids in the right
amounts, and in taking these at the right time to
meet the demands of training and competition.
Getting the food and fluid balance right should
ensure the athlete can train as hard as possible and
recover in time for competition, as well as reducing
the risk of injury or illness.

To be effective, the nutritionist needs to work closely
with coaches and medical staff in order to adjust the
athlete's diet to match their training and competition
programmes.

BIOMECHANIST

The biomechanist helps the athlete to develop better
and more efficient techniques. This should ensure a
higher level of performance and also reduces the risk
of injury.

SPORTS VISION SPECIALIST

This includes the assessment and enhancement of a
sports performer's use of vision. Most of the training
is focused on optimising visual acuity – how well a
person can see on the 20:20 scale. Other areas that

▶ *The sports nutritionist takes a scientific approach*

▶ *The biomechanist applies mechanical principles to living
organisms*

sport vision training can enhance include hand–eye
coordination, peripheral vision, perception and
reaction time.

▶ *Sport vision training can improve hand–eye coordination*

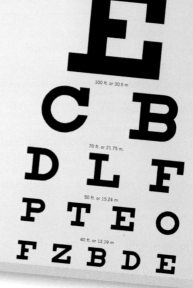

▶ *The aim is **20:20 vision***

SPORTS PODIATRIST

The podiatrist works with elite performers, analysing how their feet strike the ground. This may highlight any mechanical problems that could lead to injury. Information from analysis is used to refine the performer's technique, and possibly to add orthotic aids to the performer's footwear (orthotics are inserts that are used to control the motion of the feet).

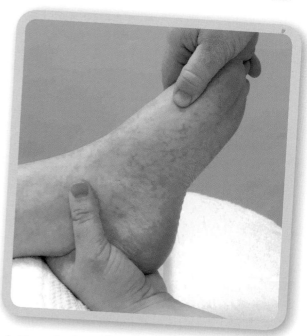

▶ *The podiatrist analyses the movement of the feet and legs*

THE ROLE OF NATIONAL AGENCIES

At the turn of the twenty-first century, the provision of high-quality coaching, science and medical support services has become essential in the preparation of elite sports performers. The former Eastern European countries were the first nations to fully develop support programmes for their elite athletes (see Chapter 8, page 153), but by the mid-1990s most governments had developed their own elite sports programmes and/or national training centres. Reasons for this include the fact that sport plays an increasingly important role in most modern global societies. The increasing level of media attention and the national honour and international prestige that global success brings are also contributory factors.

The sports science support outlined above is normally provided and funded via national sports agencies within a country. There are two main models in global sport.

- The **centralised model** – elite sports are supported via the state, which appoints a central body to oversee the management of the country's elite sports programme. Examples include the Australian and French elite sports systems. Here the majority of funding for sports science support, elite training facilities and also athletes' personal funding comes from the public sector.

- The **decentralised model** – no single agency takes control, but there is a developed system of supporting elite sport through higher education institutions. The American scholarship system is the best example of this (see Chapter 8, page 157). In this case elite athletes receive all the support mentioned above through their university or higher learning institution, and are supported financially through a scholarship.

Most elite sport programmes target performers at a young age. Any young performer who shows above-average sporting ability is generally encouraged to attend regular coaching and development sessions at regional centres of sports excellence. The objective of these satellite elite training centres is to create an environment that nurtures the performance of the young athletes. Support is given to aid the athlete with both physical and psychological development, as well as helping them to cope with the demands of global sports competitions.

Many of these training centres are classified as academies, and often represent the first step towards a career in elite sport. Academies usually focus on young people aged 14–18, and allow performers to combine elite sports training with some form of academic education. Research suggests that the average age of Olympic champions is getting younger, and at the moment the average age for most sports is in the early twenties.

▶ *Often elite athletes can combine training with education*

CASE STUDY *NEW ELITE*

India has established a country-wide system of state sports academies whose objective is to identify, select and train potential elite sports performers aged 10–13 years.

The Indian sports ministry sees the main objectives of these sports academies as to:

☐ bring glory to India in the field of sport and to inspire the youth to achieve excellence in sports

☐ provide a vast resource pool of highly skilled sports persons at national level

☐ prepare a long-term plan and produce international players through sustained scientific training from a young age

☐ obtain medals for India at international sports events.

■ Why do they target 10–13-year-olds?

HOTLINKS

Sport & Recreation New Zealand – www.sparc.org.nz

New Zealand Academy of Sport North Island – www.nzasni.org.nz

New Zealand Academy of Sport South Island – www.asi.org.nz

French Ministry of Youth, Sport and the Voluntary Sector
(for an English version click on the Union Jack) – www.jeunesse-sports.gouv.fr

French National Institute for Sport and Physical Education – www.insep.fr

United States Olympic Committee – www.usoc.org

Elite training centres and academies offer practice and training conditions that are as close as possible to the competitive environment. Their use is often exclusive to the elite teams and athletes so that there are no distractions or issues over access. As discussed above, the development of performance in these centres is also enhanced by sports science support, equipment and facilities. For more on training centres and academies, see Chapter 8, page 164.

Most national institutes and programmes also support athletes in managing their lifestyle, helping them to create an effective life–work balance combining training, competing and education or career with social life and relaxation time.

Support is also given to athletes nearing the end of their performance career. In countries such as the UK and Australia, these services are offered through programmes called Athlete Career and Education (ACE), provided by the national elite sports bodies. In Norway, for example, Olympiatoppen, the national training centre in Oslo, provides all the country's elite athletes with nutritional and training advice as well as offering a full range of medical services.

CASE STUDY *THREE NATIONAL SYSTEMS*

NEW ZEALAND

Elite sport is managed by the High Performance Sport section of Sport & Recreation New Zealand (SPARC), a government-appointed sports agency. Funding for the elite sports programme comes from two sources: the federal New Zealand Government and the New Zealand Lotteries Commission. Most of the elite sports programme is focused through the work of the New Zealand Academy of Sport, which consists of a range of regional training and support centres.

FRANCE

The elite sports system in France is coordinated by the National Commission for High-level Sport (Commission Nationale du Sport de Haut Niveau). This Commission is directly managed by the French Ministry of Youth, Sport and the Voluntary Sector. It manages a huge system of regional and national training centres, the most famous of which is the National Institute for Sport and Physical

Education (INSEP). The majority of funding for these programmes comes directly from the French Government.

USA

The USA has a developed a unique elite sports system, whereby the Federal government has allowed the management and funding of elite sport to be undertaken by independent sports agencies (see Chapter 8, page 157).

The key body is the US Olympic Committee, a private, not-for-profit organisation. It provides sports science support through its US Olympic Training Centers. The elite pathway in the USA is exclusively educational, with school and college sports programmes supported by athletic scholarships. The US Olympic Committee takes its funding from the sale of commercial and media rights.

■ Can you identify which of these global examples are centralised and which are decentralised?

CASE STUDY   AUSTRALIA'S ACE PROGRAMME

The Australian ACE programme is delivered by the Australian Sports Commission through the Australian Institute of Sport and state institutes.

The programme provides the following support.

☐ Career counselling and planning to assist athletes to identify career pathways and implement plans to achieve their career goals.

☐ Educational guidance and information on school and university education, technical and further education courses, vocational training programmes, course selection and alternative study pathways incorporating distance education and flexible delivery.

☐ Personal development training courses to help athletes develop skills in public speaking and media presentation, job interviews, resumé development, career planning and time management.

☐ Employment preparation to help athletes develop skills to become 'job ready' – writing resumés and job applications, job search and interviews.

☐ Access to career referral networks in the business community to identify potential career interests, sources of employment, work experience and sponsored courses provided by a wide range of organisations.

☐ Ongoing transitional support to guide athletes through all transition phases, including non-selection, retirement, injury, rehabilitation, move from junior to senior teams and relocation.

☐ Online services – ACEonline is an interactive career management tool for athletes. It complements the existing face-to-face service delivery provided by the ACE programme through the provision of online activities.

(Source: https://aceonline.ausport.gov.au)

■ Why is it important for elite athletes to have access to training and education programmes?

▶ *As athletes mature they need assistance with future career development*

ExamCafé
Relax, refresh, result!

Refresh your memory

Revision checklist

▷ The three traditional elements of sports science used to be physiology, psychology and biomechanics.

▷ Sports institutes and academies provide elite athletes with the optimum conditions in which to maximise their performance.

▷ Sports science support is normally provided and funded via national sports agencies in a country.

▷ There are two models of elite sport support –

   o   centralised model – elite sport is supported via the state, which appoints a central body to oversee the management of the country's elite sports programme

   o   decentralised model – no single agency takes control, but there is a developed system of supporting elite sport through higher education institutions.

▷ The key role of technology in sport is the enhancement and evaluation of sporting performance.

▷ Technology could be seen as cheating if it is available only to an exclusive group of athletes.

▷ Performance analysis is a combination of biomechanical and notational analysis techniques to study how movements relate to sports performance.

examiner's tips

Many of the topics discussed above will be covered in the questions that require longer extended answers, for more marks.

Remember to use contemporary examples in your answers to support the points you are making. Also remember that in an A2 paper, the main focus is on optimising the performance of elite athletes in sport at a global level so it is important that you research and use plenty of global examples, these should include examples from the Olympic Games, FIFA World Cup, the Commonwealth Games, international cricket and netball matches, or continental competitions such as the UEFA Champions League.

Get the result!

Sample question and answer

Examiner says:

The candidate makes a good attempt at answering the question, they make a number of good points and highlight these with relevant examples. Note how they use their examples at the end of their sentences and paragraphs to ensure they are highlighting points and not just listing examples.

Examiner says:

They do give a sound review of how technology is used to improve performance, so they are answering the question, although they sometimes don't quite go into enough depth, for example they don't fully explain how the new Speedo swimsuits improve performance.

Student answer

Athletes and coaches now use technology a lot when preparing for global competitions. Using technology gives performers a competitive edge, helping them to refine techniques and perform maybe just 1 per cent better, but this 1 per cent could mean the difference between winning and losing.

Technology can be used in two main ways to help a performer get better at their sport.

By using video feedback they can look at their technique and make this more efficient, specialist computer software packages like dartfish can be used to look at individual parts of the performer's movement and they can then work on making their skills perfect. By practising and working on their weaknesses they will be able to improve their performance. For example a decathlete like Kelly Southerton could use the feedback to work on each of the disciplines she has to compete in.

The same type of video technology can also be used by teams to analyse and prepare for matches against other teams — they will use videos of their opponents to identify weaknesses or set plays and strategies that a team uses, so the England rugby team for example will give each of the players a DVD on their opponents so they can pick out particular moves or styles of play. The players will use these DVDs in their final preparations for a game.

Technology can also be used by performers during their performance, increasingly they wear high-tech suits and clothing and a lot of research goes into their footwear. Usually in sport, clothing is designed to optimise performance by reducing factors such as drag (i.e. wind) or fluid resistance and also helping the player to thermo-regulate efficiently. Athletes often wear layers which 'wick' away sweat helping the athletes to keep cool. In some sports, like skiing and athletics, the opposite happens, their clothing is designed to retain heat especially in the hamstrings so the performers don't suffer injury again. This type of clothing may give a performer a 1 per cent improvement in performance but this might be enough to get them the gold medal. The recent news about the new Speedo Swimsuit is a good example of how technology helps performers.

Technology is now becoming more important in global sport but there is some debate about its use, some will argue that it can be seen as unfair or even illegal. Technology costs lots of money and not all performers or nations may be able to access this technology, the richer nations like the USA might get an unfair advantage in some sports. The World Anti-Doping Agency is constantly looking at the new technology and trying to decide whether it is unfair or not, recently they looked at hypoxic chambers which allow athletes to train in altitude-like conditions, but at sea level. These are very expensive, but are used extensively in sports institutes such as those in the UK. WADA has decided that they are not an unfair advantage. The other debate which the new swimsuits brought up is how much of the technology is based on marketing by the big sports clothing manufacturers. This is a huge market and they are trying to outdo each other — an important part of this is claiming that their products are scientifically better than others. Research is often inconclusive on this and it also sometimes forgets to state that the performers also have to be super fit and skilled in their sports, technology can not be a substitute for talent.

Examiner says:

They do challenge the issue in the last paragraph, and give a good summary of the issues. This answer would score 14 marks.

exam tip

Top tips for answering the extended answer questions:
▷ do these types of questions first
▷ bring in a range of global examples
▷ give both sides of the argument/debate
▷ use and show an understanding of a wide range of technical terms.

The extended answer questions towards the end of the A2 paper will very often require you to give a detailed answer to debate or discuss an issue. The trick here is to look to develop two sides of an argument. Sometimes the argument required will be clearly evident in the question set, other times you may have a choice and need to develop your own debate.

You need to take time with this type of question, firstly, reading the question through several times to ensure you fully understand what it is you are required to do. When you start such a question, plan or sketch out your answer. This will not only help you organise your answer logically, but it will also give you a checklist against which you can refer when writing out your final answer. In this way, you will be less likely to repeat yourself, wander off the subject or miss out important sections.

A basic plan to providing an answer to the extended answer questions could include the following:

INTRODUCTION: set out how you are going to answer the question

KEY TERMINOLGY: introduce any key terms or theories you think relate to the question

OVERVIEW: outline a basic background to the topic area: in a social cultural question this could include an historical overview of the Issue; in a scientific question this may include an overview of the relevant theories and research

CASE STUDY/APPLIED EXAMPLE: relate the question to a specific practical sports example or specific case study or investigation you have covered

ANSWER SPECIFIC POINTS: answer the question carefully, it may ask you to discuss or explain certain areas in particular

CONCLUSION: sum up the main points you have made in your answer and try and finish with a personal opinion or view.

Your revision plan for each topic should follow the outline given above, but remember your plan needs to flexible in the exam, don't just write out a pre-planned essay. You need to respond to the question set and make sure you are answering all the parts and debates identified in your chosen question.

Quality not quantity is the key to success in a good extended answer. The time you spend planning your answer is important and reading the question through three or four times should ensure that you are very clear what the question is asking you to do. You need to be aware of the time and divide it sensibly between the plan and the final answer.

If you do make a mistake simply put a single line through it. Don't cross your plan or any notes out, if you cross any work out the examiner will ignore it, so use labels such as 'plan', 'notes' and 'answer' to guide the examiner.

Remember that the exam paper itself can sometimes be used as a resource during the exam. If you get a mental block, look through the paper for inspiration as there will be many topic areas you can include in your answer. The other questions may also act as a good spellchecker, especially for words such as physiology and psychology (which are very often misspelt in student answers!)

UNIT 4
THE DEVELOPING SPORTS PEFORMER

On completing the AS Advanced Subsidiary course – Units 1 and 2 – you are now required to build on and extend your knowledge, understanding and experience by undertaking Unit 4: The Developing Sports Performer. This involves completing four assessed coursework tasks. Each task builds on and further develops this applied specification, which engages you in your own personal performance pathway, and in further applying your theoretical knowledge and understanding to the performance arena. In addition, you will be required to carry forward and apply the knowledge and understanding gained from the completion of Unit 3: Preparation for Optimum Sports Performance.

The performer is central to this unit. You are now required to refine a single performance role through applied experience as either a performer, a leader or an official. You will also plan, perform and evaluate a development programme specific to your chosen performance role and your Performance Analysis findings from Unit 2, Task 2.4. By completing an International Study, you are required to extend your knowledge and understanding of the impact of the globalisation of sport through the study of another nation's sporting provisions. Finally, you will complete a Life Plan that synoptically draws together your own aspirations, health trends, and the changing context of sport provisions as a result of the ageing process.

PROGRESSION FROM AS TO A2

AS – Unit 2		A2 – Unit 4
2.1 Personal Performance	⟶	4.3 Progressive Participation
2.2 Local Study and 2.3 National Study	⟶	4.2 International Study
2.4 Performance Analysis	⟶	4.1 Development Plan
Units 1–4	⟶	4.4 Life Plan

In summary, the four coursework tasks and mark allocations are:

Task		Marks
4.1	**Development Plan**	45
4.2	**International Study**	15
4.3	**Progressive Participation**	20
4.4	**Life Plan**	10

CHAPTER 10 *THE DEVELOPING SPORTS PERFORMER*

LEARNING OUTCOMES

By working through this chapter, you should:

- undertake applied experiences in order to develop your own personal sport or physical activity pathway
- develop an awareness and understanding of the sporting context of grassroots provision and elite pathways in another nation
- understand that sport and physical activity is a life-long process of involvement
- engage in the process of reflection and analysis that leads to an individually planned and performed development programme

THE PROCESS

YOUR E-PORTFOLIO

As you embark on your four coursework tasks for Unit 4, you will construct a portfolio of evidence that reflects your experiences and final task submissions. The portfolio can be in CD-ROM/DVD format. It will also contain materials from the examination board, including assessment sheets and supplementary evidence in the form of video footage, jpeg images, National Governing Body Award certifications, and any testimonial evidence that combines to form evidence of your achievements.

REMEMBER

Do not use extreme, or too many, fonts in your work. Keep it simple. Double line-space your work so that it is easier to read and assess.

The completion of the Unit 4 coursework tasks will be to a set deadline, normally in May of the final year of the award. Tasks maybe updated, amended and refined in line with individual centre course requirements prior to submission in May.

COURSEWORK TIP

The e-portfolio is a bank of evidence of your attainments, so build it up and add to it week by week – do not leave it until the very end of the course!

REFERENCING COURSEWORK AND BUILDING A BIBLIOGRAPHY

For your coursework tasks to receive academic credit and to avoid **plagiarism**, it is important that all coursework tasks are referenced accurately, and that you include an appropriate bibliography. You will have become familiar with this process from your work in Unit 2 for your AS coursework task.

Referencing, the use of footnotes and an appendix are all means of validating your research and findings, and of including additional information which, while not included in any assessment mark, supports your completed work.

KEY TERM

plagiarism
using other people's work and claiming it to be your own

REMEMBER

If you plagiarise others' work and are found out, your task will be scored zero. Avoid using large chunks of downloaded information.

It is expected that you will use the Harvard method of referencing and bibliography presentation. Importantly:

- include all sources and references that you have used in your work
- references should be listed in alphabetical order.

This should be set out as shown below.

References for books, journals and from the Internet are as follows:

Books and publications

- Give the author (including initials), the title of the book and the publishers, then the date of publication:

  Honeybourne, J., Hill, M., Moors, H., *Advanced Physical Education and Sport* (3rd edn), Nelson Thornes, 2004

Journals

- Include the author and title of the article, the name of the journal, the volume and relevant page numbers, and the date:

Wood-Martin, R., Increasing the muscle mass – making the weight, *Northern Ireland Sports Institute Newsletter*, 3 (6), 4–6, 2005

Internet sites

- Include the full URL (web address), if possible the author(s), a brief summary of the content and context of how you used the site and the date you accessed it. Do not include generic search engines such as *Yahoo*.

Peak Performance: www.pponline.co.uk Six workouts to boost your VO$_2$max: fitness journal article used to help design a training programme for improving VO$_2$max.

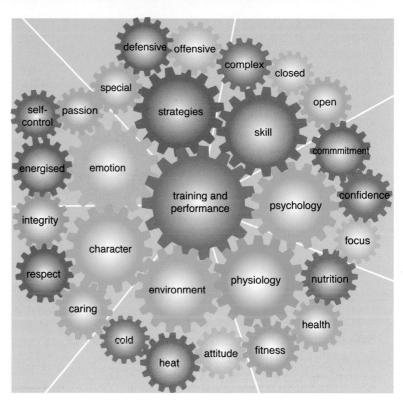

Fig. 10.2 *Which cog limits you from being an even better performer? (adapted from Wenger, 1999)*

To make progress, the performer must identify their own strengths and weaknesses, and must have an understanding of the performance expectations in the context of their own standard and level of participation.

Any performance has a number of underpinning core elements that fit together like the cogs in a machine, and combine to produce the desired cognitive and physiological outcomes. You will be aware of which elements of your performance are your strengths or good points, and which are your weaknesses or bad points (see Figure 10.2).

Strength, for instance, underpins all human movement, yet in certain sports or physical activities it may not be as important as endurance (e.g. the 3000 metres) or coordination (e.g. table tennis). Identifying the crucial elements of your own performance is the first step in building a Development Plan.

Some performers have a wide range of core physiological and technical elements in their profile, but may have a tactical or psychological weakness. You will select which aspect of your performance to concentrate on for your Development Plan in consultation with your centre staff and activity coaches.

COURSEWORK TIP

You will need to reference the work you submit from more than one source (preferably more than three). Keep an exact record as you complete your coursework.

REMEMBER

Word counts matter – if you exceed the word count you will not gain the mark you think you should!

TASK 4.1 – DEVELOPMENT PLAN

Any participant in sports builds a performance based on four fundamental components:

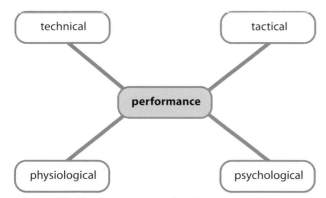

Fig. 10.1 *The four components of performance*

All performances are a combination of many integrated and dependent factors. These components of a performance can all be isolated, and for any that are considered a weakness, remedial strategies and applied methodologies can be undertaken to an appropriate schedule in order for a refinement in your performance to take place.

REMEMBER

Development has to be planned – do not guess training loads and structures, but devise them accurately. For example, for interval training you must establish the correct work-to-rest (*W:R*) ratio.

WHAT CAN I DRAW ON FROM MY AS COURSE?

You will be required to draw upon the tasks that formed the coursework content of Unit 2: The Critical Sports Performer, such as the performance history compiled for Task 2.1. By reviewing the assessment profiles created through your Personal Performance, and drawing on the knowledge and understanding gained from Task 2.4: Performance Analysis, you will have built a considerable understanding of your performances in both roles. In addition, it is vital you draw together the knowledge and understanding gained from Unit 1 (Healthy and Active Lifestyles) and Unit 3 (Short-term Preparation, Long-term Preparation and Managing Elite Performance).

In recognition of the importance of your Development Plan to your ongoing Progressive Participation (Task 4.3), you will be required to construct your Development Plan in the context of your future aspirations as either a performer, a leader or an official. These aspirations are crucial to your plan's successful completion.

THE THREE ASSESSED SECTIONS

Your Development Plan is divided into three sections that help you construct it, and form the basis of your assessment. Each section has its own assessment profile and criteria, and has a band structure for assessment that reflects the nature of applied studies. In addition, there is a final assessment profile that combines the three separate sections, allowing for a summative mark to be given.

THE KEY ASSESSMENT STATEMENTS

An understanding of the key assessment statements and criteria will enable you to fine-tune your final submission before assessment by your centre staff.

Component 1: Planning and research
Maximum marks: 20
Top band marked: 17–20

- Devise and research to a high standard.
- Clear aim(s) as appropriate to your needs.
- Make use of recognised methodologies.
- The correct use of sports science.
- Makes use of the correct technical support.
- Referenced to a high level and contains an extensive bibliography.

Component 2: Performing and recording
Maximum marks: 20
Top band marked: 17–20

- Fully completed an exacting, high-standard plan.
- Correctly performs an appropriate warm-up/cool-down.
- Accurate recording in all areas.
- Regular testing will enable you to monitor the improvements that you are making – it may be you are taking externally awarded examinations such as National Governing Body-level coaching awards.
- Works unsupervised and in safety.
- Recording reflects sports science, technical and psychological details of the plan.
- Testing, monitoring and data collection up to date and appropriate.

Component 3: Review and evaluation
Maximum marks: 5
Top band marked: 5

- A very high standard of insight.
- Established links in sports science, technical and psychological fields.
- Clear, objective judgements and conclusions drawn.
- Accurate recording with explanations of all work and testing.
- Improvements resulting from the programme have enhanced the progressive performance.
- Insightful observations on future amendments.
- You can critically discuss your plan and show an extensive understanding of the context and outcomes of the plan.

TASK

Undertake a review of your fitness components and rank them according to their importance to your organised performances. Then rank the components according to how highly you scored in each, and compare the two.

SAMPLE DEVELOPMENT PLANS

The following give concise examples of suggested development plans.

EXAMPLE 1

A physiologically-based exercise programme that enhances, for example:

- an energy system
- a recognised fitness component underpinning motor production (speed, acceleration or strength), or
- a skill-related fitness component (coordination, agility) crucial to your progressive participation.

In addition, you may wish to consider the wider context of the following development areas:

- aerobic conditioning
- anaerobic conditioning
- flexibility training
- speed combined with agility
- acceleration training
- complex training
- contrast training.

Suggested titles:

- 'The development of speed to refine my performance in netball'
- 'The enhancement of my aerobic conditioning to improve my refereeing in football'

EXAMPLE 2

A technical programme designed to eliminate a weakness in a skill fundamental to a performance.

Suggested title:

- 'The development of my backhand stroke in order to enhance my performance in badminton'

EXAMPLE 3

A programme that overcomes a biomechanical weakness in a performance.

Suggested title:

- 'The use of technology and a technical coaching programme in order to refine and develop my floor routine in gymnastics'

Those undertaking their Progressive Participation task as either a leader or an official, may wish to consider the following titles as examples of a development plan:

- 'The completion of a National Governing Body coaching course in order to develop my technical knowledge as a coach in trampolining'
- 'The study of sports injuries and their treatment in order to progress my role as a member of a sports medical team in hockey'
- 'Passing an NGB level/grade course in refereeing or umpiring in my chosen sport.'

Students can log a review of their course, including examination content and details of applied sessions.

COURSEWORK TIP

The construction of your Development Plan will be the key to its success – devote enough time to this, and seek help and advice from experts.

CONSTRUCTING YOUR DEVELOPMENT PLAN

The range of opportunities for your Development Plan are extensive and varied. But there are some common principles that will ensure you produce a well-structured plan appropriate to your performance needs in your chosen sport.

The basis of all development is to apply fundamental sporting knowledge and understanding allied to established sports training principles.

The key considerations for you to understand and apply if you are undertaking a physiologically-based Development Plan are:

- application of an appropriately designed physical activity readiness questionnaire (PARQ), warm-up and cool-down regime
- application of the most appropriate principles of training, such as overload, progression and frequency

- selection of the most suitable methods of training – understanding which training methods are best suited to you, while avoiding tedium and offering variation

- correct use of available monitoring and testing regimes – you will need to select at least two recognised tests that support your aim, which should be both valid and reliable

- the concept of **periodisation** – using the principles of macrocycles, mesocycles and microcycles

- incorporation of the additional scientific principles covered in Units 1 and 3 – e.g. undertaking an appropriate sports diet; hydration and avoiding dehydration; recovery strategies; understanding the physiological adaptations that will occur as a result of completing your plan

- application of technical information and instructions, to perform and be proficient in autonomous skill production

- use of technology, e.g. heart-rate monitoring equipment; pressure or force plates; resistance equipment

- psychological methodologies to support the performer throughout the plan, e.g. goal-setting and motivational techniques.

COURSEWORK TIP

The PARQ is designed in part to gauge whether you are ready to undertake a physically demanding Development Plan – if in doubt, consult your local GP.

KEY TERM

periodisation
a process of time management through which you divide and subdivide a period of time in order to achieve your objectives for training and performing periods. It is achieved through a structure of macrocycles, mesocycles and microcycles of allocated training times/sessions and their content.

Figure 10.3 shows an example of a heart rate record trace – what does it tell you? How hard was the performer working?

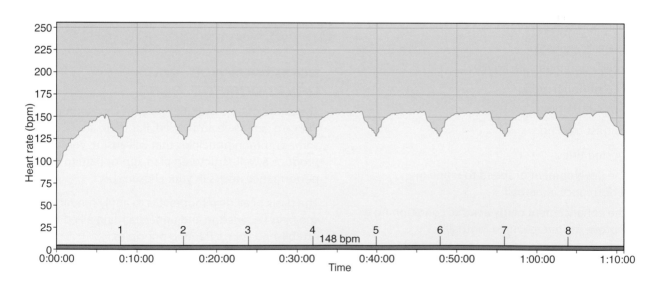

Person	A. N. OTHER	Date	12/26/00	Heart rate	148/ 160	Limits 1	146–164
Exercise	00122601	Time	10:17:03AM	Max. HR	183	Limits 2	146–164
Sport	Running	Duration	1:10:23.5			Limits 3	146–164
Note	9 x 6mins 2 rest all the way. east wind lt-med.			Selection	0:00:00 - 1:10:20 (1:10:20.0)		

Fig. 10.3 *A heart rate record trace for an internal training session*

HOW DOES THE PLAN APPLY TO A LEADER OR OFFICIAL?

If in Task 4.3 you are selecting as your single performance role that of a leader or an official, it is still possible for you to undertake the range of development programmes suggested above. For example, a referee may need to improve their own level of general aerobic fitness in order to actively control a game through mobility. You may also wish to consider the following alternatives.

- A leader may wish to undertake a **technical plan** designed to improve their specific subject knowledge and understanding through a recognised National Governing Body course. The leader may be a sports first-aider, and could undertake a sports or general injury-treatment qualification. In addition, undertaking a recognised coaching qualification in a sport or physical activity may prove central to enhancing your particular performance role.

- An official may wish to undertake a **training plan** designed to enable them to officiate physically in a chosen sport, or they may undertake a recognised National Governing Body course to qualify as a referee or other official.

It is important to remember that whichever role you select, there will be a stipulation on the minimum involvement you will have to undertake in a formal setting in order to be assessed appropriately and satisfy the examination assessment profile.

THE PROCESS

Step 1 Analysis
Your past and present performances

Step 2 Discussion
Your needs for the future – goal-setting and objective

Step 3 Construct your aims
Access the possibilities

Step 4 Devise your Development Plan
Times, dates, facilities

Step 5 Research, plan and write
Apply science in the plan

Step 6 Undertake the programme
Initial tests, mid-tests, final tests and evaluate success

Step 7 Record all work
Validate through official processes

Step 8 Final test
Evaluate, critically conclude, review attainment of objectives

Step 9 Submit
For assessment of your e-portfolio

Fig. 10.4 *The process of putting together a Development Plan*

APPLY IT!

A school or college performer identifies that they have few weaknesses in their performance – but their core and dynamic strength is not sufficiently well developed to ensure more successful performances.

How did the performer draw this conclusion?

Through the applied work undertaken for Unit 2 (Tasks 2.1, Personal Performance and 2.4, Performance Analysis), they have observed weaknesses in performances – particularly in matches against recognised higher-performing opponents, and in performances when playing in different positions. The student also undertook a battery of fitness tests to establish a performance profile as part of applying the knowledge and understanding from Unit 1, Fitness and Training. So they were able to construct a performance profile with quantifiable measurement for validation purposes that exposed this weakness.

Before you research your programme, you will need to detail the appropriate background information and how it has affected your progressive participation. You will also need to make reference to your wider sport or physical activity profile. The focus of this can centre on the following areas:

- your level of sport or physical activity performances (first level, elite or beyond) described through a performance profile over the past two years
- your performances in other sports and your commitment to them
- your level of training and personal physical and/or technical development over the past two years.

WHAT DO I NEED TO DO NEXT?

I need to:

- identify how to develop my performance and where I would like to progress to over the next 12 months
- analyse what my general sport/PE commitments give me in relation to my sports profile (e.g. circuit training gives me coordination and local muscular endurance; spin cycling sessions give me cardiovascular endurance)
- analyse what my club and/or school training provides for me.

Additional considerations when assessing my profile are to identify:

- what is missing in my sport or physical activity profile that is beyond my control (e.g. access to coaching or training facilities)
- when my Development Plan can be undertaken, and how long I will need to complete it
- where it can be carried out – what facilities do I need?
- who I will need to assist me with a programme (e.g. a gym instructor)
- what are the time and cost implications?

REMEMBER

'Sequencing strength exercises before **plyometric** exercises, and *vice versa*, will provide an added training stimulus that will ultimately produce stronger, more powerful athletes.'
Peak Performance, 2006

KEY TERM

plyometrics
a type of exercise training designed to produce fast, powerful movements and improve the functions of the nervous system, generally to improve performance in a specific sport

TIME MANAGEMENT IS THE KEY!

The most important factor for the successful completion of your Development Plan will be your ability to cope with the extra commitments and demands on your time and energy levels. This places additional pressure on you when you are also preparing the final stages of all your courses.

Fox et al. (1993) suggest that recognisable and realistic initial gains can be made after six weeks' training. This must be seen as a minimum – you should aim to time-manage your Development Plan over a longer period.

It is envisaged that you will undertake your Development Plan for a period of 8–12 weeks for recognisable gains to be measurable and to show an effect on your performances. But you may well want to carry on with your plan, once you have established the routine.

ALTERNATIVES

If you are already involved in a prescribed programme written by a National Governing Body, you can 'buy' into this programme and identify a start position and a finish date with appropriate validation.

If you become seriously injured, a rehabilitation programme to restore you to your pre-injury standard is acceptable.

If you are unfortunately unable to take part in any physical activity, the planning and research, recording, and final review and evaluation of a Development Plan for another performer would also be acceptable.

FACTORS TO CONSIDER

The additional commitments and demands on your time will make the completion of your Development Plan more difficult. You will need to take into account the issues listed below:

- your existing commitments to other sport or physical activity regimes
- travel and cost implications, if your plan cannot be undertaken on site at your school or college
- tiredness and the ability to remain energised for every session
- tedium and a general lack of motivation once the plan is a few weeks old – this will probably affect everyone!
- the possibility of becoming injured, and the recovery sessions you will need to undertake to recover from your actual performances
- school or college timetables – e.g. facilities may not always be available at the same time and place each week
- performance commitments – their impact on you both physiologically and psychologically
- external courses run by local authorities or National Governing Bodies are at their discretion – you will have to fit in with them, not the other way round!
- other commitments may get in the way – do you have a mid-week or Saturday job?

When constructing your Development Plan, describing a typical week can be a useful exercise. A simple timetable will give a visual overview of your week, and where you can best accommodate your Plan. You must allow at least one rest/recovery period of 36–48 hours, when you allow both your body and mind to recover. Rest means rest – 'down time'!

COURSEWORK TIP

Training with a partner, or at the same time as someone else, is always easier – you will encourage one another. Find someone to link in with your plan.

▶ *Don't underestimate the importance of taking some time out*

MY WEEKLY TIMETABLE							
	MON	TUE	WED	THU	FRI	SAT	SUN
School	PE School circuits				PE Spin cycle session		Recovery day
After school	Rugby practice Acceleration Drills/ technical drills		Possible match day		Strength session		
Club		Rugby practice intervals		Rugby practice or recovery session		Match day	
Own	Dynamic strength		Core strength		Recovery swim		Recovery swim

Fig. 10.5 *A timetable with built-in recovery sessions*

HOW CAN I INCORPORATE MY TRAINING WITH MY OTHER COMMITMENTS?

A typical performer may have a very full week both in and out of school. In a normal week they could plan their weekly routine as follows:

- do a strength session on Monday and Wednesday (2 × 60 minutes)
- arrive 30 minutes early on Monday to rugby training and do some speed work
- after training, stay for 20–30 minutes on a Tuesday to do some interval work
- swim for 30 minutes on Friday and Sunday to improve aerobic endurance and to act as a means of active recovery
- total extra commitment: four hours per week.

You will also be aware that there are alternatives to just doing weights, for example – gains in core and dynamic strength can be achieved by incorporating different methods of training. This will help alleviate boredom and provide variation. Alternatives could include:

- medicine ball drills
- power bags
- drag sledges
- harness work
- uphill runs
- **contrast training**
- body weight exercises – free-standing circuits
- partner resistance work
- plyometrics/power weights
- **complex training**.

> ## KEY TERMS
>
> **complex training**
> a power-developing workout that combines weights and plyometrics, e.g. three sets of 10 half-squats before three sets of 10 jump squats. Such combinations of sets are known as 'complexes'. Seventy per cent of your one-rep maximum (1RM) should be used (Peak Performance, 2006).
>
> **contrast training**
> involves alternative sets of first weights, then plyometric exercises, e.g. one set of 10 half-squats followed by one set of 10 jump-squats repeated over three sets. Seventy per cent of your 1RM should be used (Peak Performance, 2006).

When you are applying sports training principles, you should detail these in your Development Plan as evidence that you have understood the key criteria.

For example, you should condition your resistance programme (strength training) according to the following simple principles (Bompa, 1999):

- before developing muscle strength, develop joint flexibility – and in conjunction always undertake a programme designed to incorporate and develop suppleness
- aim to develop tendon strength before muscle strength
- aim to develop core strength before that of limbs
- before developing the prime movers, develop the stabilisers and fixators.

CHECKLIST

The following checklist for your Development Plan includes considerations in planning dynamic and core strength training:

- choice of exercises
- choice of equipment
- number of exercises
- order of exercises
- resistance (percentage repetition maximums)
- number of repetitions
- lifting speed – dynamic
- number of sets
- when to rest
- how to rest
- training frequency
- programme variation
- core and single joint exercises
- variation to avoid tedium
- six to 12 exercises only
- more complex exercises first – a golden rule
- start light and work up to heavier exercises
- four to 15 repetitions – depending on your aim
- varied but controlled sessions – do I need help?
- two to four sessions per week – have I the time?
- planned and regular training is best.

THE APPLIED KNOWLEDGE AND UNDERSTANDING OF SPORTS SCIENCE

Undertaking your Development Plan not only provides a significant opportunity to improve your personal performance, and a revision document for the terminal paper, but also should lead to your drawing together the scientific knowledge and understanding that underpin the physiological changes that will occur in your body. For example, if you are undertaking a cardiovascular programme, you should be prepared to ask yourself applied questions relating to your core scientific knowledge of this type of training, including the following.

■ Can you explain what are the principles of bradycardia and cardiac drift? How will they affect your Development Plan?

■ Your heart rate increases while you are in a steady state of performance, due to dehydration. What happens to the stroke volume when your heart rate rises above 145 beats?

■ How much more oxygen is needed to burn fats compared with carbohydrates?

■ How do the energy systems operate in relation to ATP resynthesis in aerobic conditioning?

■ What are the implications of this if there is limited glycogen available?

■ For how long will carbohydrate be the major source of fuel? When does the body switch to using predominantly fat as the major fuel source?

■ Can you understand, apply and discuss the concepts of **EPOC**, DOMS and OBLA?

If you are undertaking a cardiovascular or aerobic conditioning programme, you can also draw together the link between your VO_2 max and how hard your heart is working. You should use this knowledge when planning the intensity of your programme.

REMEMBER

Be cautious when performing heart rate tests to establish your maximum heart rate. Traditional calculations using 220 minus your age can be inaccurate by ±20 beats per minute, but they do provide an initial starting point.

The link between heart rate and VO_2 max	
Maximum heart rate (%)	VO_2 max (%)
35	30
60	50
80	75
90	84
100	100

APPLY IT!

When an athlete is working at 60 per cent of their maximum heart rate, they are using approximately 50 per cent of their VO_2 max and making the best use of fat as a source of fuel.

TESTING – WHAT DO I NEED TO CONSIDER?

Testing is seen as the validation of your Development Plan. By 'valid' we mean that the test selected is ethically acceptable and that it measures the specific component(s) you are aiming to develop. The multi-stage fitness test estimates your aerobic capacity, or VO_2 max, but is largely dependent on your degree of motivation relative to your ability. As an estimate, it provides only an indication of the aerobic capacity.

Tests also have to be reliable and consistent in their application. Human error will always be a factor in tests reliant on manual timekeeping (using a

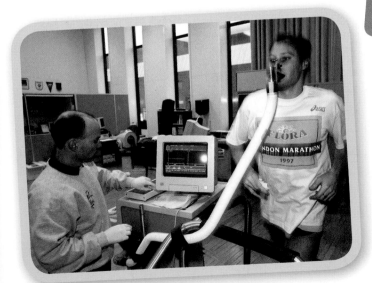

▶ *Heart rate is an important factor in your Development Plan*

stopwatch) – how valid is the test if the timekeeper makes errors? Given the available technology, it is accepted that at school and college level you may ask a member of staff to undertake the validation of your tests.

You should, if realistic, aim to include at least two tests in your Development Plan in order to cross-reference your progress. The selection of which tests to undertake should be made in conjunction with your centre staff.

Deciding on the most suitable testing procedures to use is a key consideration when formulating your Development Plan. Testing provides the following support to your plan:

- it helps measure your performance and validates the progress you have made – it provides motivation and stimulation to continue
- as a consequence, you can make appropriate adjustments to improve your current plan, to overcome tedium, and to redesign your plan if it has not been successful
- you can measure yourself against the goals you set for yourself
- you will be able to compare yourself with others and against national performance statistics.

APPLY IT!

The reality of a busy life is that training plans are interrupted. When you devise your plan, write in more potential training sessions than you need, then if you miss one there will be another opportunity that week. If you intend to train three times a week, then allow five sessions in your microcycle.

THE APPLIANCE OF SCIENCE!

With your understanding of applied scientific knowledge, your Development Plan should include details of the physiological adaptations that are expected to occur in your body. This knowledge is crucial to being able to discuss with your centre staff why you have been successful in your plan, and the physiological impact it has had.

The following box suggests the sorts of points to include – these would be expanded in your Development Plan to give fuller detail, demonstrating your level of knowledge and understanding.

APPLY IT!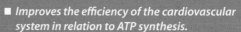

How can specific training increase an athlete's VO_2 max?

- *Improves the efficiency of the cardiovascular system in relation to ATP synthesis.*
- *Provides for hypertrophy of the heart and increased Q (cardiac output, the amount of blood the heart can expel per minute)*
- *Causes marginal increases in the surface area of the alveoli/lung capacity.*
- *Increases pulmonary diffusion.*
- *Improves the ability of muscles to utilise oxygen, fat and glycogen.*
- *Causes more myoglobin and mitochondria to be produced.*
- *Causes increased diffusion rates in tissue.*
- *Leads to an increased quantity of haemoglobin in the blood.*
- *Improves efficiency of muscles to regenerate energy.*
- *Increases the a–VO_2 difference (difference in the oxygen concentration of arterial blood leaving the heart and venous blood returning to the heart).*
- *Leads to increased vascularisation of the heart/muscles.*

KEY TERM

excess post-oxygen consumption (EPOC)
the process through which the body recovers from anaerobic energy consumption – it involves a whole series of metabolic processes, not just repaying of used oxygen in the body

DEHYDRATION

The need to maintain the correct fluid and salt balances in the body is crucial for all students undertaking a physiologically-based Development Plan. You are advised to ensure you remain hydrated at all times.

IS DEHYDRATION A SERIOUS CONSIDERATION FOR ME?

Yes! The physiological and psychological effects on your body can be serious and a hindrance to your Development Plan as well as affecting all your other sports or physical activity performances.

In the short term, dehydration causes a rapid loss in weight. The principal cause of such weight loss is the body overheating and failure to regulate this. If you become dehydrated, you will suffer from a decline in performance. This perhaps has greater significance in training, when you often work harder than in an actual performance or match situation.

As a consequence, you will suffer the following physiological and psychological effects:

- increased viscosity of the blood – it becomes thicker and harder to pump around the body
- raised blood pressure and the risk of vascular damage
- the cellular donation of water to blood increases, resulting in the shutdown of many cells and a decline in ATP production
- your body's temperature regulation fails to cope and goes 'up the wall', with the consequence that you could suffer heatstroke
- further movement leads to even greater fluid loss, severe dehydration and overheating
- increased heart rate that is not contributing to performance
- decreased stroke volume and reduced oxygen delivery to the working muscles and brain
- an overall decreased cardiac output (Q)
- dizziness, fainting and disorientation
- impaired perception and decision-making
- sensations of fatigue, then tiredness, then weakness
- changed coloration of urine
- …and above a body weight loss of 8 per cent, death could occur!

▶ *England cricketers rehydrating during a 2008 test match against South Africa*

THE PROCESS OF HYDRATION

When we exercise, up to 75 per cent of the energy used is lost as heat – we get hot!

The main way we keep cool is through sweating. By the process of evaporation, heat is taken via the vascular system from the muscles to the skin. Sweat comes from the water in our blood, so this water needs to be replaced during and after exercise. We need to drink approximately 2 litres of water a day to keep hydrated – but this will not meet our needs when performing.

APPLY IT!

Each kilogram of weight lost is equal to 1 litre of fluid. But more is lost as urine, so you need to drink 1.5 litres of fluid per kg of body weight lost. During high-intensity exercise, we will lose about 500–1000 ml of fluid per hour.

The colour of your urine is a good monitoring tool – it should be clear if you are hydrated. A 2 per cent loss of fluid affects your performance; a 4 per cent loss can cause exhaustion. While performing, for every 1 per cent drop in body weight there is about a 5 per cent drop in performance output.

Sports drinks that contain sodium are recommended – as well as containing 5–8 per cent carbohydrate, the sodium they contain is helpful if you are a 'salty sweater' – if your sweat tastes salty, is opaque, and leaves white marks on your clothes. The loss of sodium affects your performance through your neuromuscular functioning being impaired. It is not unusual for an athlete to lose up to 5 per cent of their body weight during a single event such as a match or high-intensity training session.

Don't be fooled into thinking that if you aren't thirsty, you don't need fluids. Eating stops thirst when the mouth is moistened, and you will need to keep drinking for several hours after a performance. Alcohol also causes dehydration, so avoid it unless you have rehydrated.

KEY TERM

dehydration
when fluid loss is greater than fluid input, causing impaired thermoregulation and a rise in core temperature

APPLY IT!

- A 2 per cent loss of body weight = about 10 per cent loss or deterioration in performance.
- A 5 per cent loss of body weight = 25 per cent loss or deterioration in performance.
- An 8 per cent loss of body weight may have dire consequences – what are they?

REMEMBER

To regulate your fluid intake and understand how it affects you, you need to weigh yourself before *and* after training or organised performances. Clothing holds sweat, so be as free of any clothing as you can when you weigh yourself.

HOW CAN I MAINTAIN MY ENERGY LEVELS AND OVERCOME FATIGUE?

At times you will become tired and fatigued, and less motivated to complete your Development Plan as outlined. The knowledge and understanding gained from completing Units 1 and 3 will help you to stay ahead in your plan. Correcting or modifying your diet to cope with the changes in your performance lifestyle is vital to its successful completion.

'Fuelling' is the term used to describe the process of ensuring your body has sufficient and appropriate energy to meet the demands made on it. It is expected that you will have to modify your diet as appropriate to your Development Plan and all your other commitments.

APPLY IT!

Movement requires energy. Both your training and competitive performances will need more energy in greater quantities.

THE ENERGY FUELS

Carbohydrate, fat and protein are the three main energy fuels. When broken down, these fuels provide a certain quantity of energy – measured as kilocalories (kcal) per gram (g).

1 g carbohydrate or protein = 4 kcal
1 g fat = 9 kcal.

The preferred energy fuel for muscles is glucose – especially for high-intensity exercise. Glucose is formed from the breakdown of carbohydrates (sugars and starches) in your diet, and stored as glycogen in the muscles and liver. This is a limited supply – approximately 450 g is stored in muscles and 150 g in the liver.

WHICH FUEL?

- **Anaerobic** activities depend on the alactic and lactic systems, and use **glucose** without oxygen present – high-intensity but short-lived.
- **Aerobic** activities of low intensity that use less than 300 kcal per hour burn more **fat** and less glucose.
- The fitter you are aerobically, the more fat you burn earlier in the exercise programme.
- Activities that are **moderate to high intensity** burn more glucose (500 kcal per hour).
- The more work you do, the more glucose you need!

REMEMBER

Work requires energy – ensure you have made modifications to your diet to take into account the extra demands you are placing on your body.

WHERE DOES GLUCOSE COME FROM?

Carbohydrates are divided into three groups, depending on their molecular structure:

- **monosaccharides** – single molecules of sugar, e.g.
  - o glucose – found in most sugars and starches
  - o fructose – fruit sugar from fruits, vegetables and honey
  - o galatose – part of lactose, the sugar found in milk
- **disaccharides** – two linked molecules broken down by digestion into monosaccharides, e.g.
  - o sucrose (glucose + fructose) – table sugar, and in fruits and vegetables
  - o lactose (glucose + galatose) – from milk and milk products
  - o maltose (glucose + glucose) – from malt extract and starches
- **starches** – hundreds of molecules of glucose sugar joined together. Starch is digested when broken down first into maltose, then into glucose.

The only difference between sugars and starches is the size of the molecules.

HOW MUCH CARBOHYDRATE DO I NEED?

If you are physically active, you need a diet that contains 55–70 per cent carbohydrate. But it is difficult to estimate the proportion of carbohydrate in one meal, let alone in drinks.

As most carbohydrates are eventually broken down into glucose, one type is not necessarily better than another. The key question concerns the rate at which – that is, how quickly – the carbohydrate is broken down into glucose.

This rate is known as the glycaemic index (GI).

The GI is a measure of a food's effect on blood glucose levels. It is worked out by comparing the rise in blood glucose after eating a food containing 50 g of carbohydrate. The faster the blood glucose rises, the higher the GI rating.

It is not easy to tell what GI a food has. Some sugars are high-GI (e.g. glucose) and others are low-GI (e.g. fructose). Some complex starches have a high GI (e.g. rice) and others a lower GI (e.g. pasta).

▶ *Complex carbohydrates*

THE GI GUIDE – WHAT TO EAT AND WHEN

It has been argued that low-GI foods, such as fructose, are a good thing to eat before exercise. This is because they provide a readily available energy source with minimal insulin response, and therefore encourage your body to greater fat burning. This theory is not well founded, as insulin secretion is suppressed during exercise. Also, the rate of glucose supply to the bloodstream from the digestion of low-GI food is generally not fast enough while you are exercising.

APPLY IT!

Just before, during and immediately after exercise, try to eat high- and moderate-GI foods to help stimulate glycogen synthesis.

THE PRE-PERFORMANCE ROUTINE

Allow at least 2–3 hours after a meal before your routine. Then, 5–30 minutes before exercise, have a 50 g moderate- to high-GI carbohydrate snack. Avoid bulky, fibre-rich carbohydrates.

REMEMBER

For all training or performing, even for under an hour, you will need to take a sports drink and keep drinking water to avoid dehydration.

KEY TERM

carbohydrate loading
the manipulation of a diet to maximise the body's store of glycogen, achieved by following a diet of over 70 per cent carbohydrate (known as supercompensation)

THE POST-PERFORMANCE ROUTINE

Try to eat a minimum of 50 g of carbohydrate immediately after you finish, within 20–40 minutes as a guide, and preferably 1 g per kg body weight every 2 hours for up to 6 hours after a heavy workout.

For a 60 kg person, that is three meals of 60 g carbohydrate within 6 hours of your finish. If you don't feel hungry, use a high-carbohydrate sports drink.

Between sessions, don't eat too much high-GI food. Ingest a mixture of moderate- and high-GI foods. Do not overload on pasta, potatoes or bread; butter, cakes, biscuits and cream are also high in fats.

HOW MUCH PROTEIN DO I NEED?

The average daily needs are measured as a gram per kilogram of body weight per day. If you are exercising for more than one hour per day, then your daily requirement rises from 0.75 g per day per kg body weight to 1.0–1.2 g. For a 60 kg person, that is 60–72 g protein. If you are undertaking a heavier resistance programme, this can rise to 1.6–1.7 g protein per kg body weight per day.

REMEMBER

Protein can't be stored in the body. You use the protein you need, and each day secrete any excess. The key question is – do you need to buy expensive protein supplements if you eat a healthy balanced diet?

STRETCH AND CHALLENGE

When assessing a Development Plan for the top mark award band (40–45), assessors ask the following questions when looking for a very high standard.

- *Do you have clear and concise aims appropriate to your needs as a performer?*
- *Do you demonstrate use of the appropriate physiological, technical and psychological principles?*
- *Is there a high standard in the level of planning and the quality of references used?*
- *How suitable is your time plan?*
- *Have you completed all the set sessions you intended to?*
- *Have you used appropriate tests and recorded them accurately?*
- *Have you used technology and science, and modified your diet?*
- *Are you able to discuss your Development Plan with insight?*
- *Has the Development Plan achieved your aims, and what impact has this had on your performances? How have you measured this?*
- *What level of knowledge and understanding have you acquired as a result of completing your Development Plan?*

THE ASSESSMENT PROCESS

THE FINAL MARK

The cumulative assessment of your Development Plan reflects the three individual assessed components (Planning and research; Performing and recording; Review and evaluation). The band system allows for a degree of flexibility given the extensive nature of the Development Plan and the range of contributory factors that all combine to enable you to be successful in this task. A top marked Development Plan would fall in the mark band 37–45.

SUBMISSION FORMATS: THE E-PORTFOLIO

There is no prescriptive format for the submission of your Development Plan. It is an open task. You will be free to use a variety of media that will reflect the type of plan you have undertaken and the specific nature of your training routines. There is also no set word limit for the plan – this allows you to expand and progress the plan as appropriate to your aims and abilities.

▶ *You can use other media in your e-portfolio, such as images from a mobile phone*

You may wish to consider extending your final submission beyond written documentation, perhaps including video evidence of a particular technical training session or exercise routine. Still photographs of techniques or technological aids, or a podcast or vidcast that can be used to record your ongoing and final evaluation, are all acceptable. You are free to mix and match the presentation media open to you at your own discretion.

TASK 4.2 – INTERNATIONAL STUDY

The globalisation of sport has now overtaken the self-determining developments that would normally take place internally within a country or culture. We are heading towards a 'world culture of sport' that dominates globally, and then shapes and conditions the sporting ethos and culture of every nation. Olympic Games, rugby and soccer world cups, the Commonwealth Games and world championships have become the dominant events that now dictate countries' sporting policies, structures and frameworks, in order for nations to compete globally. Success in the sporting arena brings national pride to a country and a status among the leading nations of the world. The status attained through sporting victory goes beyond just 'standing in sport'. With an explosion in worldwide media coverage, the media

are the 'prime movers' in the globalisation process and the public's apparently insatiable appetite for sports coverage.

In this global context, an understanding of another nation's unique sporting ethos, provisions and opportunities for mass participation and elite development will provide you with the opportunity to understand how sport and physical activity are constructed, and to appreciate how this reflects the cultural heritage of that particular nation. This is not a comparative study, but provides an opportunity for you to understand how and why a nation provides for and ethically decides the place of sport and recreation in its life, the role of government, and the funding processes involved.

The requirement in undertaking your International Study is research into both the grassroots provisions and the elite development pathways open to individuals and teams in your chosen nation. This study will also provide a point of reference for your synoptic answers to the externally set examination of Unit 3.

You will complete the International Study based on your single Progressive Participation choice for Task 4.3 – that is, you will focus the study on the provisions and opportunities for either a performer, a leader or an official. But while the task will focus on one activity in particular, it is envisaged that a collective review of the major sports and physical activity provisions will be made by way of references and comparisons.

WHICH NATION MAY I STUDY?

You are free to study any major sporting nation that competes globally at major championships such as the Olympic Games and profiled sports world cups or championships. These include the USA, Canada, Australia, New Zealand, European nations including Germany, Italy, France and many others, the Scandinavian countries, plus the major African, Asian and South American nations.

TASK

If your are studying a European country, there may well be a native speaker or a member of staff in your centre who has lived in that country. Undertake a recorded interview with them to find out their thoughts on that nation's sports provisions and structures.

▶ *Grassroots cricket in India*

RESEARCH

You will be required to undertake your International Study on a nation *different* from the one you studied as part of Tasks 2.2, Local Study and 2.3, National Study. While this will be largely a desktop, research-based task, you will be free to draw on the use of primary evidence and personal experiences to contribute to the completion of the task, as appropriate.

Your research will focus on the key areas within the nation being studied. A suggested series of headings might include the following areas:

- grassroots provision in both schools and the local community
- recreational and representative opportunities at local level
- the provision of competition and its formats
- elite pathways and sporting ethos
- national training structures
- provision for professional sport and the structures involved
- the nation's world standing and sports image, and political will.

▶ *Baseball is a major part of US sport*

TASK

Write to the Embassy or Consulate of your chosen country and request any resources they may have on their sports structures and funding programmes – they are usually quite willing to do this.

EXAMPLE CONTENT AREAS

If you undertook your International Study on a performer in the USA, for example, you would have to make generic statements that draw broad conclusions, given the size and diversity of the country. You may wish to consider the following questions as a focus for your research, using the USA as an example.

- What is the overall sporting ethos of the nation? Is it predominantly about 'the **win ethic**'?

- Consider the depth of sports provision in schools and the wider community – is it an elitist provision?

- What is the typical provision for a performer at grassroots level, then for first elite level performers? What is the role of junior sport?

- Do sport and physical recreation exist as a social function of the community? If so, when and where?

- What is the college system of sports scholarships, and how does this affect school and community provision?

- What is the draft system, and how does this shape college sport?

- How is the professional sports arena organised and funded?

- What roles do central and local government play in sport?

- What is the status of the Olympics to the American sporting public?

- Does the '**Americanisation**' of sport really exist?

You are also free to follow the outlined pathway through the study of one sport in particular. If your chosen role for Task 4.3 is a performer in hockey, you can base your international study on hockey in the Netherlands; if your chosen sport is rugby, on rugby union in New Zealand or South Africa; or a soccer player may choose France as the country to study and cover that sport in depth.

KEY TERM

win ethic
a term associated with the American football coach Vince Lombardi, who saw the goal of winning as the dominating principle for coaching and playing, and as the only reason for taking part. It has come to be associated with American sport and the desire to be winners first and foremost.

PRESENTATION

As with all other coursework tasks in both Units 2 and 4, you are free to present your International Study in any format or medium you wish. If the task is presented in a single continuous narrative format, then a limit of 1000 words will be applied. You are free to include photographs, charts, tables and other evidence to support your findings. You may present your task as a PowerPoint presentation, a video lecture-style presentation, a vidcast or similar.

KEY TERM

Americanisation
the concept that sport globally is now dominated by the structure, organisation and style of sport seen in the USA – characterised by private funding and media exposure

ASSESSMENT

The task will be marked against a banded set of criteria, with a final mark given out of 15.

STRETCH AND CHALLENGE

When assessing an International Study for the top mark award band (13–15), assessors ask the following questions when looking for a very high standard.

- Do you show a high level of knowledge and understanding of one nation, for one performance role?

- Have you clearly identified grassroots provisions in schools and clubs?

- Have you clearly identified the pathways for elite progression?

- Do you include full details on the nation's sporting ethos?

- Have you identified pathways for professional sport, competition formats and national training programmes?

- Do you make full reference to various schemes, funding and the roles of additional agencies?

- Do you refer to international sports issues, such as 'white flight' or '**labour migration**', as appropriate?

- Do you offer critical comments on your research findings, and significant factual information to support the task?

- Do you include an extensive bibliography?

COURSEWORK TIP

You are free to complete draft versions of this task in line with your centre's own coursework structure and deadlines.

Fig. 10.6 *Some roles of a leader*

TASK 4.3 – PROGRESSIVE PARTICIPATION

The fundamental nature of this task is to engage you in specialisation and refinement of a single sport or physical activity. Drawing on your experiences in Task 2.1, Personal Performance, you will have undertaken two roles taken from those of performer, leader and official.

Your continued involvement and participation in a single sport or physical activity will enable you to focus, producing a higher level of outcome. This will be reflected in the assessment criteria. You are free to select either of the two roles you undertook in Task 2.1, but you may wish to consider selecting the third role.

You will be expected to perform, lead or officiate in line with your abilities, and to draw together this Progressive Participation with your Development Plan (Task 4.1). This allows for a high degree of specialisation and develops a depth of knowledge and understanding in one area central to your own personal development and aspirations.

REMEMBER

The pressure on you to perform is greater at A2 level. You will need to put into practice what you have learned in sports psychology, and use strategies and methods to cope with this pressure in your organised performances. Remaining focused is of vital importance.

ASSESSMENT

The assessment process mirrors that for Task 2.1 You will be expected to become involved in a combination of structured preparation or practices, coaching or refereeing training courses, or coaching and training sessions with a technical and physiological basis, or to incorporate aspects of all of these.

TASK

Keep a log of all your organised performances and training experiences – this will allow you to build up a summary of your progress throughout the A2 course.

There is a requirement for you to have been involved in a sport or physical activity role for a minimum of 8 weeks, and to be assessed in at least three organised performances – essentially formal competitive environments for some, or a planned response to a particular set of circumstances for others. Examples could include the completion of a dance routine or finishing a timed walk/trek in an expedition.

- For the performer, this will be a straightforward process – you will be able to make progress in your performance in response to your own specific goals and objectives.

- For the leader, you will be required to be proactive and seek out opportunities to influence and direct the performance of others in your defined role.

- For the official, sitting and passing National Governing Body awards may form the crux of your Development Plan, and you will seek applied opportunities at a level appropriate to your age and experience, both within and outside your own educational establishment.

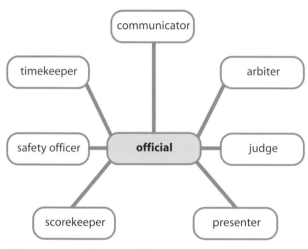

Fig. 10.7 *Some roles of an official*

KEY TERM

pressure of expectation
the expected standard to which you will perform, even when under pressure, such as in competition against performers of a similar or higher standard. A low-handicap golfer will be expected to play to that standard even in a high-level competition.

KEY TERM

first-level elite
performers who have achieved a performance standing via a selection process and are therefore considered more able than others – who represent an institution or are first-team players

TASK

Can you list three performers who consistently produce their best performances when they need to; and three who do not, but crumble under the pressure of expectation?

ASSESSMENT

The task will be marked against a banded set of criteria, with a final mark given out of 15.

HOW DO I RECORD MY PERFORMANCES?

Evidence of your progressive participation will be contained in your e-portfolio, and a range of options are open to you. The following media can be selected on a mix-and-match basis. Essentially this becomes a record of achievement for you.

- Completion of the Exam Board mark justification form.

- A testimonial from a coach, centre staff, etc.

- Fixture lists, results, competitive performance details.
- Newspaper cuttings, reports, results.
- Copies of any certification, awards.
- Personal bests – verified.
- Image files (such as jpegs) and/or video clips of performances.
- A preparation and training log of your experiences.

TASK

Ask a friend or relative to video you in action or to take still photographs when you are in organised performances, and add these to your e-portfolio.

The final assessment of your level and standard of participation can be undertaken as an ongoing process – throughout the A2 course there will be specific points when formal assessments are undertaken. The final submission will be included on your e-portfolio and internally assessed by your centre and externally moderated in the May/June of the year of award.

TASK 4.4 – LIFE PLAN

The final coursework task in Unit 4 is the formulation of a personal Life Plan. The Life Plan is an opportunity for you to draw together synoptically the relevant knowledge and understanding from all of Units 1–4. There will be physiological, psychological and sociological bases for the Life Plan. The plan will encapsulate your potential life in a sports or physical activity environment.

TASK

Using the Internet, research the participation rates in schools for the major competitive sports, and the drop-out rates post-16/18 education. What does this tell you? What does everyone else do?

The Life Plan is designed to enable you to reflect critically on the future participation opportunities open to you in the performance role you undertook for Task 4.3. It is expected that this role will change over time – for instance, opportunities to leave the performance arena as a player may lead to you being able to officiate or to be a leader in a particular sport or physical activity role. This could be part of your long-term aspirations and should be reflected in a timeline of participation.

TASK

Look at the prospective universities and colleges you hope to attend. If you visit them, find out what opportunities you will have to take part in your sport or physical activity. You may find you are not good enough to carry on performing at this new level, and decide to seek out other opportunities to participate. Most major sport at university level is very competitive, and selection is both difficult and expensive!

You should consider the following areas that you have studied in your other units:

- the ageing process and physiological degeneration rates
- health issues, onset of diseases and life-expectancy rates
- factual details on the rise in sedentary lifestyles
- the increasing dangers of obesity and other **hypokinetic disorders**
- declining participation rates in your chosen role
- opportunities post-18 in higher education or in the local community
- injury rates and recovery opportunities as you age
- cost implications and travel expectations.

KEY TERM

hypokinetic disorder
a collection of diseases brought about by insufficient movement and a lack of exercise – examples include coronary heart disease and obesity

sixth form

university → **first team/ travel home to play for money to help pay for university scholarship to USA to play for university team**

work → **continue playing for Airbus**

gap year → **travel to Australia, New Zealand USA therefore will not play for a year**

play for major league soccer franchise

Fig. 10.8 *One example of the first part of a Life Plan (Source: Steve Rosier, 2008)*

STRETCH AND CHALLENGE

When assessing the Life Plan for the top mark award band (9–10), assessors ask the following questions when looking for a very high standard.

- *Have you demonstrated a high level of knowledge and understanding of your present and future performance role?*
- *Have you detailed fully your performance history and current developments?*
- *Have you included complete and detailed research into future performance pathways?*
- *Have you considered how health, injury, disease and hypokinetic rates may affect you?*
- *Have you included an accurate timeline?*
- *Have you fully explored potential lifestyle changes with reference to provisions and opportunities both locally and nationally?*
- *Have you included full references and a bibliography?*

COURSEWORK TIP

The Life Plan requires factual evidence – visit your local health centre for information booklets on current health trends and issues.

TASK

In groups of three, list the six sports and physical activities that have the highest injury rates and shortest career spans, and match your findings to those sports that have the oldest participants.

REMEMBER

The Life Plan is by nature subjective, but you are also expected to draw heavily on objective factual data to support your findings and opinions.

ASSESSMENT

Assessment of your Life Plan is made using the established method of applying generic criteria that provide a defined expectation for the outcome of your Plan.

▶ *Some sports are more suitable for older players than others*

HOW DO I PRESENT MY LIFE PLAN?

The presentation of your Life Plan reflects the open-ended task directive for all your other coursework tasks. You may use a variety of presentation media, for example a PowerPoint presentation or a lecture-style video presentation. If your plan is in continuous narrative form, there will be a limit of 1000 words. You are free to use photographs, tables and charts to support your findings. The final submission will be included in your e-portfolio, assessed internally by your centre, and moderated externally in May/June of the year of award.

HOT LINKS

The following websites will provide you with research opportunities in order to complete your coursework tasks.

www.activeplaces.com
www.arielnet.com
www.AsktheExpert.com
www.bodybuildingforyou.com
www.brianmac.demon.co.uk
http://news.bbc.co.uk/sport1/hi/academy
www.pponline.co.uk
www.specialolympics.org
www.sportscoachuk.org
www.sport-fitness-advisor.com
www.sportsscience.org
www.teachpe.com
www.thecoachingcorner.com

▶ Use IT to prepare your Life Plan presentation

ExamCafé
Relax, refresh, result!

Relax and prepare

Ed

Train with a partner – you can motivate and encourage one another.

Charlie

Don't leave tasks until the last moment – start early and finish before the deadline!

Harley

Ask for help if you are finding things difficult.

Saskia

Keep ongoing working documents that you add to bit by bit.

Refresh your memory

▷ Do not undertake your Development Plan if the detail of the programme has not been agreed with your centre staff – this is one of the biggest areas of weakness.

▷ Use your scientific knowledge to write your training loads, dietary modifications and periodisations.

▷ Never assume you can complete your coursework on a first attempt. In the A2 course, you can build your Development Plan in three stages: Planning and Research, Performing and Recording, and Evaluation – each will take several weeks.

▷ If you are in a prescribed training programme written by a national body or club, buy into it for 8–10 weeks to form your Development Plan. (You can use an 8–10-week section of your current long-term development programme provided there is a clearly defined start and end to the period, with appropriate testing and evaluation.)

▷ Keep an ongoing daily/weekly evaluation of your Development Plan – this will make it easier at the end to write a final review.

▷ In writing the International Study, ask your centre staff about their own experiences, and write to the country's National Federation for help or use the Internet to contact them – research the facts!

▷ When doing the International Study, focus on one sport or physical activity that you are interested in.

▷ Always keep a back-up of your e-portfolio, as work often gets lost in cyberspace.

Coursework tips

For Unit 4 you can present your work in different ways – why not include still photographs and video clips of your tasks as evidence?

Time management is extremely important for you to complete your tasks successfully – plan when you can complete all your tasks and how this fits in with your centre deadlines.

If you go to another country, visit as many of the sports provisions as you can, such as schools or sports centres – take photographs and video clips, and undertake a recorded interview – mobile phones will do all this.

The Life Plan must be synoptic in nature, so revisit your notes from Unit 1 and include as many facts and figures that you can.

National Governing Bodies have fact sheets on participation levels, injury rates and details of coaches and referee statistics, so write to them and request a copy.

To gain similar marks at A2 level you must improve on last year's personal performance, so look at the assessment criteria and discuss with your centre staff how you can achieve the best marks possible – devise an action plan.

Get the result!

These might include a lack of referencing, no test validation, no video backup as evidence of progression, no bibliography, or inappropriate training loads.

Sample coursework

Development Plan (cardiovascular fitness)

How specific training increases an athlete's VO_2 max...

▷ Improves the efficiency of the CV system

▷ Hypertrophy of the heart = increased Q

▷ Marginally increases the surface area of the alveoli/lung capacity

▷ Increases pulmonary diffusion

▷ Improves ability of the muscles to utilise oxygen

▷ More myoglobin and more mitochondria

▷ Increases diffusion rates in tissue

▷ Increases quantity of haemoglobin in the blood

▷ Improves efficiency of the muscles to regenerate energy

▷ Increases vascularisation of the heart/muscles

▷ Lowers end systolic volumes in the ventricles

Examiner says:

This extract from a Development Plan on enhancing cardiovascular fitness details the physiological responses that occur in the long term as result of a planned and progressive cardiovasular training programme. The content is drawn from the student's knowledge and understanding gained from Unit 3, as well as from more specific research for this task.

Examiner says:

The factual detail is accurate, covers the core responses, and is written in appropriate language for students at A2 level.

Examiner says:

The Development Plan can also be used as a revision document for the final examination paper.

International Study

High school sport in the USA acts as a nursery for professional teams and future stars in the making. It exists, and survives, as a chance for the individual to achieve a very high social status and to 'live the dream'. Role models such as Michael Jordan have fuelled the dream that now sees sport ranked alongside Hollywood in American society. In many ways, high school sport can be seen as a substitute for professional sport, and serves as a 'production line' to the college system, and ultimately through the draft system on to professional games. It has been suggested that the US system of youth sport, which is focused almost exclusively on the school and college system, is completely different from the club-based focus in most European countries. High school sport is elitist, has superb facilities in comparison with the UK, and is of media interest, partly due to the distances between teams, which unites communities through identity and a spirit of togetherness. State championships are the number one goal to win. The lack of a club structure in the USA reinforces this provision.

Examiner says:

The student has written an introduction to the place of high school sport in the development of the individual in the USA. The paragraph forms part of the student's International Study and aims to place in context the importance of elite sport in the USA, its sociological and cultural heritage, and the sports dream held by students at high school. The extract is written at an appropriate academic level and includes a reference.

Life Plan

Student Name: John Fredericks

Examiner says:

The student has produced a PowerPoint presentation as part of his Life Plan, reviewing the options open to him at 18, once he leaves his present college. He also details his present performance levels and future aspirations.

- Currently a member of Welsh Schools' Football Under-18 Team
- Playing League of Wales Football First Team Airbus UK
- North Wales X-country Team Under-18
- Position: Striker
- Current season playing record available at www.welshfootballassociation.org.uk

Examiner says:

The student could expand the presentation further by talking in more detail about the factual information provided, and include video clips, press cuttings and jpeg images of his present participation.

Progressive Participation

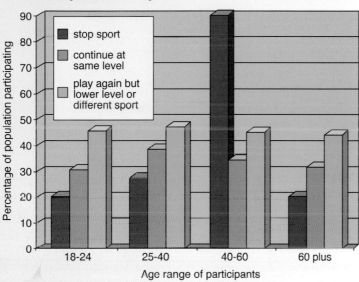

Participation in sport

Legend:
- **stop sport**
- **continue at same level**
- **play again but lower level or different sport**

Y-axis: Percentage of population participating
X-axis: Age range of participants (18-24, 25-40, 40-60, 60 plus)

- 28 per cent of the UK population do regular exercise; in Scandinavia the rate is 59 per cent.
- One in five men dies from coronary heart disease. Where I live, there are 47.12 deaths from CHD in men per 100,000.

Examiner says:

The factual information given in this slide is related to general national statistics, and then places these in the context of the student's own locality.

Examiner says:

It would be expected that the student would be able to lead a discussion on the reasons for this, and stimulate debate, drawing on both sociological and topographical explanations, to explain how the culture and lifestyle where they live influence people's sporting life.

INDEX

Bold page numbers indicate key terms, *italic* numbers indicate illustrations

ACKNOWLEDGEMENTS

Texts cited in this book are as follows:

Ahrendt, D.M., Ergogenic aids: counselling the athlete, *America Family Physician*, 63: 913–22, 2001

Atherton, C., *Skill Acquisition and Sports Psychology*, Philip Allen Updates, 2003

Atkinson, J.W., *An Introduction to Motivation*, Van Nostrand, 1964

Bale, J., *Touch Down to Home Base – Sport in the USA*, Altair Publishing, 1994

Bandura, A., *Social Learning Theory*, Prentice Hall, 1977

Barnes, S., *The Meaning of Sport,* Short Books, 2006

Bompa, T., *Total Training for Young Champions*, Human Kinetics, 1999

Carron, A.V., *Social Psychology of Sport*, Mouvement Publications, 1980

Cashmore, E. *Making Sense of Sports*, 3rd edn, Routledge, 2000

Cottrell, N.B., Social facilitation, in C. McClintock (ed.), *Experimental Social Psychology*, Holt, Rinehart & Winston, 1972

Fox, E. et al., *The Physiological Basis for Exercise and Sport*, Brown and Benchmark, 1993

Gastin, P.B., Energy system interaction and relative contribution during maximal exercise, *Sports Medicine*, 31: 725–41, 2001

Gill, D.L. and Deeter, T.E., Development of the sport orientation questionnaire, *Research Quarterly for Exercise and Sport*, 59: 191–202, 1988

Gill, D.L., *Psychological Dynamics of Sport*, Human Kinetics, 1986

Haake, S., Physics, technology and the Olympics, *Physics World* 13: 29–32, 2000

Houlihan, B. and Green, M., *Elite Sport Development*, Routledge, 2005

Jones, G. and Swain, A., Intensity and direction as dimensions of competitive state anxiety and relationships with competitiveness, *Perception and Motor Skills*, 74; 467–72, 1992

Levinson, D. and Christensen, K. (eds), *Encyclopaedia of World Sport*, ABC-CLIO, 1996

Lindsay, F.H., Hawley, J.A., Myburgh, K.H., Schomer, H.H., Noakes, T.D. and Dennis, S.C., Improved athletic performance in highly trained cyclists after interval training, *Medicine and Science in Sports and Exercise*, 28: 1427–34, 1996

Martens, R., Vealey, R.S. and Burton, D., *Competitive Anxiety in Sport*, Human Kinetics, 1998

McGuigan, M.R. and Newton, R.U., An investigation of the impact of the LineBreak Sportswear on thermoregulation during exercise in a warm and humid environment followed by recovery in a cooler environment, School of Exercise, Biomedical and Health Sciences, Edith Cowan University, 2005

Murray, H.A., *Explorations in Personality*, Oxford University Press, 1938

Noakes, T.D., Peltonen, J.E. and Rusko, H.K., Evidence that a central governor regulates exercise performance during acute hypoxia and hyperoxia, *Journal of Experimental Biology*, 204: 3225–34, 2001

Peak Performance, *Strength and Muscle Training*, Peak Performance Publishing, 2006

PriceWaterhouseCoopers, *Economic Briefing Paper: Modelling Olympic Performance*, June 2008

Smith, R.E., Smoll, F.L. and Schutz, R.W., Measurement and correlates of sport-specific cognitive and somatic trait anxiety: The Sport Anxiety Scale, *Anxiety Research*, 2: 263–80, 1990.

SportsWise, Sports Ritual Survey, October 2006

St Clair Gibson, A., Schabort, E.J. and Noakes, T.D., Reduced neuromuscular activity and force generation during prolonged cycling, *American Journal of Physiology*, R281: 187–96, 2001

Weinberg, R.S. and Gould, D., *Foundations of Sport and Exercise Psychology*, 2nd edn, Human Kinetics, 1999

Weiner, B., *Achievement Motivation and Attribution Theory*, General Learning Press, 1974

Wenger, H., *Train to Win*, Sports Coach, 1999

Williams, M.H., *The Ergogenics Edge: Pushing the Limits of Human Performance*, Human Kinetics, 1998

Zajonc, R.B., Social facilitation, *Science*, 149: 269–74, 1965

The authors and publisher would like to thank the following individuals and organisations for permission to reproduce photographs:
p3 © Pearson Education Ltd/Tudor Photography; **p4** © PhotoDisc/Photolink; **p7** © Getty Images/Stockdisc; **p10** © Corbis/Reuters/Eric Gaillard; **p16** © Science Photo Library/Gustoimages; **p18** © Getty Images/Jeff Gross; **p19** © Science Photo Library/Gustoimages; **p21** © Getty Images/Hassan Ammar; **p22** © Getty Images/AFP/Alexander Joe; **p24** © Getty Images/Mike Hewitt; **p26** © Pete Reed (www.petereed.co.uk); **p31** © PA Photos/Empics Sport/Adam Devy;**p33 TR**© Alamy/Aflo Foto Agency; **p33 MR** © Corbis/Reuters/Mike Blake; **p34** © Corbis/Wally McNamee; **p35** © Corbis/Reuters/Patrick Price; **p36** © Corbis/NewSport/Greg Fiume; **p38** © Getty Images/Allsport Concepts/Ryan McVay; **p39 BL** © Pearson Education Ltd/Jules Selmes; **p39 BR** © Getty Images/Jamie McDonald; **p43 BR** © Christa Knijff/Alamy; **p43 BL** © PhotoDisc/Steve Mason; **p44** © Corbis /Reuters; **p45 TR** © Getty Images/Julian Herbert; **p45 BR** © Alamy/Rick Decker; **p51** © PhotoDisc/jim Wehtje; **p52** © PA Photos/AP/Steve Mitchell; **p53** © Getty Images; **p55** © Getty Images/David Rogers; **p59** © PA Photos/Tom Hevezi; **p61** © Radius Images/Alamy; **p62** © iStockPhoto/Eliza Snow; **p64** © Alamy/Brand X/JupiterImages; **p65 TL** © Action Plus/Glyn Kirk; **p65 BL** © Dave Cameron/Alamy; **p66** © PhotoDisc/Lawrence M. Sawyer; **p68** © Getty Images/Touchline; **p69** © Getty Images/Allsport/Billy Stickland; **p79 TR** © Getty Images/AllSport/Shaun Botterill; **p79 BL** © Getty Images/Robert Laberge; **p81** © PhotoDisc/Karl Weatherly; **p82** © Getty Images/Jeff Brass; **p85** © PhotoDisc/Photolink; **p86 TL** © PhotoDisc/Karl Weatherly; **p86 TR** © Image Source Black/Alamy; **p87** © Digital Vision; **p88** © PhotoDisc/Photolink; **p89** © PhotoDisc; **p90** © PhotoDisc/Photolink; **p94 TR** © Tetra Images/Alamy; **p94 BR** © iStockPhoto/Eliza Snow; **p97** © Getty Images/Ian Waldie; **p106** © PA Photos/AP/Alessandro Trovati; **p107** © Getty Images/NBA/Andrew D Bernstein; **p111** © Getty Images/AFP/Nicolas Asfouri; **p114** © Corbis/Randy Faris; **p117** © Digital Stock; **p119** © Corbis/ epa/Daniel Dal Zennaro; **p120** © Corbis/Christian Liewig; **p123** © PA Photos/AP/Marc Bence; **p124** © PA Photos/Peter Byrne; **p130** © Getty Images/Gallo Images/Tertius Pickard; **p131** © PA Photos/Empics Sport/Adam Devy; **p137** © United Artists/the Kobal Collection; **p138 TL** © Corbis/Louie Psihoyos; **p138 TR** © /Getty Images/AFP/Martin Bureau; **p139** © Science Photo Library/Philippe Psaila; **p143** © Action Plus/Mike Shearman; **p144** © Alamy/imagebroker; **p145** © PhotoDisc/Photolink; **p150** © Mary Evans Picture Library; **p151** © The Illustrated London News Picture Library; **p152** © PhotoDisc/Photolink; **p154** © Getty Images/Bob Martin; **p156** © Getty Images/Hamish Blair; **p158** © Corbis/Brand X; **p158** © Alamy/George S deBlonsky; **p164** © Getty Images/Daniel Berehulak; **p165** © PA Photos/Toby Melville; **p169** © Mary Evans Picture Library; **p169** © Getty Images /Matt Cardy; **p170** © Getty Images/Sports Illustrated/Simon Bruty; **p171** © Getty Images/Mark Dadswell; **p173** © Action Plus/Glyn Kirk; **p174** © Action Plus/Neil Tingle; **p175** © Image100/Alamy; **p175** © Richard Smith; **p176 TL**© PA Photos/AP/Martin Meissner; **p176 MR** © PhotoDisc/C Squared Studios; **p176 BR** © Pearson Education Ltd/Gareth Boden; **p177** © LOOK Die Bildagentur der Fotografen GmbH/Alamy; **p179** © PhotoDisc; **p194** © Pearson Education Ltd/Tudor Photography; **p196** © Action Plus; **p198** © Getty Images/AFP/Glyn Kirk; **p200** © Pearson Education Ltd/MM Studios; **p202** © Corbis/Michael DeYoung; **p203 TL** © PhotoDisc/Photolink; **p203 BR** © Alamy/David Noble Photography; **p208** © Corbis/EPA/CJ Gunther; **p209** © Pearson Education/Ian Wedgewood

The authors and publisher would like to thank the following individuals and organisations for permission to reproduce copyright material:
P140 T Dartfish Video Software Solutions (www.dartfish.com); **p140 B** ProZone Sports Ltd (www.prozonesports.com); **p208** Steve Rosier, Edexcel presentation, 2008; **p214** Steve Rosier, Edexcel presentation, 2008; **p215** Steve Rosier, Edexcel presentation, 2008

Every effort has been made to contact copyright holders of material reproduced in this book. Any omissions will be rectified in subsequent printings if notice is given to the publishers.